Test-Driven iOS Development

Developer's Library

ESSENTIAL REFERENCES FOR PROGRAMMING PROFESSIONALS

Developer's Library books are designed to provide practicing programmers with unique, high-quality references and tutorials on the programming languages and technologies they use in their daily work.

All books in the *Developer's Library* are written by expert technology practitioners who are especially skilled at organizing and presenting information in a way that's useful for other programmers.

Key titles include some of the best, most widely acclaimed books within their topic areas:

PHP & MySQL Web Development
Luke Welling & Laura Thomson
ISBN 978-0-672-32916-6

MySQL
Paul DuBois
ISBN-13: 978-0-672-32938-8

Linux Kernel Development
Robert Love
ISBN-13: 978-0-672-32946-3

Python Essential Reference
David Beazley
ISBN-13: 978-0-672-32862-6

Programming in Objective-C
Stephen G. Kochan
ISBN-13: 978-0-321-56615-7

PostgreSQL
Korry Douglas
ISBN-13: 978-0-672-33015-5

Developer's Library books are available at most retail and online bookstores, as well as by subscription from Safari Books Online at **safari.informit.com**

**Developer's
Library**
informit.com/devlibrary

Test-Driven iOS Development

Graham Lee

✦✦ Addison-Wesley

Upper Saddle River, NJ • Boston • Indianapolis • San Francisco
New York • Toronto • Montreal • London • Munich • Paris • Madrid
Cape Town • Sydney • Tokyo • Singapore • Mexico City

The publisher offers excellent discounts on this book when ordered in quantity for bulk purchases or special sales, which may include electronic versions and/or custom covers and content particular to your business, training goals, marketing focus, and branding interests. For more information, please contact:

U.S. Corporate and Government Sales
(800) 382-3419
corpsales@pearsontechgroup.com

For sales outside the United States, please contact:

International Sales
international@pearsoned.com

Visit us on the Web: informit.com/aw

Library of Congress Cataloging-in-Publication Data is on file

ISBN-13: 978-0-32-177418-7
ISBN-10: 0-32-177418-3

Text printed in the United States on recycled paper at R.R. Donnelley in Crawfordsville, Indiana.

First printing, April 2012

Editor-in-Chief
Mark Taub

Senior Acquisitions Editor
Trina MacDonald

Managing Editor
Kristy Hart

Project Editor
Andy Beaster

Copy Editor
Barbara Hacha

Indexer
Tim Wright

Proofreader
Paula Lowell

Technical Reviewers
Richard Buckle
Patrick Burleson
Andrew Ebling
Alan Francis
Rich Wardwell

Publishing Coordinator
Olivia Basegio

Book Designer
Gary Adair

Compositor
Gloria Schurick

❖

This book is for anyone who has ever shipped a bug. You're in great company.

❖

Contents at a Glance

Table of Contents

Preface

My experience of telling other developers about test-driven development for Objective-C came about almost entirely by accident. I was scheduled to talk at a conference on a different topic, where a friend of mine was talking on TDD. His wife had chosen (I assume that's how it works; I'm no expert) that weekend to give birth to their twins, so Chuck—who commissioned the book you now hold in your hands—asked me if I wouldn't mind giving that talk, too. Thus began the path that led ultimately to the year-long project of creating this book.

It's usually the case that reality is not nearly as neat as the stories we tell each other about reality. In fact, I had first encountered unit tests a number of years previously. Before I was a professional software engineer, I was a tester for a company whose product was based on GNUstep (the Free Software Foundation's version of the Cocoa libraries for Linux and other operating systems). Unit testing, I knew then, was a way to show that little bits of a software product worked properly, so that hopefully, when they were combined into big bits of software, those big bits would work properly, too.

I took this knowledge with me to my first programming gig, as software engineer working on the Mac port of a cross-platform security product. (Another simplification—I had, a few years earlier, taken on a six-week paid project to write a LISP program. We've all done things we're not proud of.) While I was working this job, I went on a TDD training course, run by object-oriented programming conference stalwart Kevlin Henney, editor of *97 Things Every Programmer Should Know*, among other things. It was here that I finally realized that the point of test-driven development was to make me more confident about my code, and more confident about changing my code as I learned more. The time had finally arrived where I understood TDD enough that I could start learning from my own mistakes, make it a regular part of my toolbox, and work out what worked for me and what didn't. After a few years of that, I was in a position where I could say yes to Chuck's request to give the talk.

It's my sincere hope that this book will help you get from discovering unit testing and test-driven development to making it a regular part of how you work, and that you get there in less time than the five years or so it took me. Plenty of books have been written about unit testing, including by the people who wrote the frameworks and designed the processes. These are good books, but they don't have anything specifically to say to Cocoa Touch developers. By providing examples in the Objective-C language, using Xcode and related tools, and working with the Cocoa idioms, I hope to make the principles behind test-driven development more accessible and more relevant to iOS developers.

Ah, yes—the tools. There are plenty of ways to write unit tests, depending on different features in any of a small hoard of different tools and frameworks. Although I've covered some of those differences here, I decided to focus almost exclusively on the capabilities Apple supplies in Xcode and the OCUnit framework. The reason is simply one of applicability; anyone who's interested in trying out unit tests or TDD can get on straight away with just the knowledge in this book, the standard tools, and a level of determination. If you find aspects of it lacking or frustrating, you can, of course, investigate the alternatives or even write your own—just remember to test it!

One thing my long journey to becoming a test-infected programmer has taught me is that the best way to become a better software engineers is to talk to other practitioners. If you have any comments or suggestions on what you read here, or on TDD in general, please feel free to find me on Twitter (I'm @iamleeg) and talk about it.

Acknowledgments

It was Isaac Newton who said, "If I have seen a little further it is by standing on the shoulders of giants," although he was (of course!) making use of a metaphor that had been developed and refined by centuries of writers. Similarly, this book was not created in a vacuum, and a complete list of those giants on whom I have stood would begin with Ada, Countess Lovelace, and end countless pages later. A more succinct, relevant, and bearable list of acknowledgements must begin with all of the fine people at Pearson who have all helped to make this book publishable and available: Chuck, Trina, and Olivia all kept me in line, and my technical reviewers—Saul, Tim, Alan, Andrew, two Richards, Simon, Patrick, and Alexander—all did sterling work in finding the errors in the manuscript. If any remain, they are, of course, my fault. Andy and Barbara turned the scrawls of a programmer into English prose.

Kent Beck designed the xUnit framework, and without his insight I would have had nothing to write about. Similarly, I am indebted to the authors of the Objective-C version of xUnit, Sente SA. I must mention the developer tools team at Apple, who have done more than anyone else to put unit testing onto the radar (if you'll pardon the pun) of iOS developers the world over. Kevlin Henney was the person who, more than anyone else, showed me the value of test-driven development; thank you for all those bugs that I didn't write.

And finally, Freya has been supportive and understanding of the strange hours authors tend to put in—if you're reading this in print, you'll probably see a lot more of me now.

About the Author

Graham Lee's job title is "Smartphone Security Boffin," a role that requires a good deal of confidence in the code he produces. His first exposure to OCUnit and unit testing came around six years ago, as test lead on a GNUstep-based server application. Before iOS became the main focus of his work, Graham worked on applications for Mac OS X, NeXTSTEP, and any number of UNIX variants.

This book is the second Graham has written as part of his scheme to learn loads about computing by trying to find ways to explain it to other people. Other parts of this dastardly plan include speaking frequently at conferences across the world, attending developer meetings near to his home town of Oxford, and volunteering at the Swindon Museum of Computing.

1

About Software Testing
and Unit Testing

To gain the most benefit from unit testing, you must understand its purpose and how it can help improve your software. In this chapter, you learn about the "universe" of software testing, where unit testing fits into this universe, and what its benefits and drawbacks are.

What Is Software Testing For?

A common goal of many software projects is to make some profit for someone. The usual way in which this goal is realized is directly, by selling the software via the app store or licensing its use in some other way. Software destined for in-house use by the developer's business often makes its money indirectly by improving the efficiency of some business process, reducing the amount of time paid staff must spend attending to the process. If the savings in terms of process efficiency is greater than the cost of developing the software, the project is profitable. Developers of open source projects often sell support packages or use the software themselves: In these cases the preceding argument still applies.

So, economics 101: If the goal of a software project is to make profit—whether the end product is to be sold to a customer or used internally—it must provide some value to the user greater than the cost of the software in order to meet that goal and be successful. I realize that this is not a groundbreaking statement, but it has important ramifications for software testing.

If testing (also known as *Quality Assurance*, or QA) is something we do to support our software projects, it must *support the goal of making a profit*. That's important because it automatically sets some constraints on how a software product must be tested: If the testing will cost so much that you lose money, it isn't appropriate to do. But testing software can show that the product works; that is, that the product contains the valuable features expected by your customers. If you can't demonstrate that value, the customers may not buy the product.

Notice that the purpose of testing is to show that the product works, not discover bugs. It's Quality *Assurance*, not Quality *Insertion*. Finding bugs is usually bad. Why? Because it costs money to fix bugs, and that's money that's being wasted because you were being paid to write the software without bugs in in the first place. In an ideal world, you might think that developers just write bug-free software, do some quick testing to demonstrate there are no bugs, and then we upload to iTunes Connect and wait for the money to roll in. But hold on: Working like that might introduce the same cost problem, in another way. How much longer would it take you to write software that you knew, before it was tested, would be 100% free of bugs? How much would that cost?

It seems, therefore, that appropriate software testing is a compromise: balancing the level of control needed on development with the level of checking done to provide some confidence that the software works without making the project costs unmanageable. How should you decide where to make that compromise? It should be based on reducing the risk associated with shipping the product to an acceptable level. So the most "risky" components—those most critical to the software's operation or those where you think most bugs might be hiding—should be tested first, then the next most risky, and so on until you're happy that the amount of risk remaining is not worth spending more time and money addressing. The end goal should be that the customer can see that the software does what it ought, and is therefore worth paying for.

Who Should Test Software?

In the early days of software engineering, projects were managed according to the "waterfall model" (see Figure 1.1).[1] In this model, each part of the development process was performed as a separate "phase," with the signed-off output of one phase being the input for the next. So the product managers or business analysts would create the product requirements, and after that was done the requirements would be handed to designers and architects to produce a software specification. Developers would be given the specification in order to produce code, and the code would be given to testers to do quality assurance. Finally the tested software could be released to customers (usually initially to a select few, known as *beta testers*).

---

1. In fact, many software projects, including iOS apps, are still managed this way. This fact shouldn't get in the way of your believing that the waterfall model is an obsolete historical accident.

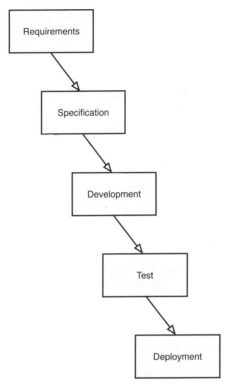

Figure 1.1   The phases of development in the waterfall
software project management process.

This approach to software project management imposes a separation between coders and testers, which turns out to have both benefits and drawbacks to the actual work of testing. The benefit is that by separating the duties of development and testing the code, there are more people who can find bugs. We developers can sometimes get attached to the code we've produced, and it can take a fresh pair of eyes to point out the flaws. Similarly, if any part of the requirements or specification is ambiguous, a chance exists that the tester and developer interpret the ambiguity in different ways, which increases the chance that it gets discovered.

The main drawback is cost. Table 1.1, reproduced from *Code Complete*, 2nd Edition, by Steve McConnell (Microsoft Press, 2004), shows the results of a survey that evaluated the cost of fixing a bug as a function of the time it lay "dormant" in the product. The table shows that fixing bugs at the end of a project is the most expensive way to work, which makes sense: A tester finds and reports a bug, which the developer must then interpret and attempt to locate in the source. If it's been a while since the developer worked on that project, then the developer must review the specifications and the code. The bug-fix version of the code must then be resubmitted for testing to demonstrate that the issue has been resolved.

Table 1.1   **Cost of Fixing Bugs Found at Different Stages of the Software Development Process**

Cost of Bugs	Time Detected				
Time Introduced	Requirements	Architecture	Coding	System Test	Post-Release
Requirements	1	3	5–10	10	10–100
Architecture	-	1	10	15	25–100
Coding	-	-	1	10	10–25

Where does this additional cost come from? A significant part is due to the communication between different teams: your developers and testers may use different terminology to describe the same concepts, or even have entirely different mental models for the same features in your app. Whenever this occurs, you'll need to spend some time clearing up the ambiguities or problems this causes.

The table also demonstrates that the cost associated with fixing bugs at the end of the project depends on how early the bug was injected: A problem with the requirements can be patched up at the end only by rewriting a whole feature, which is a very costly undertaking. This motivates waterfall practitioners to take a very conservative approach to the early stages of a project, not signing off on requirements or specification until they believe that every "i" has been dotted and every "t" crossed. This state is known as *analysis paralysis*, and it increases the project cost.

Separating the developers and testers in this way also affects the type of testing that is done, even though there isn't any restriction imposed. Because testers will not have the same level of understanding of the application's internals and code as the developers do, they will tend to stick to "black box" testing that treats the product as an opaque unit that can be interacted with only externally. Third-party testers are less likely to adopt "white box" testing approaches, in which the internal operation of the code can be inspected and modified to help in verifying the code's behavior.

The kind of test that is usually performed in a black box approach is a *system test*, or *integration test*. That's a formal term meaning that the software product has been taken as a whole (that is, the system is integrated), and testing is performed on the result. These tests usually follow a predefined plan, which is the place where the testers earn their salary: They take the software specification and create a series of test cases, each of which describes the steps necessary to set up and perform the test, and the expected result of doing so. Such tests are often performed manually, especially where the result must be interpreted by the tester because of reliance on external state, such as a network service or the current date. Even where such tests can be automated, they often take a long time to run: The entire software product and its environment must be configured to a known baseline state before each test, and the individual steps may rely on time-consuming interactions with a database, file system, or network service.

Beta testing, which in some teams is called *customer environment testing*, is really a special version of a system test. What is special about it is that the person doing the testing probably isn't a professional software tester. If any differences exist between the tester's system configuration or environment and the customer's, or use cases that users expect to use and the project team didn't consider, this will be discovered in beta testing, and any problems associated with this difference can be reported. For small development teams, particularly those who cannot afford to hire testers, a beta test offers the first chance to try the software in a variety of usage patterns and environments.

Because the beta test comes just before the product should ship, dealing with beta feedback sometimes suffers as the project team senses that the end is in sight and can smell the pizza at the launch party. However, there's little point in doing the testing if you're not willing to fix the problems that occur.

Developers can also perform their own testing. If you have ever pressed Build & Debug in Xcode, you have done a type of white-box testing: You have inspected the internals of your code to try to find out more about whether its behavior is correct (or more likely, why it isn't correct). Compiler warnings, the static analyzer, and Instruments are all applications that help developers do testing.

The advantages and disadvantages of developer testing almost exactly oppose those of independent testing: When developers find a problem, it's usually easier (and cheaper) for them to fix it because they already have some understanding of the code and where the bug is likely to be hiding. In fact, developers can test as they go, so that bugs are found very soon after they are written. However, if the bug is that the developer doesn't understand the specification or the problem domain, this bug will not be discovered without external help.

Getting the Requirements Right

The most egregious bug I have written (to date, and I hope ever) in an application fell into the category of "developer doesn't understand requirements." I was working on a systems administration tool for the Mac, and because it ran outside any user account, it couldn't look at the user settings to decide what language to use for logging. It read the language setting from a file. The file looked like this:

```
LANGUAGE=English
```

Fairly straightforward. The problem was that some users of non-English languages were reporting that the tool was writing log files in English, so it was getting the choice of language wrong. I found that the code for reading this file was very tightly coupled to other code in the tool, so set about breaking dependencies apart and inserting unit tests to find out how the code behaved. Eventually, I discovered the problem that was occasionally causing the language check to fail and fixed it. All of the unit tests pass, so the code works, right? Actually, wrong: It turned out that I didn't know the file can sometimes look at this:

```
LANGUAGE=en
```

> Not only did I not know this, but neither did my testers. In fact it took the application crashing on a customer's system to discover this problem, even though the code was covered by unit tests.

When Should Software Be Tested?

The previous section gave away the answer to the preceding question to some extent—the earlier a part of the product can be tested, the cheaper it will be to find any problems that exist. If the parts of the application available at one stage of the process are known to work well and reliably, fewer problems will occur with integrating them or adding to them at later stages than if all the testing is done at the end. However, it was also shown in that section that software products are traditionally only tested at the end: An explicit QA phase follows the development, then the software is released to beta testers before finally being opened up for general release.

Modern approaches to software project management recognize that this is deficient and aim to continually test all parts of the product at all times. This is the main difference between "agile" projects and traditionally managed projects. Agile projects are organized in short stints called *iterations* (sometimes *sprints*). At every iteration, the requirements are reviewed; anything obsolete is dropped and any changes or necessary additions are made. The most important requirement is designed, implemented, and tested in that iteration. At the end of the iteration, the progress is reviewed and a decision made as to whether to add the newly developed feature to the product, or add requirements to make changes in future iterations. Crucially, because the agile manifesto (http://agilemanifesto.org/) values "individuals and interactions over processes and tools," the customer or a representative is included in all the important decisions. There's no need to sweat over perfecting a lengthy functional specification document if you can just ask the user how the app should work—and to confirm that the app does indeed work that way.

In agile projects then, all aspects of the software project are being tested all the time. The customers are asked at every implementation what their most important requirements are, and developers, analysts, and testers all work together on software that meets those requirements. One framework for agile software projects called *Extreme Programming* (or XP) goes as far as to require that developers unit test their code and work in pairs, with one "driving" the keyboard while the other suggests changes, improvements, and potential pitfalls.

So the real answer is that software should be tested all the time. You can't completely remove the chance that users will use your product in unexpected ways and uncover bugs you didn't address internally—not within reasonable time and budget constraints, anyway. But you can automatically test the basic stuff yourself, leaving your QA team or beta testers free to try out the experimental use cases and attempt to break your app in new and ingenious ways. And you can ask at every turn whether what you're about to do will add something valuable to your product and increase the likelihood that your customers will be satisfied that your product does what the marketing text said it would.

Examples of Testing Practices

I have already described system testing, where professional testers take the whole application and methodically go through the use cases looking for unexpected behavior. This sort of testing can be automated to some extent with iOS apps, using the UI Automation instrument that's part of Apple's Instruments profiling tool.

System tests do not always need to be generic attempts to find any bug that exists in an application; sometimes the testers will have some specific goal in mind. *Penetration testers* are looking for security problems by feeding the application with malformed input, performing steps out of sequence, or otherwise frustrating the application's expectation of its environment. *Usability testers* watch users interacting with the application, taking note of anything that the users get wrong, spend a long time over, or are confused by. A particular technique in usability testing is *A/B Testing*: Different users are given different versions of the application and the usages compared statistically. Google is famous for using this practice in its software, even testing the effects of different shades of color in their interfaces. Notice that usability testing does not need to be performed on the complete application: A mock-up in Interface Builder, Keynote, or even on paper can be used to gauge user reaction to an app's interface. The lo-fi version of the interface might not expose subtleties related to interacting with a real iPhone, but they're definitely much cheaper ways to get early results.

Developers, particularly on larger teams, submit their source code for review by peers before it gets integrated into the product they're working on. This is a form of white-box testing; the other developers can see how the code works, so they can investigate how it responds to certain conditions and whether all important eventualities are taken into account. Code reviews do not always turn up logic bugs; I've found that reviews I have taken part in usually discover problems adhering to coding style guidelines or other issues that can be fixed without changing the code's behavior. When reviewers are given specific things to look for (for example, a checklist of five or six common errors—retain count problems often feature in checklists for Mac and iOS code) they are more likely to find bugs in these areas, though they may not find any problems unrelated to those you asked for.

Where Does Unit Testing Fit In?

Unit testing is another tool that developers can use to test their own software. You will find out more about how unit tests are designed and written in Chapter 3, "How to Write a Unit Test," but for the moment it is sufficient to say that unit tests are small pieces of code that test the behavior of other code. They set up the preconditions, run the code under test, and then make *assertions* about the final state. If the assertions are valid (that is, the conditions tested are satisfied), the test passes. Any deviation from the asserted state represents a failure, including exceptions that stop the test from running to completion.[2]

In this way, unit tests are like miniature versions of the test cases written by integration testers: They specify the steps to run the test and the expected result, but they do so in code. This allows the computer to do the testing, rather than forcing the developer to step through the process manually. However, a good test is also good documentation: It describes the expectations the tester had of how the code under test would behave. A developer who writes a class for an application can also write tests to ensure that this class does what is required. In fact, as you will see in the next chapter, the developer can also write tests *before* writing the class that is being tested.

Unit tests are so named because they test a single "unit" of source code, which, in the case of object-oriented software, is usually a class. The terminology comes from the compiler term "translation unit," meaning a single file that is passed to the compiler. This means that unit tests are naturally white-box tests, because they take a single class out of the context of the application and evaluate its behavior independently. Whether you choose to treat that class as a black box, and only interact with it via its public API, is a personal choice, but the effect is still to interact with a small portion of the application.

This fine granularity of unit testing makes it possible to get a very rapid turnaround on problems discovered through running the unit tests. A developer working on a class is often working in parallel on that class's tests, so the code for that class will be at the front of her mind as she writes the tests. I have even had cases where I didn't need to run a unit test to know that it would fail and how to fix the code, because I was still thinking about the class that the test was exercising. Compare this with the situation where a different person tests a use case that the developer might not have worked on for months. Even though unit testing means that a developer is writing code that won't eventually end up in the application, this cost is offset by the benefit of discovering and fixing problems before they ever get to the testers.

Bug-fixing is every project manager's worst nightmare: There's some work to do, the product can't ship until it's done, but you can't plan for it because you don't know how many bugs exist and how long it will take the developers to fix them. Looking back at Table 1.1, you will see that the bugs fixed at the end of a project are the most expensive to fix, and that there is a large variance in the cost of fixing them. By factoring the time for writing unit tests into your development estimates, you can fix some of those bugs as you're going and reduce the uncertainty over your ship date.

Unit tests will almost certainly be written by developers because using a testing framework means writing code, working with APIs, and expressing low-level logic: exactly the things that developers are good at. However it's not necessary for the same developer to write a class and its tests, and there are benefits to separating the two tasks.

---

2. The test framework you use may choose to report assertion failures and "errors" separately, but that's okay. The point is that you get to find out the test can't be completed with a successful outcome.

A senior developer can specify the API for a class to be implemented by a junior developer by expressing the expected behavior as a set of tests. Given these tests, the junior developer can implement the class by successively making each test in the set pass.

This interaction can also be reversed. Developers who have been given a class to use or evaluate but who do not yet know how it works can write tests to codify their assumptions about the class and find out whether those assumptions are valid. As they write more tests, they build a more complete picture of the capabilities and behavior of the class. However, writing tests for existing code is usually harder than writing tests and code in parallel. Classes that make assumptions about their environment may not work in a test framework without significant effort, because dependencies on surrounding objects must be replaced or removed. Chapter 11, "Designing for Test-Driven Development" covers applying unit testing to existing code.

Developers working together can even switch roles very rapidly: One writes a test that the other codes up the implementation for; then they swap, and the second developer writes a test for the first. However the programmers choose to work together is immaterial. In any case, a unit test or set of unit tests can act as a form of documentation expressing one developer's intent to another.

One key advantage of unit testing is that running the tests is automated. It may take as long to write a good test as to write a good plan for a manual test, but a computer can then run hundreds of unit tests per second. Developers can keep all the tests they've ever used for an application in their version control systems alongside the application code, and then run the tests whenever they want. This makes it very cheap to test for *regression* bugs: bugs that had been fixed but are reintroduced by later development work. Whenever you change the application, you should be able to run all the tests in a few seconds to ensure that you didn't introduce a regression. You can even have the tests run automatically whenever you commit source code to your repository, by a *continuous integration* system as described in Chapter 4, "Tools for Testing."

Repeatable tests do not just warn you about regression bugs. They also provide a safety net when you want to edit the source code without any change in behavior— when you want to *refactor* the application. The purpose of refactoring is to tidy up your app's source or reorganize it in some way that will be useful in the future, but without introducing any new functionality, or bugs! If the code you are refactoring is covered by sufficient unit tests, you know that any differences in behavior you introduce will be detected. This means that you can fix up the problems now, rather than trying to find them before (or after) shipping your next release.

However, unit testing is not a silver bullet. As discussed earlier, there is no way that developers can meaningfully test whether they understood the requirements. If the same person wrote the tests and the code under test, each will reflect the same preconceptions and interpretation of the problem being solved by the code. You should also appreciate that no good metrics exist for quantifying the success of a unit-testing strategy. The only popular measurements—code coverage and number of passing tests—can both be changed without affecting the quality of the software being tested.

Going back to the concept that testing is supposed to reduce the risk associated with deploying the software to the customer, it would be really useful to have some reporting tool that could show how much risk has been mitigated by the tests that are in place. The software can't really know what risk you place in any particular code, so the measurements that are available are only approximations to this risk level.

Counting tests is a very naïve way to measure the effectiveness of a set of tests. Consider your annual bonus—if the manager uses the number of passing tests to decide how much to pay you, you could write a single test and copy it multiple times. It doesn't even need to test any of your application code; a test that verifies the result `"1==1"` would add to the count of passing tests in your test suite. And what is a reasonable number of tests for any application? Can you come up with a number that all iOS app developers should aspire to? Probably not—I can't. Even two developers each tasked with writing the same application would find different problems in different parts, and would thus encounter different levels of risk in writing the app.

Measuring code coverage partially addresses the problems with test counting by measuring the amount of application code that is being executed when the tests are run. This now means that developers can't increase their bonuses by writing meaningless tests— but they can still just look for "low-hanging fruit" and add tests for that code. Imagine increasing code coverage scores by finding all of the `@synthesize` property definitions in your app and testing that the getters and setters work. Sure, as we'll see, these tests do have value, but they still aren't the most valuable use of your time.

In fact, code coverage tools specifically weigh against coverage of more complicated code. The definition of "complex" here is a specific one from computer science called *cyclomatic complexity*. In a nutshell, the cyclomatic complexity of a function or method is related to the number of loops and branches—in other words, the number of different paths through the code.

Take two methods: `-methodOne` has twenty lines with no `if`, `switch`, `?:` expressions or loops (in other words, it is minimally complex). The other method, `-methodTwo:(BOOL)flag` has an `if` statement with 10 lines of code in each branch. To fully cover `-methodOne` only needs one test, but you must write two tests to fully cover `-methodTwo:`. Each test exercises the code in one of the two branches of the `if` condition. The code coverage tool will just report how many lines are executed—the same number, twenty, in each case—so the end result is that it is harder to improve code coverage of more complex methods. But it is the complex methods that are likely to harbor bugs.

Similarly, code coverage tools don't do well at handling special cases. If a method takes an object parameter, whether you test it with an initialized object or with nil, it's all the same to the coverage tool. In fact, maybe both tests are useful; that doesn't matter as far as code coverage is concerned. Either one will run the lines of code in the method, so adding the other doesn't increase the coverage.

Ultimately, you (and possibly your customers) must decide how much risk is present in any part of the code, and how much risk is acceptable in the shipping product. Even if the test metric tools worked properly, they could not take that responsibility away from you. Your aim, then, should be to test while you think the tests are being helpful—and conversely, to stop testing when you are not getting any benefit from the tests. When asked the question, "Which parts of my software should I test?" software engineer and unit testing expert Kent Beck replied, "Only the bits that you want to work."

What Does This Mean for iOS Developers?

The main advantage that unit testing brings to developers of iOS apps is that a lot of benefit can be reaped for little cost. Because many of the hundreds of thousands of apps in the App Store are produced by micro-ISVs, anything that can improve the quality of an app without requiring much investment is a good thing. The tools needed to add unit tests to an iOS development project are free. In fact, as described in Chapter 4, the core functionality is available in the iOS SDK package. You can write and run the tests yourself, meaning that you do not need to hire a QA specialist to start getting useful results from unit testing.

Running tests takes very little time, so the only significant cost in adopting unit testing is the time it takes you to design and write the test cases. In return for this cost, you get an increased understanding of what your code should do *while you are writing the code*. This understanding helps you to avoid writing bugs in the first place, reducing the uncertainty in your project's completion time because there should be fewer show-stoppers found by your beta testers.

Remember that as an iOS app developer, you are not in control of your application's release to your customers: Apple is. If a serious bug makes it all the way into a release of your app, after you have fixed the bug you have to wait for Apple to approve the update (assuming they do) before it makes its way into the App Store and your customers' phones and iPads. This alone should be worth the cost of adopting a new testing procedure. Releasing buggy software is bad enough; being in a position where you can't rapidly get a fix out is disastrous.

You will find that as you get more comfortable with test-driven development—writing the tests and the code together—you get faster at writing code because thinking about the code's design and the conditions it will need to cope with become second nature. You will soon find that writing test-driven code, including its tests, takes the same time that writing the code alone used to take, but with the advantage that you are more confident about its behavior. The next chapter will introduce you to the concepts behind test-driven development: concepts that will be used throughout the rest of the book.

2

Techniques for Test-Driven Development

You have seen in Chapter 1, "About Software Testing and Unit Testing," that unit tests have a place in the software development process: You can test your own code and have the computer automatically run those tests again and again to ensure that development is progressing in the right direction. Over the past couple of decades, developers working with unit testing frameworks—particularly practitioners of Extreme Programming (XP), a software engineering methodology invented by Kent Beck, the creator of the SUnit framework for SmallTalk (the first unit testing framework on any platform, and the progenitor of Junit for Java and OCUnit for Objective-C)—have refined their techniques, and created new ways to incorporate unit testing into software development. This chapter is about technique—and using unit tests to improve your efficiency as a developer.

Test First

The practice developed by Extreme Programming aficionados is *test-first* or *test-driven* development, which is exactly what it sounds like: Developers are encouraged to write tests *before* writing the code that will be tested. This sounds a little weird, doesn't it? How can you test something that doesn't exist yet?

Designing the tests before building the product is already a common way of working in manufacturing real-world products: The tests define the *acceptance criteria* of the product. Unless all the tests pass, the code is not good enough. Conversely, assuming a comprehensive test suite, the code is good enough as soon as it passes every test, and no more work needs to be done on it.

Writing all the tests before writing any code would suffer some of the same problems that have been found when all the testing is done after all the code is written. People tend to be better at dealing with small problems one at a time, seeing them through to completion before switching context to deal with a different problem. If you were to write all the tests for an app, then go back through and write all the code, you would need to address each of the problems in creating your app twice, with a large gap in between each go. Remembering what you were thinking about when you wrote any particular group of tests a few months earlier would not be an easy task. So test-driven developers do not write all the tests first, but they still don't write code before they've written the tests that will exercise it.

An additional benefit of working this way is that you get rapid feedback on when you have added something useful to your app. Each test pass can give you a little boost of encouragement to help get the next test written. You don't need to wait a month until the next system test to discover whether your feature works.

The idea behind test-driven development is that it makes you think about what the code you're writing needs to do while you're designing it. Rather than writing a module or class that solves a particular problem and then trying to integrate that class into your app, you think about the problems that your application has and then write code to solve those problems. Moreover, you demonstrate that the code actually does solve those problems, by showing that it passes the tests that enumerate the requirements. In fact, writing the tests first can even help you discover whether a problem exists. If you write a test that passes without creating any code, either your app already deals with the case identified by the new test, or the test itself is defective.

The "problems" that an app must solve are not, in the context of test-driven development, entire features like "the user can post favorite recipes to Twitter." Rather they are microfeatures: very small pieces of app behavior that support a little piece of a bigger feature. Taking the "post favorite recipes to Twitter" example, there could be a microfeature requiring that a text field exists where users can enter their Twitter username. Another microfeature would be that the text in that field is passed to a Twitter service object as the user's name. Yet another requires that the Twitter username be loaded from NSUserDefaults. Dozens of microfeatures can each contribute a very small part to the use case, but all must be present for the feature to be complete.

A common approach for test-driven working is to write a single test, then run it to check that it fails, then write the code that will make the test pass. After this is done, it's on to writing the next test. This is a great way to get used to the idea of test-driven development, because it gets you into the mindset where you think of every new feature and bug fix in terms of unit tests. Kent Beck describes this mindset as "test infection"— the point where you no longer think, "How do I debug this?" but "How do I write a test for this?"

Proponents of test-driven development say that they use the debugger much less frequently than on non–test-driven projects. Not only can they show that the code does what it ought using the tests, but the tests make it easier to understand the code's behavior without having to step through in a debugger. Indeed, the main reason to use a debugger is because you've found that some use-case doesn't work, but you can't work out where the problem occurs. Unit tests already help you track down the problem by testing separate, small portions of the application code in isolation, making it easy to pinpoint any failures.

So test-infected developers don't think, "How can I find this bug?" because they have a tool that can help locate the bug much faster than using a debugger. Instead, they think, "How can I demonstrate that I've fixed the bug?" or, "What needs to be added or changed in my original assumptions?" As such, test-infected developers know when they've done enough work to fix the problem—and whether they accidentally broke anything else in the process.

Working in such a way may eventually feel stifling and inefficient. If you can see that a feature needs a set of closely related additions, or that fixing a bug means a couple of modifications to a method, making these changes one at a time feels artificial. Luckily, no one is forcing you to make changes one test at a time. As long as you're thinking, "How do I test this?" you're probably writing code that can be tested. So writing a few tests up front before writing the code that passes them is fine, and so is writing the code that you think solves the problem and then going back and adding the tests. Ensure that you do add the tests, though (and that they do indeed show that the freshly added code works); they serve to verify that the code behaves as you expect, and as insurance against introducing a regression in later development.

Later on, you'll find that because writing the tests helps to organize your thoughts and identify what code you need to write, the total time spent in writing test-driven code is not so different than writing code without tests used to take. The reduced need for debugging time at the end of the project is a nice additional savings.[1]

Red, Green, Refactor

It's all very well saying that you should write the test before you write the code, but how do you write that test? What should the test of some nonexistent code look like? Look at the requirement, and ask yourself, "If I had to use code that solved this problem, how would I want to use it?" Write the method call that you think would be the perfect way to get the result. Provide it with arguments that represent the input needed to solve the problem, and write a test that asserts that the correct output is given.

Now you run the test. Why should you run the test (because we both know it's going to fail)? In fact, depending on how you chose to specify the API, it might not even compile properly. But even a failing test has value: It demonstrates that there's something the app needs to do, but doesn't yet do. It also specifies what method it would be good to use to satisfy the requirement. Not only have you described the requirement in a repeatable, executable form, but you've designed the code you're going to write to meet that requirement. Rather than writing the code to solve the problem and then working out how to call it, you've decided what you want to call, making it more likely that you'll come up with a consistent and easy-to-use API. Incidentally, you've also demonstrated

---

1. Research undertaken by Microsoft in conjunction with IBM (http://research.microsoft.com/ en-us/groups/ese/nagappan_tdd.pdf) found that although teams that were new to TDD were around 15–35% slower at implementing features than when "cowboy coding," the products they created contained 40–90% fewer bugs—bugs that needed to be fixed after the project "completed" but before they could ship.

that the software doesn't yet do what you need it to. When you're starting a project from scratch, this will not be a surprise. When working on a legacy application[2] with a complicated codebase, you may find that it's hard to work out what the software is capable of, based on visual inspection of the source code. In this situation, you might write a test expressing a feature you want to add, only to discover that the code already supports the feature and that the test passes. You can now move on and add a test for the next feature you need, until you find the limit of the legacy code's capabilities and your tests begin to fail.

Practitioners of test-driven development refer to this part of the process—writing a failing test that encapsulates the desired behavior of the code you have not yet written—as the *red stage*, or *red bar stage*. The reason is that popular IDEs including Visual Studio and Eclipse (though not, as you shall see shortly, the newest version of Xcode) display a large red bar at the top of their unit-testing view when any test fails. The red bar is an obvious visual indicator that your code does not yet do everything you need.

Much friendlier than the angry-looking red bar is the peaceful serenity of the green bar, and this is now your goal in the second stage of test-driven development. Write the code to satisfy the failing test or tests that you have just written. If that means adding a new class or method, go ahead: You've identified that this API addition makes sense as part of the app's design.

At this stage, it doesn't really matter how you write the code that implements your new API, as long as it passes the test. The code needs to be Just Barely Good Enough™ to provide the needed functionality. Anything "better" than that doesn't add to your app's capabilities and is effort wasted on code that won't be used. For example, if you have a single test for a greeting generator, that it should return "Hello, Bob!" when the name "Bob" is passed to it, then this is perfectly sufficient:

```
- (NSString *)greeter: (NSString *)name {
    return @"Hello, Bob!";
}
```

Doing anything more complicated *right now* might be wasteful. Sure, you *might* need a more general method later; on the other hand, you might not. Until you write another test demonstrating the need for this method to return different strings (for example, returning "Hello, Tim!" when the parameter is "Tim"), it does everything that you know it needs to. Congratulations, you have a green bar (assuming you didn't break the result of any other test when you wrote the code for this one); your app is demonstrably one quantum of awesomeness better than it was.

You might still have concerns about the code you've just written. Perhaps there's a different algorithm that would be more efficient yet yield the same results, or maybe

---

2. I use the same definition of "legacy code" as Michael Feathers in *Working Effectively with Legacy Code* (Prentice Hall, 2004). Legacy code is anything you've inherited—including from yourself—that isn't yet described by a comprehensive and up-to-date set of unit tests. In Chapter 11 you will find ways to incorporate unit testing into such projects.

your race to get to the green bar looks like more of a kludge than you're comfortable with. Pasting code from elsewhere in the app in order to pass the test—or even pasting part of the test into the implementation method—is an example of a "bad code smell" that freshly green apps sometimes give off. *Code smell* is another term invented by Kent Beck and popularized in Extreme Programming. It refers to code that *may* be OK, but there's definitely something about it that doesn't seem right.[3]

Now you have a chance to "refactor" the application—to clean it up by changing the implementation without affecting the app's behavior. Because you've written tests of the code's functionality, you'll be able to see if you do break something. Tests will start to fail. Of course, you can't use the tests to find out if you accidentally add some new unexpected behavior that doesn't affect anything else, but this should be a relatively harmless side-effect because nothing needs to use that behavior. If it did, there'd be a test for it.

However, you may not need to refactor as soon as the tests pass. The main reason for doing it right away is that the details of the new behavior will still be fresh in your mind, so if you do want to change anything you won't have to familiarize yourself with how the code currently works. But you might be happy with the code right now. That's fine; leave it as it is. If you decide later that it needs refactoring, the tests will still be there and can still support that refactoring work. Remember, the worst thing you can do is waste time on refactoring code that's fine as it is (see "Ya Ain't Gonna Need It" later in the chapter).

So now you've gone through the three stages of test-driven development: You've written a failing test (red), got the test to pass (green), and cleaned up the code without changing what it does (refactor). Your app is that little bit more valuable than it was before you started. The microfeature you just added may not be enough of an improvement to justify releasing the update to your customers, but your code should certainly be of release candidate quality because you can demonstrate that you've added something new that works properly, and that you haven't broken anything that already worked. Remember from the previous chapter that there's still additional testing to be done. There could be integration or usability problems, or you and the tester might disagree on what needed to be added. You can be confident that if your tests sufficiently describe the range of inputs your app can expect, the likelihood of a logic bug in the code you've just written will be low.

Having gone from red, through green, to refactoring, it's time to go back to red. In other words, it's time to add the next microfeature—the next small requirement that represents an improvement to your app. Test-driven development naturally supports iterative software engineering, because each small part of the app's code is developed to production quality before work on the next part is started. Rather than having a dozen features

---

3. An extensive list of possible code smells was written by Jeff Atwood and published at http://www.codinghorror.com/blog/2006/05/code-smells.html.

that have all been started but are all incomplete and unusable, you should either have a set of completely working use cases, or one failing case that you're currently working on. However, if there's more than one developer on your team, you will each be working on a different use case, but each of you will have one problem to solve at a time and a clear idea of when that solution has been completed.

Designing a Test-Driven App

Having learned about the red-green-refactor technique, you may be tempted to dive straight into writing the first feature of your app in this test-driven fashion, then incrementally adding the subsequent features in the same way. The result would be an app whose architecture and design grow piecemeal as small components aggregate and stick themselves to the existing code.

Software engineers can learn a lot by watching physical engineering take place. Both disciplines aim to build something beautiful and useful out of limited resources and in a finite amount of space. Only one takes the approach that you can sometimes get away with putting the walls in first then hanging the scaffolding off of them.

An example of an aggregate being used in real-world engineering is concrete. Find a building site and look at the concrete; it looks like a uniformly mucky mush. It's also slightly caustic. Touch it while you're working with it and you'll get burned. Using test-driven development without an overall plan of the app's design will lead to an app that shares many of the characteristics of concrete. There'll be no discernible large-scale structure, so it'll be hard to see how each new feature connects to the others. They will end up as separate chunks, close together but unrelated like the pebbles in a construction aggregate. You will find it hard to identify commonality and chances to share code when there's no clear organization to the application.

So it's best to head into a test-driven project with at least a broad idea of the application's overall structure. You don't need a detailed model going all the way down to lists of the classes and methods that will be implemented. That fine-grained design does come out of the tests. What you will need is an idea of what the features are and how they fit together: where they will make use of common information or code, how they communicate with each other, and what they will need to do so. Again, Extreme Programming has a name for this concept: It's called the *System Metaphor*. More generally in object-oriented programming it's known as the Domain Model: the view of what users are trying to do, with what services, and to what objects, in your application.

Armed with this information, you can design your tests so that they test that your app conforms to the architecture plan, in addition to testing the behavior. If two components should share information via a particular class, you can test for that. If two features can make use of the same method, you can use the tests to ensure that this happens, too. When you come to the refactoring stage, you can use the high-level plan to direct the tidying up, too.

More on Refactoring

How does one refactor code? It's a big question—indeed it's probably open-ended, because I might be happy with code that you abhor, and vice versa. The only workable description is something like this:

- Code needs refactoring if it does what you need, but you don't like it. That means you may not like the look of it, or the way it works, or how it's organized. Sometimes there isn't a clear signal for refactoring; the code just "smells" bad.
- You have finished refactoring when the code no longer looks or smells bad.
- The refactoring process turns bad code into code that isn't bad.

That description is sufficiently vague that there's no recipe or process you can follow to get refactored code. You might find code easier to read and understand if it follows a commonly used object-oriented design pattern—a generic blueprint for code that can be applied in numerous situations. Patterns found in the Cocoa frameworks and of general use in Objective-C software are described by Buck and Yacktman in *Cocoa Design Patterns* (Addison-Wesley 2009). The canonical reference for language-agnostic design patterns is *Design Patterns: Elements of Reusable Object-Oriented Software* by Gamma, Helm, Johnson, and Vlissides (Addison-Wesley 1995), commonly known as the "Gang of Four" book.

Some specific transformations of code are frequently employed in refactoring, because they come up in a variety of situations where code could be made cleaner. For example, if two classes implement the same method, you could create a common superclass and push the method implementation into that class. You could create a protocol to describe a method that many classes must provide. The book *Refactoring: Improving the Design of Existing Code* by Martin Fowler (Addison-Wesley, 1999) contains a big catalog of such transformations, though the example code is all in Java.

Ya Ain't Gonna Need It

One feature of test-driven development that I've mentioned in passing a few times deserves calling out: If you write tests that describe what's needed of your app code, and you only write code that passes those tests, *you will never write any code that you don't need.* Okay, so maybe the requirements will change in the future, and the feature you're working on right now will become obsolete. But *right now*, that feature is needed. The code you're writing supports that feature and does nothing else.

Have you ever found that you or a co-worker has written a very nice class or framework that deals with a problem in a very generic way, when you only need to handle a restricted range of cases in your product? I've seen this happen on a number of projects; often the generic code is spun out into its own project on Github or Google Code as a "service to the community," to try to justify the effort that was spent on developing unneeded code. But then the project takes on a life of its own, as third-party users discover that the library isn't actually so good at handling the cases that weren't needed by the original developers and start filing bug reports and enhancement requests. Soon enough, the application developers realize that they've become framework developers as they spend more and more effort on supporting a generic framework, all the while still using a tiny subset of its capabilities in their own code.

Such gold plating typically comes about when applications are written from the inside out. You know that you'll need to deal with URL requests, for example, so you write a class that can handle URL requests. However, you don't yet know how your application will use URL requests, so you write the class so that it can deal with any case you think of. When you come to write the part of the application that actually needs to use URL requests, you find it uses only a subset of the cases handled by the class. Perhaps the application makes only GET requests, and the effort you put into handling POST requests in the handler class is wasted. But the POST-handling code is still there, making it harder to read and understand the parts of the class that you actually use.

Test-driven development encourages building applications from the outside in. You know that the user needs to do a certain task, so you write a test that asserts this task can be done. That requires getting some data from a network service, so you write a test that asserts the data can be fetched. That requires use of a URL request, so you write a test for that use of a URL request. When you implement the code that passes the test, you need to code only for the use that you've identified. There's no generic handler class, because there's no demand for it.

Testing Library Code

In the case of URL request handlers, there's an even easier way to write less code: find some code somebody else has already written that does it and use that instead. But should you exhaustively test that library code before you integrate it into your app?

No. Remember that unit tests are only one of a number of tools at your disposal. Unit tests—particularly used in test-driven development—are great for testing your own code, including testing that your classes interact with the library code correctly. Use integration tests to find out whether the application works. If it doesn't, but you know (thanks to your unit tests) that you're using the library in the expected way, you know that there's a bug in the library.

You could then write a unit test to exercise the library bug, as documentation of the code's failure to submit as a bug report. Another way in which unit tests can help with using third-party code is to explore the code's API. You can write unit tests that express how you expect to use somebody else's class, and run them to discover whether your expectations were correct.

Extreme programmers have an acronym to describe gold-plated generic framework classes: YAGNI, short for Ya Ain't Gonna Need It™. Some people surely do need to write generic classes; indeed, Apple's Foundation framework is just a collection of general-purpose objects. However, most of us are writing iOS applications, not iOS itself, and applications have a much smaller and more coherent set of use cases that can be satisfied without developing new generic frameworks. Besides which, you can be sure that Apple studies the demand and potential application of any new class or method before adding it to Foundation, which certainly isn't an academic exercise in providing a functionally complete API.

It saves time to avoid writing code when YAGNI—you would basically be writing code that you don't use. Worse than that, unnecessary code might be exploitable by an attacker, who finds a way to get your app to run the code. Or you might decide to use it yourself at some future point in the app's development, forgetting that it's untested code you haven't used since it was written. If at this point you find a bug in your app, you're likely to waste time tracking it down in the new code you've written—of course, the bug wasn't present before you wrote this code—not realizing that the bug actually resides in old code. The reason you haven't discovered the bug yet is that you haven't used this code before.

A test-driven app should have no unused code, and no (or very little) untested code. Because you can be confident that all the code works, you should experience few problems with integrating an existing class or method into a new feature, and you should have no code in the application whose only purpose is to be misused or to cause bugs to manifest themselves. All the code is pulling its weight in providing a valuable service to your users. If you find yourself thinking during the refactoring stage that there are some changes you could make to have the code support more conditions, stop. Why aren't those conditions tested for in the test cases? Because those conditions don't arise in the app. So don't waste time adding the support: Ya Ain't Gonna Need It.

Testing Before, During, and After Coding

If you're following the red-green-refactor approach to test-driven development, you're running tests before writing any code, to verify that the test fails. This tells you that the behavior specified by the test still needs to be implemented, and you may get hints from the compiler about what needs to be done to pass the test—especially in those cases when the test won't even build or run correctly because the necessary application code is missing. You're also running tests while you're building the code, to ensure you don't break any existing behavior while working toward that green bar. You're also testing after you've built the functionality, in the refactoring stage, to ensure that you don't break anything while you're cleaning up the code. In a fine-grained way this reflects the suggestion from Chapter 1 that software should be tested at every stage in the process.

Indeed, it can be a good idea to have tests running automatically during the development life cycle so that even if you forget to run the tests yourself, it won't be long before they get run for you. Some developers have their tests run every time they build, although when it takes more than a few seconds to run all the tests this can get in the way. Some people use continuous integration servers or buildbots (discussed in Chapter 4, "Tools for Testing") to run the tests in the background or even on a different computer whenever they check source into version control or push to the master repository. In this situation it doesn't matter if the tests take minutes to run; you can still work in your IDE and look out for a notification when the tests are completed. Such notifications are usually sent by email, but you could configure your build system to post a Growl notification or send an iChat message. I have even worked on a team where the build server was hooked up to a microcontroller, which changed the lighting between green and red depending on the test status. A reviewer of an early draft of this chapter went one better: He described a workspace where test failure triggered a flashing police light and siren! Everybody on the team knew about it when a test failed, and worked to get the product back into shape.

Another important backstop is to ensure that the tests are run whenever you prepare a release candidate of your product. If a test fails at this point, there's no reason to give the build to your testers or customers. It's clear something is wrong and needs fixing. Your release process should ideally be fire-and-forget, so you just press a button and wait for the release build to be constructed. A failing test should abort the build process. At this point it doesn't really matter how long the tests take, because preparing a release candidate is a relatively infrequent step, and it's better for it to be correct than quick. If you have some extra-complicated tests that take minutes or longer to run, they can be added at this stage. Admittedly, these tend not to be true unit tests: The longer tests are usually integration tests that require environmental setup such as a network connection to a server. Those situations are important to test, but are not suitable for inclusion in a unit test suite because they can fail nondeterministically if the environment changes.

In general, as long as you don't feel like you spend longer waiting for the tests than you do working, you should aim to have tests run automatically whenever possible. I run my tests whenever I'm working with them, and additionally have tests run automatically when I commit code to the "master" branch in my git repository (the same branch in subversion and other source control systems is called "trunk"). The shorter a delay between adding some code and discovering a failure, the easier it is to find the cause. Not only are there fewer changes to examine, but there's more of a chance that you're still thinking about the code relevant to the new failure. That is why you should test as you go with the red-green-refactor technique: You're getting immediate feedback on what needs to happen next, and how much of it you've done so far.

3

How to Write a Unit Test

You've now seen what we're trying to achieve by testing software, and how test-driven software and unit tests can help to achieve that. But how exactly is a unit test written? In this chapter you'll see a single unit test being built from first principles. You'll see what the different components of a test are, and how to go from a test or collection of tests to production code. The code in this chapter is not part of a project: It just shows the thought process in going from requirement to tested app code. You do not need to run the code in this chapter.

The Requirement

Remember, the first step in writing a unit test is to identify what the application needs to do. After I know what I need, I can decide what code I would like to use to fulfill that need. Using that code will form the body of the test.

For this chapter, the example will be that perennial favorite of sample-code authors throughout history: the temperature converter. In this simple version of the app, guaranteed not to win an Apple Design Award, the user enters a temperature in Celsius in the text field and taps the Go button on the keyboard to see the temperature in Fahrenheit displayed below. This user interaction is shown in Figure 3.1.

This gives me plenty of clues about how to design the API. Because the conversion is going to be triggered from the text field, I know that it needs to use the `UITextFieldDelegate`'s `-textFieldShouldReturn:` method. The design of this method means that the text field—in this case, the field containing the Celsius temperature—is the parameter to the method. Therefore, the signature of the method I want to use is

```
- (BOOL)textFieldShouldReturn: (id)celsiusField;
```

Figure 3.1   Screenshot of the completed Temperature Converter app.

Running Code with Known Input

An important feature of a unit test is that it should be repeatable. Whenever it's run, on whatever computer, it should pass if the code under test is correct and fail otherwise. Environmental factors such as the configuration of the computer on which the tests are running, what else is running, and external software such as databases or the contents of the computer's file system should not have an effect on the results of the test. For this example, this means that the temperature-conversion method cannot be tested by presenting the user interface and having a tester type a number in and look for the correct result. Not only would that fail whenever the tester wasn't present or made a mistake, it would take too long to run as part of a build.

Thankfully, this method requires very little setup to run (just the required `celsiusField` parameter), so I can configure a repeatable case in code. I know that −40°C is the same as −40°F, so I'm going to test that case. I identified while thinking about the method's API that I just need the text from the text field as input, so rather than configuring a whole `UITextField` object, I think I can just create a simple object that has the same `text` property. I Ain't Gonna Need all the additional complexity that comes with a full view object. Here's the fake text field class.

```
@interface FakeTextContainer : NSObject
@property (nonatomic, copy) NSString *text;
@end

@implementation FakeTextContainer
@synthesize text;
@end
```

Now I can start to write the test. I know what input I need, so I can configure that and pass it to my (as yet unwritten) method. I'm going to give the test method a very long name: In unit tests just as in production code, they're very useful to succinctly capture the intention of each method.

```
@interface TemperatureConversionTests : NSObject
@end

@implementation TemperatureConversionTests

- (void)testThatMinusFortyCelsiusIsMinusFortyFahrenheit {
    FakeTextContainer *textField = [[FakeTextContainer alloc] init];
    textField.text = @"-40";
    [self textFieldShouldReturn: textField];
}
@end
```

Notice that I've assumed that the method I'm writing is going to be on the same object as the test code, so I can call it via `self`. This is almost never the case—you will usually keep the test code and application code separate. However, it's good enough to start testing and building the method. I can move it into a production class (probably a `UIViewController` subclass) later. I don't need to refactor until I've got to the green bar. But right now I still have the red bar, because this code won't even compile without warnings[1] until I provide an implementation of the action method.

```
- (BOOL)textFieldShouldReturn: (id)celsiusField {
    return YES;
}
```

I don't (yet) need a more capable implementation than that. In fact, I've had to make a decision for something that isn't even specified: Should I return YES or NO? We'll revisit that decision later in the chapter.

---

1. The implication here is that I have Treat Warnings as Errors enabled. You should enable this setting if you haven't already, because it catches a lot of ambiguities and potential issues with code that can be hard to diagnose at runtime, such as type conversion problems and missing method declarations. To do so, search your Xcode target's Build Settings for the Warnings as Errors value and set it to Yes.

Seeing Expected Results

Now that I can call my method with input under my control, I need to inspect what that method does and ensure that the results are consistent with the app's requirements. I know that the result of running the method should be to change the text of a label, so I need a way to discover what happens to that label. I can't pass that label in as a parameter to the method, because the API contract for the UITextFieldDelegate method doesn't allow for it. The object that provides my temperature conversion method will need a property for the label so that the method can find it.

As with the input text field, it looks like the only part of the label this method will need to deal with is its text property, so it seems I can reuse the `FakeTextContainer` class I've already built. The test case now looks like this:

```
@interface TemperatureConversionTests
@property (nonatomic, strong) FakeTextContainer *textField;
@property (nonatomic, strong) FakeTextContainer *fahrenheitLabel;
- (BOOL)textFieldShouldReturn: (id)celsiusField;
@end


@implementation TemperatureConversionTests

@synthesize fahrenheitLabel; // a property containing the output label

- (void)testThatMinusFortyCelsiusIsMinusFortyFahrenheit {
    FakeTextContainer *textField = [[FakeTextContainer alloc] init];
    fahrenheitLabel = [[FakeTextContainer alloc] init];
    textField.text = @"-40";
    [self convertToFahrenheit: textField];
}
@end
```

The pattern of using special objects to provide the method's input and see its output is common to many tests. The pattern is known as Fake Objects or Mock Objects. This pattern will be seen throughout the book, but you can see what it gets us in this test. We've created an object we can use in place of the real application's text label; it behaves in the same way, but we can easily inspect to find out whether the code that uses it is doing the correct thing.

Verifying the Results

I now have a way to see what the outcome of the -convertToFahrenheit: method is, by looking at what happens to the `fahrenheitLabel` property. Now is the time to make use of that capability. It would not be appropriate to just print out the result and expect the user to read through, checking that each line of output matches a list of successful results; that's really inefficient and error prone. A key requirement for unit tests is that they should be *self-testing*: Each test should discover whether its postconditions were met and report on whether it was a success or a failure. The user just needs to know whether any tests failed, and if so, which ones. I'll change the test I'm working on to automatically discover whether it was successful.

```
- (void)testThatMinusFortyCelsiusIsMinusFortyFahrenheit {
    FakeTextContainer *textField = [[FakeTextContainer alloc] init];
    textField.text = @"-40";
    fahrenheitLabel = [[FakeTextContainer alloc] init];
    [self textFieldShouldReturn: textField];
    if ([fahrenheitLabel.text isEqualToString: @"-40"]) {
        NSLog(@"passed: -40C == -40F");
    } else {
        NSLog(@"failed: -40C != -40F");
    }
}
```

Now the test is complete. It sets up the input conditions for the method it's testing, calls that method, then automatically reports whether the expected postconditions occur. However, should you run it now, it will fail. The method doesn't set the label's text correctly. A quick change to the method fixes that:

```
- (BOOL)textFieldShouldReturn: (id)celsiusField {
    fahrenheitLabel.text = @"-40";
    return YES;
}
```

That may not seem like a good implementation of a temperature converter, but it does pass the one test. As far as the specification has been described, this method does everything required of it.

How Many Tests Could a Unit Test Test If a Unit Test Could Test Tests?

You'll notice that the -testThatMinusFortyCelsiusIsMinusFortyFahrenheit method tests only a single condition. It would be very easy to add extra tests here—for example, setting different values for the input text field and ensuring that each gets converted to the correct value in the output label, or testing the Boolean return value that we have so far been ignoring. That is not a good way to design a test and I recommend against it.

If any one of the conditions in the test fails, you will have to spend some time working out which part failed—more time than would be needed if each test evaluated only one condition. The worst problem occurs when results from the beginning of a test are used later on. In tests designed this way, one failure can cause a cascade of failures in code that would work if its preconditions were met, or can hide real failures in the later part of the test. You either spend time looking for bugs where they don't exist, or not looking for bugs in code where they do.

A well-designed test does just enough work to set up the preconditions for one scenario, then evaluates whether the app code works correctly in that one scenario. Each test should be independent, and atomic—it can pass or fail, but there are no intermediate states.

Making the Tests More Readable

The test constructed previously already has a name that explains what is being tested, but it's not as easy as it could be to see how the test works. One particular problem is that the test itself is buried in that `if` statement: It's the most important part of the test, but it's hard to find. It would be more obvious if the "machinery" surrounding the test—the condition, and the act of reporting success or failure—could be collapsed into a single line, making it obvious that this is where the test happens and making the tested expression easier to find. I can make that change by defining a macro to put the condition and test on one line.

```
#define FZAAssertTrue(condition) do {\
    if (condition) {\
        NSLog(@"passed: " @ #condition);\
    } else {\
        NSLog(@"failed: " @ #condition);\
    }\
} while(0)

// ...

- (void)testThatMinusFortyCelsiusIsMinusFortyFahrenheit {
    FakeTextContainer *textField = [[FakeTextContainer alloc] init];
    textField.text = @"-40";
    fahrenheitLabel = [[FakeTextContainer alloc] init];
    [self textFieldShouldReturn: textField];
    FZAAssertTrue([fahrenheitLabel.text isEqualToString: @"-40"]);
}
```

It can still be made better. For a start, it would be useful to have a custom message that appears if the test fails, to remind you why this test exists. Also, there's no need to have a message when tests pass, because that should be the normal case most of the time—it's not something you particularly need to read about. Both of these changes can be made to the `FZAAssertTrue()` macro.

```
#define FZAAssertTrue(condition, msg) do {\
    if (!condition) {\
        NSLog(@"failed: " @ #condition @" " msg);\
    }\
} while(0)

//...
```

```
    FZAAssertTrue([fahrenheitLabel.text isEqualToString: @"-40"], @"-40C should
➥equal -40F");
//...
```

Jumping ahead slightly, the `FZAAssertTrue()` macro now looks a lot like the
OCUnit `STAssertTrue` macro. The framework uses the developer-supplied message in
its output when the test fails:

```
[...]/TestConverter.m:34: error: -[TestConverter

testThatMinusFortyCelsiusIsMinusFortyFahrenheit] : "[fahrenheitText
➥isEqualToString:

@"-40"]" should be true. In both Celsius and Fahrenheit -40 is the same
➥temperature
```

That message gives me some more information about why I created this test, which
should help to understand something about the failure. The specific condition being
tested can still be made more obvious, though. If all your application's tests used
`STAssertTrue()`, every test—whether it checks for equality, for an object being `nil`, or
for a method throwing an exception—will look similar. In fact OCUnit provides different macros for each of these cases, so the condition in any test can be pulled to the front
of the line where the test occurs, making it more obvious. These macros are described in
more detail in the next chapter.

Organizing Multiple Tests

The test constructed throughout this chapter doesn't really do much: It confirms that a
temperature converter will output −40°F when the input is −40°C. But a temperature
converter must do much more than that. It must provide accurate output across its
whole input domain, so there should be tests with various input conditions. The bounds
of its acceptable input must be defined, and the behavior when faced with input outside
these definitions must be specified. For example, what happens if the input Celsius temperature would result in a Fahrenheit temperature outside the range of an `NSInteger`?
What happens when the input is not a number?

In addition to thorough testing of the temperature converter component, other components to the application will need testing. If the user's input in the Celsius text field is
sanitized or interpreted before being passed to the converter, you would want to test that
code, too. Similarly, you would test code that formats the output from the converter, and
any error-handling behavior in the app.

Each of these conditions should be evaluated by a different test (see the preceding
sidebar), which even for a trivial app like this temperature converter will mean dozens of
different test methods. For a "real" application with complicated functionality and multiple features, there could be a couple of thousand unit tests. It would clearly be beneficial
to have some organization strategy for unit tests, in the same way that application code is
organized into methods and classes.

In fact, a good way to organize your unit tests is to mirror the class organization in your app. Each class in the application has an associated unit test class that tests the methods of that particular class. So one way to lay out the tests in this temperature-conversion app would be that shown in Figure 3.2. Notice that although there may be connections indicating dependencies between the application classes, no such dependencies exist between the test classes. Being *unit* tests, each test class relies only on the particular unit that it is testing. It can use fake and mock objects like the `FakeTextContainer` used previously to avoid dependencies on other classes. Avoiding dependencies on other code cuts down on spurious or unexpected failures, because a failure in one test class means that a problem resides in the one class that it tests. If one test class depended on more application classes, you would need to examine more source code to find the cause of any one test failure.

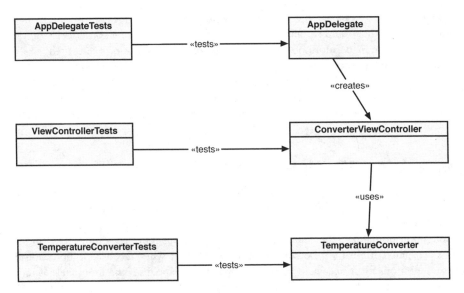

Figure 3.2   Mapping of unit test organization to
organization of application classes.

With multiple test methods on a single class all testing different aspects of the behavior of one application class, it seems likely that there will be code duplicated across the tests in a class. Indeed, looking back to the temperature converter, I can see that I might want to test conversions at absolute zero (−273.15°C/−459.67°F) and the boiling point of water (100°C/212°F) to ensure that the conversion method works across a wide choice of input values. Each of these tests will work in the same way: A fake text field is set up with the required input, a fake label to receive the output, then the conversion method is called. Only the input and output values need to change.

Unit testing frameworks like OCUnit help you to avoid duplication in these similar test methods by creating a *test fixture* for each class: a common environment in which each of the tests run. Aspects of the environment that are needed across multiple tests go into the fixture, and each test is run in its own copy of the fixture. In this way, each test gets its own version of the environment that is unaffected by the execution of other tests.[2] In OCUnit, a fixture is created by subclassing `SenTestCase` and providing two methods: `-setUp` to configure the fixture and `-tearDown` to clean up after the test has run. I will change the test I've written previously to make it part of a fixture.

```
- (void)setUp {
    [super setUp];
    textField = [[FakeTextContainer alloc] init];
    fahrenheitLabel = [[FakeTextContainer alloc] init];
}


- (void)testThatMinusFortyCelsiusIsMinusFortyFahrenheit {
    textField.text = @"-40";
    [self textFieldShouldReturn: textField];
    FZAAssertTrue(fahrenheitLabel.text, @"-40", @"In both Celsius and Fahrenheit
➥-40 is the same temperature");
}
```

Notice that the test now really is minimally brief: The initial conditions specific to the test are created, then the method under test is called, then the postconditions are evaluated. All the "plumbing" related to creating the fake objects and managing their memory is separated out into the fixture setup and teardown methods. This means that the plumbing can be reused in a different test. In fact, we might want to add a couple here. First, what about that return value from `-textFieldShouldReturn:`? Reading the documentation, that method should return `YES` to get the usual text field behavior, and there's no reason to change that behavior. It happens that this is already the case, but it's still good to document the requirement in the form of a test.

```
- (void)testThatTextFieldShouldReturnIsTrueForArbitraryInput {
    textField.text = @"0";
    FZAAssertTrue([self textFieldShouldReturn: textField], @"This method should
➥return YES to get standard textField behaviour");
}
```

Notice that this test automatically gets all the same setup code as the existing test, so there's no need to duplicate that. The test method just needs to do the work specific to executing that test. For the sake of completeness, let's add another test method that

---

2. Incidentally, this is another reason to require that a test doesn't rely on the results of previous tests. Each test gets its own copy of the fixture—a separate instance of the class, fresh from having run `-setUp`—and can neither see the results of nor influence the execution of other tests, even from the same class.

ensures 100°C is converted to 212°F: meaning that the previous, extremely limited implementation of the -textFieldShouldReturn: method will need changing.

```
- (void)testThatOneHundredCelsiusIsTwoOneTwoFahrenheit {
    textField.text = @"100";
    [self textFieldShouldReturn: textField];
    STAssertTrue([fahrenheitLabel.text isEqualToString: @"212"], @"100 Celsius is
➡212 Fahrenheit");
}


// ...


- (BOOL)textFieldShouldReturn: (id)celsiusField {
    double celsius = [[celsiusField text] doubleValue];
    double fahrenheit = celsius * (9.0/5.0) + 32.0;
    fahrenheitLabel.text = [NSString stringWithFormat: @"%.0f", fahrenheit];
    return YES;
}
```

Refactoring

We have a working method now, but it's implemented on the same class as the test cases for that method. The temperature converter and the tests of its behavior are separate concerns, so should be defined in separate classes. In fact, dividing the responsibilities between two different classes means we don't need to ship the test class at all, which is beneficial because the user doesn't particularly need our test code. Because the converter method needs to use the text field and the label from the converter view, it makes sense to put it into a view controller that will manage the view.

```
@interface TemperatureConverterViewController : UIViewController
➡<UITextFieldDelegate>
@property (strong) IBOutlet UITextField *celsiusTextField;
@property (strong) IBOutlet UILabel *fahrenheitLabel;
@end


@implementation TemperatureConverterViewController


@synthesize celsiusTextField;
@synthesize fahrenheitLabel;


- (BOOL)textFieldShouldReturn: (id)celsiusField {
    double celsius = [[celsiusField text] doubleValue];
    double fahrenheit = celsius * (9.0/5.0) + 32.0;
    fahrenheitLabel.text = [NSString stringWithFormat: @"%.0f", fahrenheit];
```

```
    return YES;
}

@end
```

Moving the method from the test class to the new `UIViewController` subclass stops the tests from working: They all call [`self textFieldShouldReturn`], which no longer exists. The test class's `-setUp` method should configure an instance of the new view controller, and the tests need to use that.

```
@interface TestConverter ()
@property (nonatomic, strong) FakeTextContainer *textField;
@property (nonatomic, strong) FakeTextContainer *fahrenheitLabel;
@property (nonatomic, strong) TemperatureConverterViewController
➡*converterController;
@end

@implementation TestConverter

@synthesize textField;
@synthesize fahrenheitLabel;
@synthesize converterController;

- (void)setUp {
    [super setUp];
    converterController = [[TemperatureConverterViewController alloc] init];
    textField = [[FakeTextContainer alloc] init];
    fahrenheitLabel = [[FakeTextContainer alloc] init];
    converterController.celsiusTextField = (UITextField *)textField;
    converterController.fahrenheitLabel = (UILabel *)fahrenheitLabel;
}

- (void)testThatMinusFortyCelsiusIsMinusFortyFahrenheit {
    textField.text = @"-40";
    [converterController textFieldShouldReturn: textField];
    STAssertEqualObjects(fahrenheitLabel.text, @"-40", @"In both Celsius and
➡Fahrenheit -40 is the same temperature");
}

- (void)testThatOneHundredCelsiusIsTwoOneTwoFahrenheit {
    textField.text = @"100";
    [converterController textFieldShouldReturn: textField];
    STAssertTrue([fahrenheitLabel.text isEqualToString: @"212"], @"100 Celsius is
➡212 Fahrenheit");
}
```

```
- (void)testThatTextFieldShouldReturnIsTrueForArbitraryInput {
    textField.text = @"0";
    STAssertTrue([converterController textFieldShouldReturn: textField], @"This
➥method should return YES to get standard textField behaviour");
}
```

@end

You could take this refactoring further; for example, the converter method currently has multiple responsibilities. It parses text from the Celsius text field, converts the parsed value into Fahrenheit, then converts that back into a string to display in the Fahrenheit label. These responsibilities could be separated into different classes. Indeed, the temperature conversion logic could go into a separate class from the view manipulation behavior. You can take this refactoring process as far as you like, until you have a design you're happy with. The tests will always be there, allowing you to find out if you make a change that breaks the application logic.

Summary

So that's how a unit test is designed and written. Along the way you've seen how a real part of an iOS app—an interface builder action method—can be tested, how to create fake objects to stand in for more complicated classes (such as the UIKit text field and label classes I otherwise would have needed to use), and how tests make it easy to refactor the design of your app by checking that everything still works after your changes. In the next chapter you'll see how to set up an Xcode project to support unit tests, and how the OCUnit framework helps you to write more succinct test cases and get better reports from your test runs.

4

Tools for Testing

Now that you've seen what test-driven development can do for you and have learned how to write test-first code, it's time to look at the tools available. In this chapter, you'll learn more about the OCUnit framework that is bundled with Apple's developer tools, and about some alternatives and their advantages and disadvantages. You'll also find out about a framework for creating mock objects and Continuous Integration tools that help you run your tests automatically.

OCUnit with Xcode

Now that you know how to design a unit test, it's time to set up your Xcode project for test-driven development. In this section, you'll learn how to use OCUnit, a framework developed by Sen:Te (hence the assertion macros using the ST prefix). OCUnit has been around since 1998, when Mac OS X was still a beta operating system distributed under the code name "Rhapsody." OCUnit is a straightforward port of Kent Beck's SUnit framework to Objective-C.

The main advantage of OCUnit is that Apple has integrated it into Xcode ever since version 2.1, so OCUnit is the easiest unit testing framework to start working with and get quick results. It's also cross-platform, which is useful if you're using Objective-C on platforms other than iOS or the Mac. Alternative choices to OCUnit are discussed in later sections of this chapter.

In the previous chapter, I built a single unit test from scratch, using features from OCUnit to make the test more readable and to enable code reuse. In this section I'll demonstrate how the project that test is part of was set up.

Start by launching Xcode and creating a new project. At the project configuration sheet (see Figure 4.1), choose the project template most suited for your needs. In the case of the temperature converter app, that's View-Based Application. Click Next, and then enter the details of the project, including your company name and the product name, such as "Temperature Converter." For this project, choose the iPhone device family. Unit tests work in the same way for iPad and Universal apps (and for Mac OS X apps, too). Most importantly for configuring the project for test-driven development, ensure the Include Unit Tests box (shown in Figure 4.2) is checked. Click Next again, then choose where to save your project. Xcode asks at this stage whether you want to create a git repository; see the sidebar "Configuring a Source Control System" for more information. Your project will open in Xcode's main window, looking like Figure 4.3.

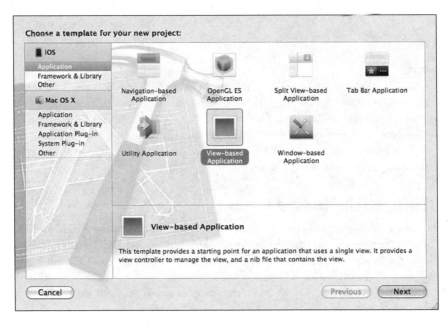

Figure 4.1   Configuring an Xcode project.

Figure 4.2   Telling Xcode to include unit tests in an iOS app project.

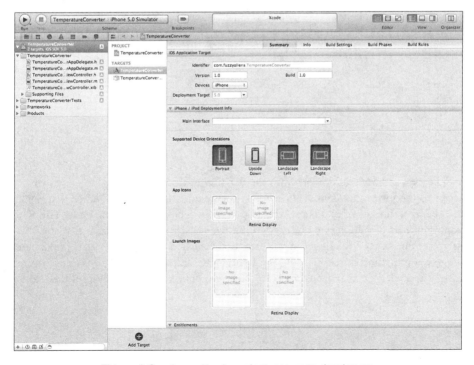

Figure 4.3   A new Xcode project, set up to develop an
iOS app with associated unit tests.

Configuring a Source Control System

While you are creating a new project, Xcode will ask whether you want to set up a local git repository to provide source control. While source control is not necessary to work with test-driven development, I strongly recommend using source control with your project.

Used in its simplest way, source control can act as an additional safety net for your development work. If you're using test-driven development, you're already carefully adding incremental improvements to your code, rather than plowing ahead without a plan or a definition of what it means to be "done." With source control in place, you can take a snapshot of your project after each increment is added. If you decide that you don't need some specific behavior after all, it's easy to go back and remove it using the source control. Similarly, if you get lost implementing a particular test case and end up with a complete mess of your code, you can quickly revert to the last clean state and pick up from there.

More complex use cases for source control include maintaining separate branches of your code relating to different versions of the product, merging changes between different branches, and integrating work from multiple developers. Those are beyond the scope of this book. See *Pragmatic Version Control Using Git* (Swicegood, Pragmatic Programmers 2008). Suffice it to say that if you are not yet using source control to manage your projects, now is a good time to start.

Have a look at the source files that Xcode provides in the new project. In addition to the app delegate and view controller templates, there is a group called Temperature ConverterTests that contains a single class, called `Temperature_ConverterTests`. This is where your first tests can go. Here's the class interface.

```
#import <SenTestingKit/SenTestingKit.h>

@interface Temperature_ConverterTests : SenTestCase {
@private

}

@end
```

The class imports the headers from the SenTestingKit framework, which gives you access to the various `STAssert*()` macros, documented in Table 4.1. Notice that rather than being a subclass of `NSObject`, this test class is a subclass of `SenTestCase`. This is an important part of running unit tests. OCUnit detects at runtime all classes that are derived from `SenTestCase` and instantiates each one as a fixture. If the class implements the `-setUp` method for configuring the fixture, OCUnit automatically runs that before each test; similarly, it will detect and run the `-tearDown` method afterward if that exists.

Table 4.1   **The Macros Made Available to Unit Tests by OCUnit, and the Conditions Needed to Pass the Test in Each Case**

Test Macro	Success Criteria
`STAssertTrue(expression, msg, ...)`	Expression does not evaluate to 0.
`STAssertEqualObjects (a1, a2, msg, ...)`	Either the object pointers a1 and a2 refer to the same object (a1 == a2), or [a1 isEqual: a2] == YES.
`STAssertEquals(a1, a2, msg, ...)`	The arguments a1 and a2 are C datatypes (for example, primitive values or structs) of the same type with equal values.
`STAssertEqualsWithAccuracy (a1, a2, accuracy, msg, ...)`	The C scalar values a1 and a2 are of the same type and have the same value to within ±accuracy.
`STFail(msg, ...)`	Never successful.
`STAssertNil(a1, msg, ...)`	The object a1 is nil.
`STAssertNotNil(a1, msg, ...)`	The object a1 is not nil.
`STAssertTrueNoThrow(expression, msg, ...)`	Expression does not evaluate to 0 and does not throw an exception.
`STAssertFalse(expression, msg, ...)`	Expression does evaluate to 0.
`STAssertFalseNoThrow(expression, msg, ...)`	Expression evaluates to 0 and does not throw an exception.
`STAssertThrows(expression, msg, ...)`	Expression must throw an exception.
`STAssertThrowsSpecific (expression, exception, msg, ...)`	Expression must throw an exception of the same class as the exception parameter, or a subclass of that class. In other words, [expression isKindOfClass: exception] must be true.
`STAssertThrowsSpecificNamed (expression, exception, name, msg, ...)`	Expression must throw an exception of the same class as or a subclass of the exception parameter, and with the name passed in the name parameter.
`STAssertNoThrow(expression, msg, ...)`	Expression does not throw an exception.
`STAssertNoThrowSpecific (expression, exception, msg, ...) or its subclasses.`	Expression either doesn't throw an exception, or if it does, the exception isn't an instance of the exception parameter
`STAssertNoThrowSpecificNamed (expression, exception, name, msg, ...)`	Expression either doesn't throw an exception or throws one that does not have the same type and name as the exception and name parameters.

> **Note**
>
> In each case the mandatory `msg` parameter is interpreted as a format string suitable for passing to `+[NSString stringWithFormat:]`, and the variable-length argument list is used as the parameters to the format string.

OCUnit also automatically detects all the unit tests implemented by each fixture and runs all of them, recording the number of successes and failures to report once the tests have run. To have OCUnit discover your test methods, you must declare them as methods with no return value and no parameters, with their names starting with the word "test" in lowercase. This is why the test case defined in the last chapter was called `-(void) testThatMinusFortyCelsiusIsMinusFortyFahrenheit`. Add a very simple test case to the `Temperature_ConverterTests.m` implementation now, so that you can test out OCUnit.

```
- (void)testThatOCUnitWorks {
    STAssertTrue(YES, @"OCUnit should pass this test.");
}
```

You do not need to declare this method in the class interface: OCUnit is going to detect the test method using the Objective-C runtime library. Run the test by pressing Cmd-U in Xcode, or select Test from Xcode's Product menu. Xcode compiles the application target, then launches the iOS Simulator to run your tests.

You will probably see a test failure at this point: Apple's template unit test fixture includes the following method:

```
- (void)testExample
{
    STFail(@"Unit tests are not implemented yet in Temperature_ConverterTests");
}
```

This method isn't helpful; it gets in the way by giving the impression that your tests are broken. Remove the `-testExample` method and run the test again.

This time, no news is good news: Xcode doesn't have the green bar of other IDEs, and the result of all tests passing is that Xcode doesn't report any errors. If you want to confirm that no errors have occurred, you can inspect the detailed output of the test process, available in Xcode's Log navigator (the right-most icon in the navigator bar, or press Cmd-7). You can also have your unit tests run on an iOS device, if you have one enabled for development and attached to your Mac. Click the Scheme drop-down at the top left of the Xcode project window, and select your device as the target. Running the tests on a device works in the same way as running them on the simulator—although it usually takes a bit longer both to deploy the tests over the USB cable and then to run them on the slower CPU of the iOS device.

In order to have something to look at, and because knowing what a test failure looks like is an important part of test-driven development, change the YES in the test you just wrote to NO, and test the product again. Now you should see a red error message in the source editor at the line where the failure occurred; the message includes your custom text and explains why the assertion failed. If you click in the sidebar of Xcode's editor at this line, you can set a breakpoint at the location where the test fails. Run the tests again, and Xcode will break into the debugger at the failing line so you can investigate the failing test in more detail.

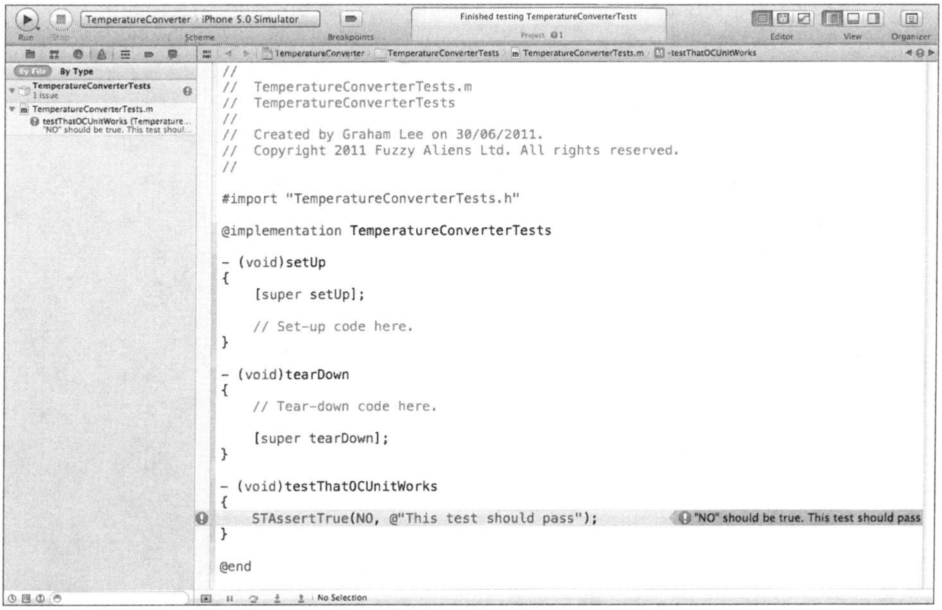

Figure 4.4   A failed unit test in Xcode.

You can make Xcode more vocal about the test results: In the Behaviors pane of Xcode's preferences, you can configure a custom alert when testing succeeds or fails. This alert can be a sound or spoken announcement, an image that appears over the Xcode editor, or an AppleScript of your own construction. You can even configure whether Xcode reacts to a test failure by jumping to the line of code that contains the failing assertion.

Warning

Remember to change the failing test back so that it passes before you carry on building your unit tests, or you can delete it. Either way, it's not needed for the rest of the examples.

Because there will be multiple components to test in your application, you need to be
able to create more test fixtures—in other words, more SenTestCase subclasses. To add a
new test class, go to the project navigator in Xcode (in the navigation view's toolbar, the
left-most icon shows the project navigator; alternatively you can press Cmd-1) and
control-click or right-click the group containing the existing fixture files. Select New
File from the menu, and then add a new Objective-C Test Case Class (see Figure 4.5).
Name the class as you like, and make sure you add it to the test case target but not to
the target for your application, as shown in Figure 4.6. Now when you run the tests by
pressing Cmd-U, the tests in this new class get run in addition to any existing tests.

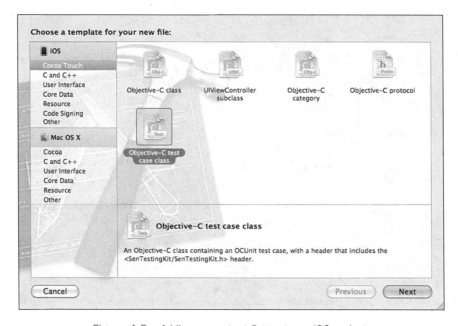

Figure 4.5   Adding a new test fixture to an iOS project.

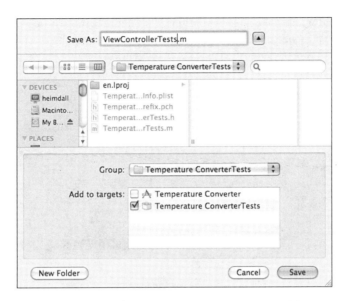

Figure 4.6   Adding the test fixture to the test case build target.

Notice that some of the unit test templates created by Xcode include a preprocessor macro to selectively compile different parts of the test fixture:

```
// Application unit tests contain unit test code that must be
   injected into an application to run correctly.
// Define USE_APPLICATION_UNIT_TEST to 0 if the unit test code is
   designed to be linked into an independent test executable.
#define USE_APPLICATION_UNIT_TEST 1
```

Xcode's test procedure injects the test bundle into your app, so you should ensure that your tests are defined in the section of the implementation file marked `#if USE_APPLI-CATION_UNIT_TEST`. Otherwise, the tests will not be compiled or run. Or remove all the preprocessor statements about `USE_APPLICATION_UNIT_TEST` from the files and all tests in the fixture will always be available. The alternative case, which Apple calls "logic tests," is suitable for testing library code where you don't have a host app in which to inject the tests. Xcode injects logic tests into its own host process running in the iOS Simulator.

As you build up the number of tests in your project, it will take longer to compile and run the tests. If you've managed to get yourself deep into development mode, this can be distracting. You have to stop working for half a minute or so every time you want to see the results of your work. If you're working on one particular feature, it would be useful to see results from tests that exercise that feature, but the rest are just taking time to run while their results are unlikely to change. In Xcode, you can configure which

tests get run and which are skipped by editing the build scheme. Choose Edit Scheme
from the Product menu to see the scheme editor. The editor for the test phase is shown
in Figure 4.7. From here you can enable or disable testing whole fixtures or individual
tests within a fixture.

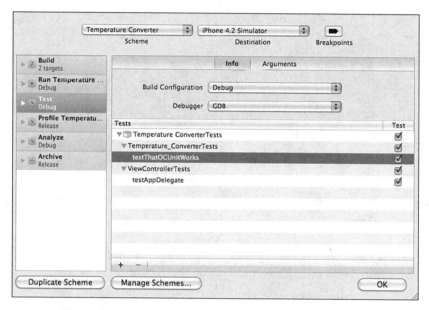

Figure 4.7   The Xcode scheme editor configuring which tests
get executed in the test phase.

Don't forget that those tests you have disabled are not being run! If you see no failures, it
doesn't mean there might not be any problems if you're not running all the tests. It's a
good idea to duplicate the build scheme in Xcode's scheme editor and keep one scheme
with all the tests enabled. Then you can run selected tests while you're working and
switch back to running all tests every so often to ensure you haven't introduced a bug in
a test you weren't looking at.

One important time when you should run your unit tests is when you prepare a
build. There's no point trying out your app when problems can be detected by the unit
tests, and giving such a build to your customers could be disastrous. One of the build
settings you can configure for your app target (or at the project level, for all targets in the
project) is that the tests run automatically after any successful build, highlighted in Figure
4.8. Enabling this setting means that even if you forget to run the tests yourself when
you prepare a build, Xcode will have you covered.

One of the technical reviewers reading an early draft of this chapter recommended
leaving automatic tests off for Debug builds so they don't slow you down when you
don't need them, but enabling the setting for Release builds so you definitely run the
tests before submitting a binary to iTunes Connect.

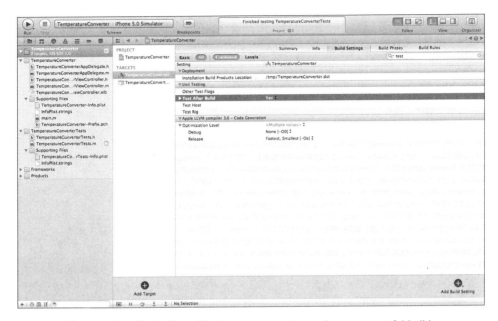

Figure 4.8   The build setting to always run tests after a successful build.

It's useful to be able to run tests from the command line, either in the Terminal application or as part of a shell script. Indeed, you will need to execute the tests from a script to make use of a continuous integration system, described in detail at the end of this chapter.

Xcode includes a command-line tool, xcodebuild, suitable for using in scripts and Terminal. Unfortunately, you cannot just tell it to test your build scheme in a way analogous to pressing Cmd-U inside the Xcode GUI, so you have to do a little digging to find the command line you must provide.

The first step is to find out the names of all the targets in your project. This is done with xcodebuild's -list option:

```
heimdall:Temperature Converter leeg$ xcodebuild -list
Information about project "Temperature Converter":
    Targets:
        Temperature Converter
        Temperature ConverterTests

    Build Configurations:
        Debug
        Release

    If no build configuration is specified "Release" is used.
```

In this case, there are two targets. Temperature Converter is my app, and Temperature ConverterTests is the target for the unit tests. To get Xcode to execute the tests, you need to build the target. You can do that with this command:

```
heimdall:Temperature Converter leeg$ xcodebuild -target Temperature\
➥ConverterTests build
```

The xcodebuild tool outputs all the commands it runs to build and execute the test targets, including any test failure reports. Reading this to find out the results would not be a good way to deal with test failures, so your script can instead make use of the numeric return value from xcodebuild, available in the script environment as the $? variable. If the tests are built correctly and all succeed, xcodebuild returns 0. Any other number means that the tests failed, or could not be compiled correctly.

Alternatives to OCUnit

Although OCUnit is perfectly adequate for test-driven development, and its integration with Xcode has come a long way since it was first bundled in version 2.1 of the IDE, it isn't everyone's cup of tea. Independent developers have written other testing frameworks for applying TDD to Objective-C projects, each with its own features.

Google Toolkit for Mac

The Google Toolkit for Mac (GTM) is a grab bag of interesting and useful utilities for Mac and iOS developers. The iOS unit testing capabilities described at http://code.google.com/p/google-toolbox-for-mac/wiki/iPhoneUnitTesting are just one of its features. GTM's testing capabilities extend OCUnit's features by providing a collection of extra macros, described in Table 4.2. These macros allow the some test methods to be shorter and more expressive than they are when written for OCUnit's macro set. It also provides a mock object for verifying that log messages match what you would expect, and has convenience categories for testing graphics and image code.

Table 4.2   Test Assertion Macros Provided by GTM's Unit Testing Capabilities

Test Macro	Success Criteria
`STAssertNoErr(expression, msg, ...)`	Expression is an `OSStatus` or `OSErr` equal to the constant noErr.
`STAssertErr(expression, err, msg, ...)`	Expression is an `OSStatus` or `OSErr` equal to the value of `err`.
`STAssertNotNULL(expression, msg, ...)`	Expression is a pointer, the value of which is not `NULL`.
`STAssertNULL(expression, msg, ...)`	Expression is a pointer, the value of which is `NULL`.
`STAssertNotEquals(a1, a2, msg, ...)`	The C types `a1` and `a2` are not equal.

Table 4.2   **Continued**

Test Macro	Success Criteria
STAssertNotEqualObjects(a1, a2, msg, ...)	The Objective-C objects a1 and a2 are not equal.
STAssertOperation(a1, a2, op, msg, ...)	The expression a1 op 'a2' must be true, where a1 and a2 are simple C types. E.g. if op is &, then a1 & a2 must not be equal to 0.
STAssertGreaterThan(a1, a2, msg, ...)	a1 > a2
STAssertGreaterThanOrEqual (a1, a2, msg...)	a1 >= a2
STAssertLessThan(a1, a2, msg, ...)	a1 < a2
STAssertLessThanOrEqual (a1, a2, msg)	a1 <= a2
STAssertEqualStrings (a1, a2, msg, ...)	The NSString instances a1 and a2 represent the same sequence of characters.
STAssertNotEqualStrings(a1, a2, msg, ...)	The NSString instances a1 and a2 represent different sequences of characters.
STAssertEqualCStrings(a1, a2, msg, ...)	The C strings a1 and a2 represent the same sequence of characters.
STAssertNotEqualCStringsx (a1, a2, msg, ...)	The C strings a1 and a2 represent different sequences of characters.

GHUnit

The GHUnit framework, at https://github.com/gabriel/gh-unit, is designed with OCUnit and Google Toolkit compatibility in mind. Indeed, it is possible to take test fixtures written for either framework and use them in GHUnit without modification. GHUnit's main feature is a custom front-end for both Mac and iOS, which provides the capability to filter test results based on keywords, and offers more control over presentation of the test results than Xcode allows. Originally, running in an application made it easier to debug unit tests than was possible with OCUnit's bundle-based tests, but this is no longer the case. The GHUnit GUI for iOS is shown in Figure 4.9.

Figure 4.9   The GHUnit app for iOS running a project's unit tests.

To present this GUI, tests are not injected into your own app. Instead, you create a new application target containing your test code, the GHUnit framework which detects and runs your tests, and a file called GHUnitIOSTestMain.m, which configures the user interface. This means that to run your tests, rather than choosing the Test option for your app's build scheme, you have to build and run the test app target. Full instructions on using GHUnit are available from the git project page at the preceding URL.

CATCH

CATCH, short for C++ Adaptive Test Cases in Headers, is the newest of the unit testing frameworks described here. It can be downloaded from its github project page at https://github.com/philsquared/Catch.

CATCH takes a different approach from the others, which are all based on OCUnit. CATCH is implemented in C++, but can be used from any C, C++, or Objective-C code. As the name suggests, it is entirely implemented in headers. Rather than the collection of assertion macros in the OCUnit-style frameworks, CATCH defines a protocol containing the setup and teardown methods, and a couple of macros to mark the test methods and wrap an expression in an assertion handler. Any expression, such as an Objective-C method call or a C comparison, that results in a value can be used in the REQUIRE() macro. The macro automatically discovers which parts of the expression are the left side, the right side, and the operator, so it still provides meaningful failure messages like the other frameworks.

To use CATCH for your unit tests, you must ensure that the test fixtures are compiled as Objective-C++ files. Although you can implement all your fixtures in Objective-C, the internals of CATCH are written in C++. To tell Xcode that a file is an Objective-C++ file, name it with the .mm extension. Fixtures in CATCH do not need to subclass any particular class like SenTestCase, because the CATCH runner searches through all classes to find test methods. Adopting the `OcFixture` protocol in fixture classes is useful as an annotation that the class is a test fixture, although this is not necessary, and all the `OcFixture` methods are optional.

The temperature converter test from the previous chapter would look like this if implemented using CATCH:

```
#import "catch_objc_main.hpp"
#import "ConverterTests.h"

@interface ConverterTests : NSObject <OcFixture>
@property (nonatomic, strong) id textField;
@property (nonatomic, strong) id fahrenheitLabel;
@end

@implementation ConverterTests
@synthesize textField;
@synthesize fahrenheitLabel;

- (void)setUp {
    textField = [[FakeTextContainer alloc] init];
    fahrenheitLabel = [[FakeTextContainer alloc] init];
}

OC_TEST_CASE("ConverterTests/minusFortyTest", "Ensure that -40C is converted to
➡-40F") {
    [textField setText: @"-40"];
    [self convertToFahrenheit: textField];
    REQUIRE([[fahrenheitLabel text] isEqualToString: @"-40"]);
}

@end
```

The `catch_objc_main.hpp` header includes a `main()` function that lets you build the tests as a Mac OS X command-line tool (which could also be run in the iOS Simulator). The API for discovering and running tests is very simple, so it would be straightforward to create a custom test runner for iOS.

The `OC_TEST_CASE` macro defines the test method that will be discovered by the runner. The name of the test is not the method name, which is created by the framework, but a string that you pass as the first parameter to the macro. That allows you to choose more expressive names. Here I've included the fixture name in addition to a camelCase identifier for the test. The description of the test is also provided as a parameter to the test definition, rather than being a parameter of the assertion statement as it is in OCUnit.

OCMock

In Chapter 3, "How to Write a Unit Test," I created a very simple mock object to inspect whether the temperature conversion method I was writing would set the text property on a label. Mock objects are crucial to test-driven development: Without them you could not automatically test methods that have side-effects.

A side-effect is any result of a method other than its return value. It's a good idea to avoid surprising side-effects in your code, because it's much easier to understand what "pure functions"—those whose behavior depends only on their inputs and don't have any side-effects—do and to trace code flow through multiple pure functions. However, apps and the devices they run on are inherently stateful, so at some point you need to read or modify app state, such as the content of a UI object, user defaults, or the file system. To test these, you need to provide mock implementations of the objects that will be affected.

There is no library for mock objects distributed with Xcode. A long-standing popular choice for Objective-C developers is OCMock, available from Mulle Kybernetik at http://www.mulle-kybernetik.com/software/OCMock/.

OCMock is a framework for simple creation of mock objects. It uses the Objective-C runtime's introspection capabilities to automatically create mocks that can stand in for instances of any other Objective-C class. To use OCMock's mock objects in a test case, you create the mocks that must stand in for other classes and configure them by telling them what methods you expect to be called, what the parameters should be, and what value should be returned, if applicable. After the body of the test has been performed, you tell the mock objects to verify their state. In the verification phase, they will evaluate whether the expected methods were called (and that nothing else happened) with the parameters you previously configured. If not, they raise a test failure.

The following listing demonstrates the tests from Chapter 3, rewritten to use the OCMock framework (the method under test has been elided but would be the same as that shown in Chapter 3).

```
#import <OCMock/OCMock.h>
#import <SenTestingKit/SenTestingKit.h>

@interface TestConverter : SenTestCase {
}
/*
 * Notice that the properties are defined as type 'id', rather than
 * specific UIKit classes. This is to avoid undefined selector warnings
 * when compiling the test cases, as this code will call OCMock methods
```

```
 * on the stand-ins for these properties.
 */
@property (nonatomic, strong) id textField;
@property (nonatomic, strong) id fahrenheitLabel;
@end

@implementation TestConverter

@synthesize textField;
@synthesize fahrenheitLabel;

- (void)setUp {
    [super setUp];
    textField = [OCMockObject mockForClass: [UITextField class]];
    fahrenheitLabel = [OCMockObject mockForClass: [UILabel class]];
}

- (void)testThatMinusFortyCelsiusIsMinusFortyFahrenheit {
    [[[textField stub] andReturn: @"-40"] text];
    [[fahrenheitLabel expect] setText: @"-40"];
    [self convertToFahrenheit: textField];
    [fahrenheitLabel verify];
    [textField verify];
}

- (void)tearDown {
    [super tearDown];
}

@end
```

Both the input text field and the output label are set up as mock objects for the specific classes that will be used in the real app. These are no longer the fake text containers created in Chapter 3. These objects are fully capable of standing in for any of the functionality offered by the `UITextField` and `UILabel` classes.

The test case method tells the mock objects what should happen during the test. The mock `UITextField` is instructed to return the string `@"-40"` when its `-text` method is called. OCMock arranges this by "swizzling" the method: Calling `-stub` replaces the real `-[UITextField text]` implementation with a "stub" method that returns the value specified in the test. The `-expect` call on the `UILabel` mock tells OCMock that a side-effect of the test is to call the `-setText:` method on the label, and that the parameter should be `@"-40"`.

Notice that this capability for mocks to replace methods with stubs returning supplied values, and to express expectations about the methods called on a mock, is independent of the class being mocked. OCMock uses the Objective-C runtime to discover and replace the mocked class's behavior, so although this test demonstrated its use only with `UIKit` objects, you can use OCMock with any classes, including your own custom classes.

There aren't any assertion macros in the test anymore: The side-effect result is tested by OCMock using the `-verify` calls at the end of the test method, and because the `-convertToFahrenheit:` method doesn't return a value, there is nothing else to do. In a more complicated test you would need to call `-verify` on every mock object to ensure that all the expected events have occurred. In this case, OCMock checks that the text on the label is set correctly, and that nothing else happens. If the expectations are not met, OCMock throws an exception describing the problem:

```
2011-02-01 14:55:25.475 otest[2006:903] *** Terminating app due to uncaught
➥exception
'NSInternalInconsistencyException', reason: 'OCMockObject[UILabel]: unexpected
➥method
invoked: setText:@"0"
    expected:    setText:@"-40"'
```

Unfortunately, this exception aborts the test runner, so no other failures get reported. The obvious solution may appear to be to wrap the call in `STAssertNoThrow()`, so that OCUnit handles the exception. This does not work, because the test runner will still abort. Even wrapping the test method in a `@try/@catch` block does not stop OCMock from aborting the test suite.

Even with this limitation in mind, OCMock provides a very powerful implementation of mock objects that makes it easy to replace even complicated classes with mocks suitable for test-driven development. Alex Vollmer has much more information about the specific capabilities of OCMock over at http://alexvollmer.com/posts/2010/06/28/making-fun-of-things-with-ocmock/.

Continuous Integration

Continuous Integration tools do not change the way you write unit tests. They are tools to support test-driven development by automatically running your tests whenever you change the code. Continuous Integration servers watch your source code repository, and when a change is committed, they check out that change and run the tests. You could get them to do anything: prepare a build for your testers, publish the revision message to a website, or post to a mailing list about the new change. In this section, you will find out about using two popular (and free) Continuous Integration tools to support your testing.[1]

---

1. Continuous Integration itself is a broad topic and this section will only cover the bare essentials. For a more complete discussion, see the book *Continuous Integration: Improving Software Quality and Reducing Risk*, Duvall, Matyas, and Glover, Addison-Wesley 2007.

Typically, developers do not run the Continuous Integration server on their own development workstation, but instead it is deployed on a standalone system. However, when developing iOS apps this system still needs to be a Mac so that Xcode and the iOS SDK are available. In addition to not taking resources away from their own development work, having continuous integration on a different machine helps to identify dependencies—for example on third-party frameworks or Interface Builder plug-ins—that must be satisfied to build the app.

"You broke the build"

Continuous Integration servers are particularly useful for teams of multiple developers. One programmer working alone on a feature might be confident that he has not introduced any regressions, only to find that when he shares his work with the rest of the team it conflicts with something another developer has added. In other words, a problem arises at *integration* time.

Continuous Integration helps the team discover and react to this problem quickly. I have also found it very useful for discovering and reacting rapidly to a different issue: A developer creates a new file but doesn't commit it to the repository along with the changes that use this file. The continuous integration server builds the team's product and runs the tests as soon as any developer integrates new code, providing fast notification of any failures. The tools described in this section can identify which developers have committed changes since the last successful build, and send them messages explaining what has broken.

Some development teams operate a penalty system for developers who break the build—that is, who commit changes that cause tests to start failing. The penalty is usually small and light-hearted: The developer might have to wear a silly hat until he fixes the problems or buy the donuts at the next team meeting. It's a small incentive to be careful when coders integrate their work with the team's.

Hudson

Important note: As this section was being written, the project team behind Hudson voted to fork the project. Hudson, available at http://hudson-ci.org, is maintained by Oracle, Inc., whereas Jenkins, available at http://jenkins-ci.orgs, is a community-run project. At time of writing, there is no functional difference between the two tools. Here I will use the name Hudson throughout, though the instructions should apply to Jenkins, too.

Hudson is a web application written in Java. In addition to running builds and collecting the results, it provides a comprehensive browser-based user interface, including a dashboard that lets you see summary information on the "health" of all your projects. Hudson was primarily designed to work with Java projects, but you can use it to build and test iPhone apps, too.

Download the Hudson software as a WAR package from http://hudson-ci.org. In Terminal, navigate to the folder where you downloaded the file, and launch Hudson with this command:[2]

```
$ java -jar hudson.war
```

As Hudson starts up it logs a series of status messages, including the following:

```
INFO: Completed initialization
```

When this line appears, Hudson is ready to use. Point your browser at http://local-host:8080 to see the Hudson dashboard, shown in Figure 4.10. Now you can create a job that will run your unit tests.

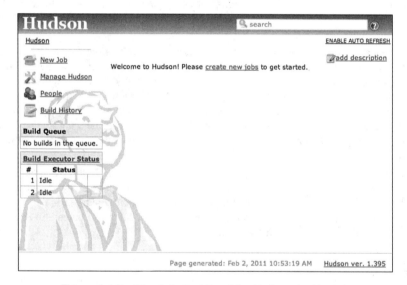

Figure 4.10   The default state of the Hudson dashboard.

Click the New Job item in the menu on the left of Hudson's dashboard. Now give your job a name: The name should give specific information about the job so that you can distinguish the jobs in Hudson's dashboard. If you intend to have one only job for a project, the project's name is sufficient; otherwise, including information about which branch is being built and in what configuration (for example, Debug, Release, or

---

2. If you want continuous integration via Hudson, CruiseControl, or any other tool to become part of your regular workflow, you will need to arrange for that tool to run automatically so that even when you reboot your continuous integration server, the service is still available. A great way to do this is to create a launch agent: See the Mac OS X manual page for launchd.plist for more information.

Deployment) will be useful, too. Choose Build a Free-Style Software Project, and click OK.

On the next form you configure the new job. The project description allows you to provide more information about the job than would fit in a name of reasonable length. The important parts to configure are the source code management, build triggers, and build steps.

At time of writing, Hudson supports only a couple of centralized source code management tools: CVS and subversion, with plug-ins available for some other version control systems. If you're using the git version control system bundled with Xcode, use the git plug-in on the Hudson website: http://wiki.hudson-ci.org/display/HUDSON/Git+Plugin. If you use a different tool that Hudson does not have support for, you will need to configure the project without source code management support. You can create a shell script to check out the source as a build step. Consult the manual for your source code management tool of choice to find out how to do that.

For your first Hudson job, you cannot set up project dependencies (there is nothing else for it to be dependent on) so there are three options for triggering builds. From Hudson's interface, you can configure it to poll source control (if configured) and build whenever a new commit is discovered, or you can set up periodic builds. Periodic builds are useful for projects that provide nightly releases to beta testers. In each case, the configuration is the same: specify a range of times at which the poll or build should occur using the UNIX `crontab` format. For example, to configure a build every 10 minutes, enter

```
*/10 * * * *
```

The final option you have is not to configure automatic builds in Hudson, and to rely on external triggers. The build can be triggered by manually pressing the build button in Hudson's dashboard, or a "post-commit hook" in source code management tools that support hooks. The post-commit hook is a good way to integrate Hudson with unsupported version control systems like git. From your project's post-commit hook, you would execute a command like this:

```
curl http://your-build-server:8080/job/job-name/build
```

After you have configured the build triggers as desired, add a build step to run a shell script. This is the script that Hudson will run when it comes time to build the project. As a rule, this script should not be very long or complicated. You do not want build failures to be caused by errors in the script that invokes the build, only by errors in building the software and running the tests. If building your application depends on a lot of logic in the build script, then create the build script as a file in your version control system and call that script from Hudson's shell script step. In that way you can track changes to the script's logic alongside changes to the app source code. Running unit tests in a target set up by Xcode requires only a one-line script. Check the name of the test target in Xcode; it's usually the name of your app followed by "Tests," as in "Temperature

ConverterTests" earlier in this chapter. The script to build and run your tests from
Hudson is:[3]

```
#!/bin/bash
```

```
xcodebuild -configuration Debug -target "Temperature ConverterTests" build
```

That's all there is to it. Save your job's configuration, and it's good to go. Rather than
waiting for the next scheduled build, you may want to press the Build Now button to
check that you configured everything correctly. Hudson saves the console logs of its
builds, so if anything goes wrong you can inspect the logs for error messages and address
the problem. After your job has been built at least once, its page on Hudson will show
the history and status of the project, as shown in Figure 4.11. The "weather" icon
over the build history summarizes the project's stability: to bring sunshine into your life,
you need a project that rarely fails a test.

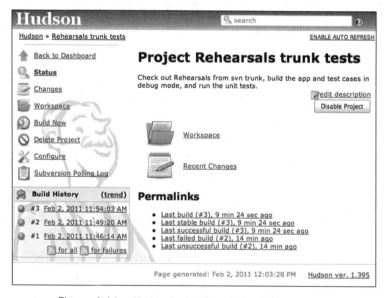

Figure 4.11   Hudson's dashboard showing the status
and stability of a project.

---

3. This script assumes that the Xcode project file for your app gets checked out into the top level
of Hudson's workspace for the build. If this is not the case, you will need to modify the script to
`cd` to the appropriate folder before running `xcodebuild`. The `WORKSPACE` environment variable
points to the top-level folder in Hudson's workspace, so if your project is in a folder called
Source you would need to `cd  ${WORKSPACE}/Source`.

Hudson offers a couple of options for notifying you about your build status. In Figure 4.11 you will see icons in the build history box for RSS feeds, allowing you to subscribe to a list of every build result or just the failed builds. Additionally, if you configure an outgoing mail server in Hudson's settings, you can set up each job to email developers about failed builds.

CruiseControl

CruiseControl is not a single continuous integration tool. The name "CruiseControl" is given by the ThoughtWorks company to two different continuous integration products.[4] CruiseControl.net is designed for developers working with Microsoft's platform, so in this section I'll concen trate on the cross-platform product written in Ruby, CruiseControl.rb. You can download the latest version of CruiseControl.rb from http://cruisecontrolrb.thoughtworks.com/. After you have done so, navigate to the folder where you downloaded the tool using Terminal.app, and decompress the package before changing directory to the folder containing the unpacked CruiseControl:

```
$ tar xzf cruisecontrol-1.4.0.tar.gz
$ cd cruisecontrol-1.4.0
```

Now you can add a project to CruiseControl. You do this with the following command:

```
$ ./cruise add project-name --source-control git --repository
http://yourserver/path/to/repository.git
```

where you should replace the project name and the contents of the **--source-control** and **--repository** arguments with values applicable to your project. CruiseControl is compatible with a more modern subset of version control systems than Hudson: subversion, git, mercurial, and bazaar are all supported.

Before you can launch CruiseControl, you must tell it how to run your tests. CruiseControl project configurations are stored as Ruby source code in files named `~/.cruise/projects/project-name/cruise_config.rb`. Open this file in your favorite text editor and set the project's `build_command` variable to the command needed to run your tests:

```
Project.configure do |project|
  project.build_command = 'xcodebuild -configuration Debug -target "Temperature\
ConverterTests" build'
end
```

You can configure other options here, such as the interval at which CruiseControl polls your version control system (the default is 30 seconds), and email addresses to

---

4. Matthew Foemmel at ThoughtWorks was one of the pioneers of Continuous Integration and coined the term along with Martin Fowler in their article "Continuous Integration": http://martinfowler.com/articles/continuousIntegration.html.

notify when builds fail. After you have set the project up according to your needs, save `cruise_config.rb` and launch CruiseControl.

```
$ ./cruise start
```

Like Hudson, CruiseControl's output is exposed via a browser-based dashboard. Go to http://localhost:3333/ to see the CruiseControl dashboard (Figure 4.12). The status and history of each project is listed, and you can click each build result to see details like the console log and the commit message that triggered the build. You can subscribe to an RSS feed for each project to see up-to-date build results.

Figure 4.12   The CruiseControl.rb dashboard,
showing the status of a project.

Summary

Apple's developer tools come with powerful and mature support for test-driven development. As with every aspect of software development, developers have their own requirements and preferences, which may not be met by the built-in tools. Plenty of third-party alternatives and extensions exist so you can set up an environment suited to your project and way of working.

Throughout the rest of this book, the examples will focus on capabilities provided by OCUnit. By all means investigate the alternatives presented in this chapter; whether you find something that suits you better than OCUnit or not, you'll be able to follow the rest of this book without needing to install any additional tools.

5

Test-Driven Development of an iOS App

Over the next few chapters, you'll see an iOS app developed from initial specification to functional product. Of course, with this book being about test-driven development, the app will be written in a test-first fashion. This chapter defines the application's specification and sets out the strategy for developing the functionality. At the end of this part of the book, you'll have a fully working—though by no means full-featured—app, supported by a suite of unit tests. You'll also have seen how the tests help to design and implement the app code. The full project is available from https://github.com/iamleeg/BrowseOverflow, should you want to build the app yourself or even extend it.

Product Goal

The app, called BrowseOverflow, gives users access to recent questions about iOS development on the stackoverflow.com website. Users can easily find recently asked questions on relevant topics and see the answers that visitors to the site have contributed.

StackOverflow

I'm not associated with the company behind Stack Overflow: Stack Overflow Internet Services, Inc. I just think that stackoverflow.com is a great resource for iOS developers. It also happens to have a simple API, making it easy to create a nontrivial demo app in the limited space available in a book like this, and the content is made available under a Creative Commons license. If you have questions about iOS app programming or any other coding topic, stackoverflow.com ought to be your first port of call.

You can use Stack Overflow's API without registering for an API key. Your app will be limited in the number of requests it can make per unit time, so if you intend to distribute a (test-driven!) app based on the code here, you should register and get an API key from http://stackapps.com/.

Use Cases

On launching BrowseOverflow, the user sees a list of topics, shown in Figure 5.1. Each topic represents a tag on Stack Overflow. Questions are tagged to indicate what subjects they address.

Figure 5.1   As a stack overflow browser, I want to see a list of topics
related to iOS development.

Tapping on a topic in the list loads a list of the 20 most recently asked questions tagged with that topic, presented in chronological order. A sample list is shown in Figure 5.2. In addition to the titles of the questions, users can see who asked each question (including an avatar image) and the question's score (how many times it has been voted up and down on the website).

Figure 5.2   As a stack overflow browser, given that I have tapped on a
topic, I want to see a list of questions that have been asked on that topic.

Retrieving the list of questions clearly requires a network connection, and even if the
app has a Wi-Fi or 3G data network available, it's still possible for the connection to
stackoverflow.com to fail. If it does, BrowseOverflow should show a message explaining
that current questions are not available (demonstrated in Figure 5.3).

Figure 5.3   As a stack overflow browser, given that the app encountered
a problem, I want to be told about it.

Tapping on a question title in one of the lists of questions presents a view showing more information about this question. The full question text is available, along with each of the answers. The accepted answer (if there is one) is indicated with a tick and appears directly below the question. Following this, the other answers are presented in descending order of score. The name and avatar of the writer of each answer is presented along with that answer, as shown in Figure 5.4. As with the question list, BrowseOverflow should display a message explaining that answers aren't available if it cannot retrieve the information from the Stack Overflow website.

Figure 5.4   As a stack overflow browser, given that I have tapped on a question, I want to see answers people have provided to that question.

Because the preceding views represent a master-detail presentation of the information on the website, the overall flow through the app should use standard iOS navigation controls, starting from the tag list, navigating through the question list, to an individual question and its answers.

Plan of Attack

There are numerous approaches to implement an app like this one. Many developers would develop a single feature at a time, ensuring that all the functionality behind one button works completely before moving on to the next button. Others would work on each view separately, getting all of the functionality in the topics view working before working on the questions list view. In each case, it's common to take an "outside-in" approach, in which you put the view together first, then enough controller code to allow users to interact with the view as it is envisaged to behave in the app, then finally to flesh out the functionality until the requirement is fully satisfied.

Whichever way you slice the cake, it's usual in agile development teams to work on a single story or small collection of stories for a short period of time (usually known as an iteration or a sprint), with the aim of providing satisfactory implementations of those stories at the end of the sprint. I'm going to take a different approach: My goal here is to show how you can work with test-driven development on code that uses the various parts of the iOS APIs. To support that goal, I'm going to develop this app thematically, starting with the model in Chapters 6 and 7, then the controllers in Chapters 8 and 9 (BrowseOverflow does not contain any custom views). Finally, in Chapter 10, I'll put the classes together to form the complete app.

In this example, the preceding limited and well-defined specification should help to avoid any YAGNI[1] that would normally arise from building an app "from the inside out." If I do find that things go a little weird along the way, I can always refactor! That's one of the benefits of supporting the code with tests; you can make any changes you want and get fast feedback on whether anything broke (and if so, what).

Getting Started

It's time to set up the project to manage the BrowseOverflow application and test case sources. Launch Xcode and create a new project based on the Master-Detail Application iOS app template. In the project options, you'll want to check the Include Unit Tests box, but you won't need Core Data, so leave that option unchecked. This app will provide only iPhone views, so choose iPhone for the device family. Choose somewhere to save the project, and create a local git repository if you want to work with that version control system.

If you followed along with that paragraph you'll already have a working app, although it doesn't really do much. You can build and run it, and enjoy your lovingly crafted product: an empty table as shown in Figure 5.5.

---

1. YAGNI is short for "Ya Ain't Gonna Need It," a concept introduced in Chapter 2.

Figure 5.5   A new project, ready to be turned into
BrowseOverflow.app.

Apple's Template Code

Now that you've created a new project, you'll see that there's a lot of code in it already.
The Master-Detail app target contains a few classes: the app delegate and the view controllers. The BrowseOverflow app could make use of both of these classes. Should you go
through and create tests for all that template code?

The answer is no—or not yet, anyway. Because you haven't yet gotten around to implementing any of the app's behavior, no requirements exist yet for what that code should do.
It can't possibly be correct or broken (as long as it compiles); it's just there.

When you come to add features to the app, you'll find that you want to create some behavior in these classes. That's the time to write the tests that test the behavior you want. If
you find that the template code already does what you need, that's great; there's nothing
to write. If the tests fail, you can edit the code until it does what you need. There's an old
hacker maxim that seems appropriate here: "If it ain't broke, fix it 'til it is."

One thing you will need to change is Apple's test fixture, which is named
BrowseOverflowTests by default. The template code includes a call to STFail( ), which
means that the tests automatically fail even though you haven't written any bugs yet! You
won't need that fixture at all, so it's safe to delete the BrowseOverflowTests.h and
BrowseOverflowTests.m files from your project.

6

The Data Model

The first thing I want to implement is the model layer, the objects that represent the information in the BrowseOverflow app. I'll take another look at the app description from Chapter 5, "Test-Driven Development of an iOS App," this time with a requirements engineering hat on. Specifically, I'll use a technique called *domain analysis* to see what classes and objects are required in the app.

In domain analysis, you look at the requirements with a view to deciding what objects exist in the problem domain and what their responsibilities are. Nouns in the software requirements represent either objects or properties of some object. Verbs represent actions (that is, methods), and the object and subject of the verb tell you which object calls the method on which other object.

The idea is that you can identify the classes and interactions in the problem domain, and then design your software classes and objects to reflect the domain model. Because the software model is based on the problem domain, it's unlikely that you'll write code that doesn't or can't satisfy the problem conditions. It also has the benefit that it's easier for coders to talk to users and other stakeholders about the software because you're all using the same terminology to talk about the same parts of the problem.

An example from a different problem domain is an email application. Email has almost completely replaced postal mail, in which a sender wrote a message and addressed it to the reader so that the postal service could determine how to deliver it to—in the context of a business anyway—the recipient's inbox. Having read the message, the recipient could throw it away or file it into a labeled folder. It is easy to see how the various objects—message, address, inbox and so on—and verbs—writing, reading, delivering—from the problem domain found their way into the software.

Topics

Enough talk; let's look at an example from the BrowseOverflow problem domain. One sentence from Chapter 5 says:

> On launching BrowseOverflow, the user sees a list of topics... Each topic represents a tag on Stack Overflow. Questions are tagged to indicate what subjects they address.

I shall assume that the user is not part of the software system (it's hard to sell an app if the only user is the app itself). However, the list of topics should be part of the system. It seems that a "topic" is an object in the problem domain. It's time to write a test to prove that the app provides a `Topic` class. In fact, because `Topic` will be a class in the app, I'll create a new `TopicTests` fixture in the BrowseOverflowTests target (not the app target), and add the test to that:

```
@implementation TopicTests

- (void)testThatTopicExists {
    Topic *newTopic = [[Topic alloc] init];
    STAssertNotNil(newTopic,
        @"should be able to create a Topic instance");
}

@end
```

You can't run that test; it won't even compile. That's because there isn't yet a `Topic` class at all. Add a new `NSObject` subclass called `Topic` to the project. When Xcode asks which targets to add the new file to, check both the app target and the test bundle target. (This is required to work around a problem with unit test bundles: They don't link symbols from their host apps correctly.) Now the class exists, and you can tell the test fixture about it:

```
#import "TopicTests.h"
#import "Topic.h"

@implementation TopicTests

- (void)testThatTopicExists {
    Topic *newTopic = [[Topic alloc] init];
    STAssertNotNil(newTopic,
        @"should be able to create a Topic instance");
}

@end
```

Run the test again: That change was sufficient to get this test to pass.

The user needs to see the topics, so the `Topic` class needs some property that can represent it in the UI—a textual name seems appropriate. The list of topics is presented to the user at launch, so the objects can be created with the names they'll have throughout the lifetime of the app. I would like to be able to do this:

```
- (void)testThatTopicCanBeNamed {
    Topic *namedTopic = [[Topic alloc] initWithName: @"iPhone"];
    STAssertEqualObjects(namedTopic.name, @"iPhone",
        @"the Topic should have the name I gave it");
}
```

That won't compile, because the compiler finds that `Topic` doesn't have a `name` property. Add it to the class interface:

```
@property (readonly) NSString *name;[1]
```

and to the implementation:

```
@synthesize name;
```

Try running the tests again. That last change lets the tests compile, but the sweet smell of success is still beyond our grasp. In fact, the test runner crashes. Why?

```
2011-02-17 16:04:33.463 BrowseOverflow[3146:207] -[Topic initWithName:]:
unrecognized selector sent to instance 0x4e3f980
```

Add that initializer method to the `Topic` class.

```
- (id)initWithName:(NSString *)newName {
    if ((self = [super init])) {
        name = [newName copy];
    }
    return self;
}
```

Testing Memory Management

The code examples throughout this book rely on Automatic Reference Counting (ARC), a compiler-supported memory management technique introduced with Xcode 4.2 for iOS developers using the iOS 4 and 5 SDKs. Test-driven development doesn't require ARC, so it's possible to use the techniques described here with manual memory management (or garbage collected Objective-C on the Mac OS X SDK) should you need to.

However, memory management doesn't really lend itself to automated testing. The only method Foundation classes provide to inspect memory-management code is the reference count, and this is not trustworthy enough to form the basis of a repeatable test. Sometimes the Foundation or UIKit library might want to retain an object; sometimes an object's reference count doesn't change when it's released; sometimes something happens on a different thread to change the retain count. Because of this, asking an object for its reference count or using a mock to find out when retain or release are called is not going to lead to repeatable results.

The rules for memory management in an iOS app are very straightforward, and described by Apple at http://developer.apple.com/library/ios/#documentation/cocoa/conceptual/MemoryMgmt/MemoryMgmt.html. Following those rules, and testing for problems using Instruments, are both good ways to ensure that your objects live for the correct amount of time in your app.

---

1. Notice that we have no requirements describing whether this property should be atomic or nonatomic, so I have used the default behavior. On the other hand, there doesn't appear to be a need to change a `Topic`'s name after it's been created, so it's appropriate to create a read-only property: The application doesn't need the (untested) setter method.

Now the test succeeds, and BrowseOverflow's topic objects have a name property that works in the way specified by the tests. The one thing we've yet to address from the preceding sentence is that a `Topic` object should identify a tag from the stackoverflow.com question tags. It happens that a tag is just another string, so it can be handled in the same way as the name property. I'll add another parameter to the initializer, so the test for the tag looks like this:

```
- (void)testThatTopicHasATag {
    Topic *taggedTopic = [[Topic alloc] initWithName: @"iPhone"
        tag: @"iphone"];
    STAssertEqualObjects(taggedTopic.tag, @"iphone",
        @"Topics need to have tags");
}
```

The procedure to get this test passing is the same as with the name: Add the property and the new initializer.

This seems like a good time to stand back and look for opportunities to refactor. Currently, each test uses a different initializer: `-init`, `-initWithName:` and `-initWithName:tag:`. In fact, if each test used the "full" two-argument initializer, all the tests would still work and there would be less code in the `Topic` class. It doesn't seem like there's a need for the `-initWithName:` initializer at all. Change the tests so that the fixture uses only one initializer for `Topic`:

```
@implementation TopicTests

- (void)testThatTopicExists {
    Topic *newTopic = [[Topic alloc] initWithName: @"iPhone"
        tag: @"iphone"];
    STAssertNotNil(newTopic,
        @"should be able to create a Topic instance");
}

- (void)testThatTopicCanBeNamed {
    Topic *namedTopic = [[Topic alloc] initWithName: @"iPhone"
        tag: @"iphone"];
    STAssertEqualObjects(namedTopic.name, @"iPhone",
        @"the Topic should have the name I gave it");
}

- (void)testThatTopicHasATag {
    Topic *taggedTopic = [[Topic alloc] initWithName: @"iPhone"
        tag: @"iphone"];
    STAssertEqualObjects(taggedTopic.tag, @"iphone",
        @"Topics need to have tags");
}

@end
```

Now that there's no need for the `-initWithName:` initializer, you can delete it from the `Topic` class.[2] The recent changes bring an interesting observation: It looks like all the tests work with identical `Topic` instances. They could all use the same instance, defined as part of the fixture. In other words, we could create a single topic instance in `-setUp`, use it in every test, and then clean it up in `-tearDown`. Make that change, and the test fixture interface will look like this:

```
#import <SenTestingKit/SenTestingKit.h>
#import <UIKit/UIKit.h>

@class Topic;

@interface TopicTests : SenTestCase {
    Topic *topic;
}

@end
```

and the implementation like this:

```
#import "TopicTests.h"
#import "Topic.h"

@implementation TopicTests

- (void)setUp {
    topic = [[Topic alloc] initWithName: @"iPhone" tag: @"iphone"];
}

- (void)tearDown {
    topic = nil;
}

- (void)testThatTopicExists {
    STAssertNotNil(topic, @"should be able to create a Topic instance");
}

- (void)testThatTopicCanBeNamed {
    STAssertEqualObjects(topic.name, @"iPhone",
        @"the Topic should have the name I gave it");
}

- (void)testThatTopicHasATag {
    STAssertEqualObjects(topic.tag, @"iphone",
        @"the Topic should have the tag I gave it");
}

@end
```

2. And indeed you should. Because it's no longer being tested, you don't want users of the `Topic` class to rely on it working properly in the future.

In the -tearDown method, the test fixture's Topic is set to nil so that the different tests each get a fresh instance (in fact, that's guaranteed by OCUnit itself; destroying the variable in -tearDown documents that fact explicitly). There's one remaining thing that a Topic needs. Examine this sentence from the requirements:

> Tapping on a topic in the list loads a list of the 20 most recently asked questions tagged with that topic, presented in chronological order.

There should be a way to get from a topic to "a list of...questions." Reading on, it appears that questions have a number of different properties associated with them. This suggests that questions should be represented as a class in the problem domain, and that this should be reflected in the software domain by having the Topic class provide access to a list of Questions. The relationship is shown in Figure 6.1 as a UML[3] diagram.

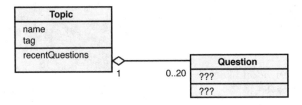

Figure 6.1   UML diagram showing the relationship between Topics and Questions.

The topic object needs to do something to give us "a list" of something. Because we haven't investigated the requirements about questions yet, we can't say anything about what objects in that list should do. For now, it's enough to ensure that Topics can provide a list:

```
- (void)testForAListOfQuestions {
    STAssertTrue([[topic recentQuestions] isKindOfClass:
        [NSArray class]],
        @"Topics should provide a list of recent questions");
}
```

Of course, that test fails, so implement a new method on Topic to pass the test (and don't forget to declare the method in Topic.h, too).

```
- (NSArray *)recentQuestions {
    return [NSArray array];
}
```

Now the test passes, but it doesn't seem very satisfying. The requirements call for a "list of questions," and all the code does is provide a list. Not a list of anything, just an empty list. Before defining the list of questions in more detail, it will be useful to have a better idea of what a question is.

---

3. UML, the Unified Modeling Language, is a standardized way to graphically model object-oriented systems. More information is available at www.uml.org/.

Questions

Let's put the Topic class on one side for the moment, because we've gotten to a point in implementing the app's requirements that needs us to think about what's required of a question. In fact, we need to do that in order to complete the implementation of Topic. The first thing to notice is the definition of a Topic's list that we used in the last section. That specified that the list must be "in chronological order," so questions must need a date property that can be used for sorting. Question is a new class, so create a new QuestionTests fixture to test it in the BrowseOverflowTests target, and add the first test:

```
@implementation QuestionTests

- (void)testQuestionHasADate {
    Question *question = [[Question alloc] init];
    STAssertTrue([question.date isKindOfClass: [NSDate class]],
        @"Question needs to provide its date");
}

@end
```

However, this test doesn't compile because there isn't a Question class yet. Here's the implementation of that class, to be added to both the app and test case targets. For brevity's sake the corresponding header file has been left out.

```
@implementation Question

- (NSDate *)date {
    return [NSDate date];
}

@end
```

That allows the test to pass, but it looks fishy. The iOS SDK documentation tells us that +[NSDate date] returns the *current* date, but what we want to know is the date the question was *asked*. Evidently the test is wrong. What we really need is some way for the code that creates a Question object to set the date at which it was asked. A setter would do the trick,[4] so I'll update the test:

```
- (void)testQuestionHasADate {
    Question *question = [[Question alloc] init];
    NSDate *testDate = [NSDate distantPast];
    question.date = testDate;
    STAssertEqualObjects(question.date, testDate,
        @"Question needs to provide its date");
}
```

---

4. As would an initializer parameter, in the same way that the Topic class was designed. This goes to show that testing doesn't limit the ways in which you can implement required behavior.

A simple read/write property on the `Question` class is sufficient to pass this test, and can replace the previous implementation of `-date`. You may be thinking that this represents a lot of work just to add a one-line property declaration to a class; can't we assume that Apple's implementation of `@synthesize` works properly? The point of the preceding test is not to show that the property works, but to demonstrate that the property is *needed* in the application. Test-driven development is helping to design the classes in the app by making us think about how we should fulfill the app's requirements in code. As a side effect, we get some safety against breaking things in the future. Should we decide later that these classes should provide a dynamic or hand-crafted implementation of the property, this test will ensure we keep the basic requirement that we can get and set the value.

What are the other requirements of question objects? Here's a relevant quote from the requirements:

> [...]in addition to the titles of the questions, users can see who asked each question (including an avatar image) and the question's score (how many times it has been voted up and down on the website).

Okay, titles must be easy to do. I'll move the question instance that was created in the `-testQuestionHasADate` test into the fixture, and add a test that ensures it has a title string. Similarly with scores, except that a score will be a `NSInteger` rather than a string.

```
#import "Question.h"
@implementation QuestionTests
{
    Question *question;
}

- (void)setUp {
    question = [[Question alloc] init];
    question.date = [NSDate distantPast];
    question.title = @"Do iPhones also dream of electric sheep?";
    question.score = 42;
}

- (void)tearDown {
    question = nil;
}

- (void)testQuestionHasADate {
    NSDate *testDate = [NSDate distantPast];
    question.date = testDate;
    STAssertEqualObjects(question.date, testDate,
        @"Question needs to provide its date");
}
```

```
- (void)testQuestionsKeepScore {
    STAssertEquals(question.score, 42,
        @"Questions need a numeric score");
}

- (void)testQuestionHasATitle {
    STAssertEqualObjects(question.title,
        @"Do iPhones also dream of electric sheep?",
        @"Question should know its title");
}

@end
```

As with the date test, getting this test to pass is trivial because you just need to add a read-write property with the correct name and type to `Question`.

The next stage is to decide what to do with the asker's name and image, and this is going to require a little more thought. On the face of it, it would appear that a `Person` is a different thing than a `Question` in the problem domain. However, the app needs only a couple of properties related to people: a name and an image. Wouldn't it be easy just to add those properties to `Question`, so we could ask for `question.askerName` and `question.askerImage`? Yes, it would, but read on a little in the requirements:

The name and avatar of the writer of each answer is presented along with that answer…

So the app will also need the name and an image of the Person who provides an answer. I'm jumping ahead a little here, but it's obvious that if the code for the asker's name and avatar go into `Question`, we'll just need to write the same code again for the class that describes answers later. I could have added the properties to `Question` and then refactored them out to a `Person` class later, but spotting this association now lets me shortcut that process. This is an example of applying the System Metaphor idea introduced in Chapter 2, "Techniques for Test-Driven Development"; it seems clear that a `Person` is a top-level concept in this app so should be treated as such during development.

People

Unless the artist formerly known as Prince changes career and becomes an iOS developer, it seems likely that the name of a `Person` can be represented as a string. Deciding what to do about a `Person`'s avatar needs a little more thought. There are many ways to represent an image in an iOS app: a URL that can be used to retrieve the image, the image data, or a `CGImageRef` or `UIImage` that represents the image directly. Which should the `Person` class provide?

This is to a large extent a matter of personal preference. My opinion is that the URL is a good fit here. It means that the data model is kept comparatively simple, and the logic over when and how to retrieve image contents is dealt with at the controller level.

With that decision made, the `PersonTests` fixture is easy to design:

```
@implementation PersonTests

- (void)setUp {
    person = [[Person alloc] initWithName: @"Graham Lee"
        avatarLocation: @"http://example.com/avatar.png"];
}

- (void)tearDown {
    person = nil;
}

- (void)testThatPersonHasTheRightName {
    STAssertEqualObjects(person.name, @"Graham Lee",
        @"expecting a person to provide its name");
}

- (void)testThatPersonHasAnAvatarURL {
    NSURL *url = person.avatarURL;
    STAssertEqualObjects([url absoluteString],
        @"http://example.com/avatar.png",
        @"The Person's avatar should be represented by a URL");
}

@end
```

The Person class itself is two straightforward read-only properties, along with this code to initialize the properties:

```
- (id)initWithName:(NSString *)aName avatarLocation:(NSString *)location {
    if ((self = [super init])) {
        name = [aName copy];
        avatarURL = [[NSURL alloc] initWithString: location];
    }
    return self;
}
```

Connecting Questions to Other Classes

The reason I originally left the `Topic` alone to start work on `Question` was that I needed to see what a `Question` looked like before I could say what a list of questions in chronological order looked like. I didn't need to go quite as far as I did with `Question` before turning back to the interaction with `Topic`: It's just easier for you, my beloved readers, if I don't keep changing the subject all over the place. But speaking of changing the subject, let's add a new feature to `Topic`.

So, how would I like to use code that returns an ordered list of questions, and how should I test that the questions are in the correct order? Unfortunately, although we're told that the list must be "in chronological order," the requirements don't specify *in which direction*—that is, whether earlier questions should appear before later questions, or vice versa. I'll follow convention offered by the iOS Mail app, and a number of third-party apps, in putting newer questions near the top of the list: I should make a note to talk to the customer about that requirement.[5]

Okay, first I'll make sure that I can tell a `Topic` that it has a `Question` and see the list of questions for a `Topic`. In fact, before that, I'll want to check that a `Topic` to which no questions have been added actually does contain no questions. Here are both additions to `TopicTests`:

```
- (void)testForInitiallyEmptyQuestionList {
    STAssertEquals([[topic recentQuestions] count], (NSUInteger)0,
        @"No questions added yet, count should be zero");
}


- (void)testAddingAQuestionToTheList {
    Question *question = [[Question alloc] init];
    [topic addQuestion: question];
    STAssertEquals([[topic recentQuestions] count], (NSUInteger)1,
        @"Add a question, and the count of questions should go up");
}
```

The casts are necessary in these tests because OCUnit compares the type of arguments to `STAssertEquals()` in addition to their values. Notice that the test to add a question to the list modifies the topic's list of questions. Won't that break other tests that expect an empty list? No. Remember that each test is executed in its own instance of the fixture class, fresh from having run `-setUp`. The outcome of one test can't affect the behavior of another.

Recall the implementation of `-[Topic recentQuestions]` provided in a previous section: It always returns an empty list. That means that the first of these two tests already passes (the empty list has zero members), but the other test does not pass because there's no `-addQuestion:` method yet. Add that method and somewhere for it to put the questions:

```
@implementation Topic
{
    NSArray *questions;
}
// ...
- (id)initWithName:(NSString *)newName tag: (NSString *)newTag {
```

5. Because the customer is me, I doubt there'll be an issue. The point I'm making here is that because test-driven development makes you think about the app requirements in detail, you uncover problems like this before you get too far into coding up the objects that implement the problematic requirements.

```
    if ((self = [super init])) {
        name = [newName copy];
        tag = [newTag copy];
        questions = [[NSArray alloc] init];
    }
    return self;
}


- (void)addQuestion: (Question *)question {
    questions = [questions arrayByAddingObject: question];
}


@end
```

Now the test doesn't throw an "unrecognized selector" exception, but it still doesn't pass. That's because we still need to get the existing -recentQuestions method to return the list of questions.

```
- (NSArray *)recentQuestions {
    return questions;
}
```

Any list with zero or one objects is always guaranteed to be in chronological order. What about a list of two objects? Let's try it.

```
- (void)testQuestionsAreListedChronologically {
    Question *q1 = [[Question alloc] init];
    q1.date = [NSDate distantPast];

    Question *q2 = [[Question alloc] init];
    q2.date = [NSDate distantFuture];

    [topic addQuestion: q1];
    [topic addQuestion: q2];

    NSArray *questions = [topic recentQuestions];
    Question *listedFirst = [questions objectAtIndex: 0];
    Question *listedSecond = [questions objectAtIndex: 1];

    STAssertEqualObjects([listedFirst.date laterDate:
        listedSecond.date], listedFirst.date,
        @"The later question should appear first in the list");
}
```

The test fails. This is unsurprising, because we didn't do anything yet to control the order of the question list. Let's change the -recentQuestions method so that it sorts the questions by date.

```
- (NSArray *)recentQuestions {
    return [questions sortedArrayUsingComparator: ^(id obj1, id obj2) {
        Question *q1 = (Question *)obj1;
        Question *q2 = (Question *)obj2;
        return [q2.date compare: q1.date];
    }];
}
```

There—that works. (You can convince yourself of that by writing the complementary test, where the later question is added before the earlier question. It should pass.) That's nearly everything, but we need to ensure that only the newest 20 questions are shown:

```
- (void)testLimitOfTwentyQuestions {
    Question *q1 = [[Question alloc] init];
    for (NSInteger i = 0; i < 25; i++) {
        [topic addQuestion: q1];
    }
    STAssertTrue([[topic recentQuestions] count] < 21,
        @"There should never be more than twenty questions");
}
```

That doesn't work. We can see as many questions as have ever been added. There are two obvious ways to limit the number: Either put some logic into -addQuestion: to remove the twenty-first question if too many get added; or return only the first 20 questions in -recentQuestions no matter how many there really are. The second way is the easiest to get the test to pass, so let's try that:

```
- (NSArray *)recentQuestions {
    NSArray *sortedQuestions =  [questions sortedArrayUsingComparator:
    ^(id obj1, id obj2) {
        Question *q1 = (Question *)obj1;
        Question *q2 = (Question *)obj2;
        return = [q2.date compare: q1.date];
    }
    }];
    if ([sortedQuestions count] < 21) {
        return sortedQuestions;
    }
    else {
        return [sortedQuestions subarrayWithRange: NSMakeRange(0, 20)];
    }
}
```

That does work, but it doesn't seem very nice to me. The number of questions stored for any Topic could grow endlessly, and although the app would only see 20 of them, the rest would stay around, consuming memory. That's not a memory leak, but it is a stale reference problem. Because this app needs to run in the limited-memory environment of an iOS device, it would be good to address this problem straight away. I'll refactor the `Topic` class by reverting the last change and implementing the other option—namely, throwing away the earliest question in `-addQuestion:`. This will require using the same sorting logic that's in `-recentQuestions`, so my first refactoring step is to pull that out into a method that can be used from both of the other methods.

```
- (NSArray *)sortQuestionsLatestFirst: (NSArray *)questionList {
    return [questionList sortedArrayUsingComparator:
    ^(id obj1, id obj2) {
        Question *q1 = (Question *)obj1;
        Question *q2 = (Question *)obj2;
        return [q2.date compare: q1.date];
    }];
}


- (NSArray *)recentQuestions {
    return [self sortQuestionsLatestFirst: questions];
}
```

Now I can use that method to find the earliest question and discard it if there are too many questions.

```
- (void)addQuestion: (Question *)question {
    NSArray *newQuestions = [questions arrayByAddingObject: question];
    if ([newQuestions count] > 20) {
        newQuestions = [self sortQuestionsLatestFirst: newQuestions];
        newQuestions = [newQuestions subarrayWithRange:
            NSMakeRange(0, 20)];
    }
    questions = newQuestions;
}
```

Running the (unmodified) test suite shows that I haven't broken anything, so this implementation is just as useful as the first: I just happen to prefer it. Test-driven development motivates rapid addition of new functionality to your code, because you are free to make any change you want to your code and can rapidly get feedback on whether the change introduced any problems. It still gives you a chance to take a step back and change things to make them look, perform, or smell better.

This last section shows a very powerful benefit of test-driven development. At the beginning, we had two tests that worked using a very trivial implementation of the app code. The implementation was significantly modified, both to provide new functionality and to clean up the code. In each case, the tests of the original behavior were still present and demonstrated that the new changes had not broken existing code—that no regressions had been introduced by refactoring or by adding new features.

Answers

There's not much point in having questions that don't get answered (or is there?). The BrowseOverflow app calls for the ability to see the list of answers for any question. Many of the properties on `Answer` objects will be very similar to those already found on other classes, so to save a bit of time and a few trees, here's the test fixture for the familiar parts:

```
@implementation AnswerTests

- (void)setUp {
    answer = [[Answer alloc] init];
    answer.text = @"The answer is 42";
    answer.person = [[[Person alloc] initWithName: @"Graham Lee"
        avatarLocation: @"http://example.com/avatar.png"] autorelease];
    answer.score = 42;
}

- (void)tearDown {
    answer = nil;
}

- (void)testAnswerHasSomeText {
    STAssertEqualObjects(answer.text, @"The answer is 42",
        @"Answers need to contain some text");
}

- (void)testSomeoneProvidedTheAnswer {
    STAssertTrue([answer.person isKindOfClass: [Person class]],
        @"A Person gave this Answer");
}

- (void)testAnswersNotAcceptedByDefault {
    STAssertFalse(answer.accepted, @"Answer not accepted by default");
}

- (void)testAnswerCanBeAccepted {
    STAssertNoThrow(answer.accepted = YES,
        @"It is possible to accept an answer");
}

- (void)testAnswerHasAScore {
    STAssertTrue(answer.score == 42,
        @"Answer's score can be retrieved");
}

@end
```

You'll have enough experience now with implementing code based on test fixtures like this to fill in the implementation of `Answer` so far yourself. The interesting bit comes when linking `Answers` to `Questions`. We need the answers to be ranked in descending order of score, except that an accepted answer (if there is one) must come first. Let's add some tests to the `AnswerTests` fixture to show what those comparisons should look like.

```
- (void)setUp {
    answer = [[Answer alloc] init];
    answer.text = @"The answer is 42";
    answer.person = [[Person alloc] initWithName: @"Graham Lee"
        avatarLocation: @"http://example.com/avatar.png"];
    answer.score = 42;
    otherAnswer = [[Answer alloc] init];
    otherAnswer.text = @"I have the answer you need";
    otherAnswer.score = 42;
}


- (void)testAcceptedAnswerComesBeforeUnaccepted {
    otherAnswer.accepted = YES;
    otherAnswer.score = answer.score + 10;

    STAssertEquals([answer compare: otherAnswer], NSOrderedDescending,
        @"Accepted answer should come first");
    STAssertEquals([otherAnswer compare: answer], NSOrderedAscending,
        @"Unaccepted answer should come last");
}

- (void)testAnswersWithEqualScoresCompareEqually {
    STAssertEquals([answer compare: otherAnswer], NSOrderedSame,
        @"Both answers of equal rank");
    STAssertEquals([otherAnswer compare: answer], NSOrderedSame,
        @"Each answer has the same rank");
}

- (void)testLowerScoringAnswerComesAfterHigher {
    otherAnswer.score = answer.score + 10;
    STAssertEquals([answer compare: otherAnswer], NSOrderedDescending,
        @"Higher score comes first");
    STAssertEquals([otherAnswer compare: answer], NSOrderedAscending,
        @"Lower score comes last");
}
```

Notice the symmetric requirements in each test: If we require that a<b is true, we also need b>a to be true. You may choose to write those as separate tests, but I didn't, because they're testing identical requirements but in different ways. Here's an implementation of `-[Answer compare:]` that addresses all the requirements in the test fixture.

```
- (NSComparisonResult)compare:(Answer *)otherAnswer {
    if (accepted && !(otherAnswer.accepted)) {
        return NSOrderedAscending;
    } else if (!accepted && otherAnswer.accepted){
        return NSOrderedDescending;
    }
    if (score > otherAnswer.score) {
        return NSOrderedAscending;
    } else if (score < otherAnswer.score) {
        return NSOrderedDescending;
    } else {
        return NSOrderedSame;
    }
}
```

With a working comparison method, it should be easy to provide the list of answers for any question in the correct order.

```
@interface QuestionTests : SenTestCase {
    Question *question;
    Answer *lowScore;
    Answer *highScore;
}

@end

- (void)setUp {
    question = [[Question alloc] init];
    question.date = [NSDate distantPast];
    question.title = @"Do iPhones also dream of electric sheep?";
    question.score = 42;

    Answer *accepted = [[Answer alloc] init];
    accepted.score = 1;
    accepted.accepted = YES;
    [question addAnswer: accepted];

    lowScore = [[Answer alloc] init];
    lowScore.score = -4;
    [question addAnswer: lowScore];

    highScore = [[Answer alloc] init];
    highScore.score = 4;
    [question addAnswer: highScore];
}
```

```
- (void)tearDown {
    question = nil;
    lowScore = nil;
    highScore = nil;
}

- (void)testQuestionCanHaveAnswersAdded {
    Answer *myAnswer = [[Answer alloc] init];
    STAssertNoThrow([question addAnswer: myAnswer],
        @"Must be able to add answers");
}

- (void)testAcceptedAnswerIsFirst {
    STAssertTrue([[question.answers objectAtIndex: 0] isAccepted],
        @"Accepted answer comes first");
}

- (void)testHighScoreAnswerBeforeLow {
    NSArray *answers = question.answers;
    NSInteger highIndex = [answers indexOfObject: highScore];
    NSInteger lowIndex = [answers indexOfObject: lowScore];
    STAssertTrue(highIndex < lowIndex,
        @"High-scoring answer comes first");
}
```

There are a few problems with getting this to compile. I decided I wanted to use the
-[Answer isAccepted] method here, but it doesn't exist: I previously created a
@property for whether answers are accepted, but it doesn't provide that method.
Creating it is a simple refactoring exercise on the **Answer** class:

```
@property (getter=isAccepted) BOOL accepted;
```

The remaining compile problems relate to providing the methods we want to implement on **Question**: the new implementation follows:

```
@class Answer;
@interface Question : NSObject {
    NSMutableSet *answerSet;
}

@property (retain) NSDate *date;
@property (copy) NSString *title;
@property NSInteger score;
@property (readonly) NSArray *answers;

- (void)addAnswer: (Answer *)answer;

@end
```

```
#import "Question.h"
#import "Answer.h"
@implementation Question

@synthesize date;
@synthesize title;
@synthesize score;

- (id)init {
    if ((self = [super init])) {
        answerSet = [[NSMutableSet alloc] init];
    }
    return self;
}

- (void)addAnswer:(Answer *)answer {
    [answerSet addObject: answer];
}

- (NSArray *)answers {
    return [[answerSet allObjects]
        sortedArrayUsingSelector: @selector(compare:)];
}

@end
```

Notice that although the requirements on the list of questions in a topic and the list of answers are fairly similar, the implementations of each are quite different. Test-driven development still gives you lots of flexibility in how you write application code. You are not constrained to follow particular patterns or methods.

That's actually all we need from the data model, as far as it's possible to tell from the requirements. In the next chapter, we'll look at the application logic.

7

Application Logic

Now that I can create and manipulate objects that the user cares about working with in BrowseOverflow, it's time to think about hooking up with the real StackOverflow service so that the objects created in the app reflect the content of the site. This means going to the Stack Exchange API documentation at http://api.stackoverflow.com/1.1/usage and finding out how to consume their data.

Plan of Attack

According to the API documentation, StackOverflow has methods for requesting the questions in a topic, and the details for a question including the list of answers for that question. This does not validate the design for the domain model from Chapter 6, "The Data Model," but indicates that because it's a good fit for the data coming from the service, creating the objects we've designed from StackOverflow's data should be straightforward. The data will be sent in JSON format;[1] we need objects that can retrieve that, and construct our domain objects from the encoded data.

It's always good to have an endgame in mind. Remember the system metaphor described in Chapter 2, "Techniques for Test-Driven Development." The way in which I want to develop this application's logic is depicted in Figure 7.1. The app has a `StackOverflowManager`, which it can ask for questions associated with a particular Topic instance. That object fetches the JSON using a `StackOverflowCommunicator` object, and passes it to a `QuestionBuilder` that constructs the `Question` object. The `StackOverflowManager` communicates with the app via a delegate to find out whether to additionally fetch the answers and people associated with the question, before finally passing the completed `Question` object to the delegate. Similar interactions exist for an `AnswerBuilder` and `PersonBuilder` class.

---

1. JSON is the JavaScript Object Notation, a lightweight data markup format that's very similar to Apple's property list format. JSON is described in more detail at http://json.org.

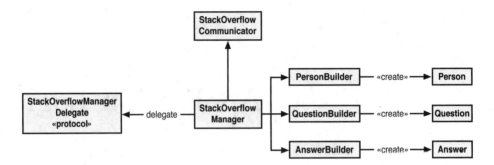

Figure 7.1   Class diagram for the proposed app logic classes.

In this interaction, the `StackOverflowManager` acts as a Façade to the domain logic. The app's controller can work with the model objects created here, without needing to know any of the details about the network connection, the object notation or how the objects are constructed. The various `Builder` classes encapsulate the creation of the model objects, to avoid making the manager too complicated. If the details of constructing a `Question`, for instance, were to change, then finding the relevant code in `Question Builder` is easier than grubbing through all the manager class's source to find the methods to update.

However, the tests could end up taking us in a different direction. We might find while implementing the code that the design planned previously is not suitable or that a better design presents itself. This is fine; all we need now is a high-level goal to aim for.

Design Patterns

Both the Façade and Builder patterns employed in this design are described in the classic book on the topic, *Design Patterns* by Gamma, Helm, Johnson, and Vlissides (also known as the "Gang of Four"). This book, and the general topic of design patterns, was introduced in Chapter 2.

Creating a Question

The first piece of the puzzle to implement is the ability to build a question. Let's start at the beginning: The application will ask the `StackOverflowManager` to provide its delegate with questions on a particular topic. That means that the `StackOverflowManager` class must have a delegate. It seems like it's time to create a `StackOverflowManagerTests` fixture, but because I'm concentrating on this workflow of creating questions, I'm going to call it `QuestionCreationTests` instead. The `QuestionCreationTests` class should be an Objective-C test case class, added to the `BrowseOverflowTests` target but not the `BrowseOverflow` app target.

```
#import "QuestionCreationTests.h"
#import "StackOverflowManager.h"

@implementation QuestionCreationTests
{
@private
    StackOverflowManager *mgr;
}

- (void)setUp {
    mgr = [[StackOverflowManager alloc] init];
}

- (void)tearDown {
    mgr = nil;
}

- (void)testNonConformingObjectCannotBeDelegate {
    STAssertThrows(mgr.delegate =
        (id <StackOverflowManagerDelegate>)[NSNull null],
        @"NSNull should not be used as the delegate as doesn't"
        @" conform to the delegate protocol");
}

- (void)testConformingObjectCanBeDelegate {
    id <StackOverflowManagerDelegate> delegate =
        [[MockStackOverflowManagerDelegate alloc] init];
    STAssertNoThrow(mgr.delegate = delegate,
        @"Object conforming to the delegate protocol should be used"
        @" as the delegate");
}

@end
```

Try running the tests now (Cmd-U), and you'll find quite a number of errors and warnings. For a very simple pair of tests, this puts a lot of requirements onto the product before the tests will pass. Even to get the code to compile it will need three additions:

- A `StackOverflowManager` class with a delegate property must be added to both the app and the test target. (It's usual to use a weak relationship between an object and its delegate, to avoid a retain cycle.)

- A `StackOverflowManagerDelegate` protocol, which the manager's delegate must conform to, must also be added to both targets. The `StackOverflow ManagerDelegate` protocol should extend the NSObject protocol.

- A `MockStackOverflowManagerDelegate` class. This will not be part of the product; it gives us a way to detect how the manager interacts with its delegate. It should just be added to the test case target.

Here's a first attempt at the interface and implementation of `StackOverflowManager`. The `#import` directives have been left out for clarity.

```
@interface StackOverflowManager : NSObject

@property (weak) id<StackOverflowManagerDelegate> delegate;

@end

@implementation StackOverflowManager

@synthesize delegate;

@end
```

This is, unfortunately, not a successful implementation. The `-testNonConforming ObjectCannotBeDelegate` test fails: It's possible to set objects that do not conform to the delegate protocol as delegates for the `StackOverflowManager` class. I want to forbid that so that I don't forget the protocol conformance—and therefore the methods I need to implement—on the real application's delegate. The benefit of enforcing the protocol conformance at runtime is that if someone does try to hook up an instance of the manager to the wrong delegate object, the error will be reported in the setup code rather than at an indeterminate time later in the running of the app.

Override the `-[StackOverflowManager setDelegate:]` accessor in the implementation. This also means changing the property's declaration from `@property (weak)` to `@property (weak, nonatomic)` so that you don't have to supply a matching get accessor implementation.

```
- (void)setDelegate:(id<StackOverflowManagerDelegate>)newDelegate {
    if (![newDelegate conformsToProtocol:
        @protocol(StackOverflowManagerDelegate)]) {
        [[NSException exceptionWithName: NSInvalidArgumentException
            reason:
            @"Delegate object does not conform to the delegate protocol"
            userInfo: nil] raise];
    }
    delegate = newDelegate;
}
```

Is that a complete implementation? There's one thing left to test: What happens if the application uses `nil` as the delegate? That should be supported, because maybe the app wants to fetch the content but doesn't care about the results. Another test on `QuestionCreationTests` shows that it currently isn't supported:

```
- (void)testManagerAcceptsNilAsADelegate {
    STAssertNoThrow(mgr.delegate = nil,
        @"It should be acceptable to use nil as an object's delegate");
}
```

Running the tests confirms that this test fails: `nil` cannot currently be used as the delegate. A small fix (highlighted in the following code) corrects this.

```
- (void)setDelegate:(id<StackOverflowManagerDelegate>)newDelegate {
    if (newDelegate &&
        ![newDelegate conformsToProtocol:
            @protocol(StackOverflowManagerDelegate)]) {
        [[NSException exceptionWithName: NSInvalidArgumentException
    reason: @"Delegate object does not conform to the delegate protocol"
        userInfo: nil] raise];
    }
    delegate = newDelegate;
}
```

Now that the manager has a delegate, it can start doing some real work. The first thing that ought to happen is that if the manager is asked to provide questions for some topic, it should contact the communicator class and tell it to download the JSON.

A little aside: I don't want to have to develop the `StackOverflowCommunicator` class now—I'm just trying to find out how the `StackOverflowManager` should behave. But it looks like the communicator class is already needed. The way to deal with this is to define the `StackOverflowCommunicator` class in both the app and the test target, and at the same time create a mock—a subclass called `MockStackOverflow Communicator`—just in the test case's target that implements the same methods. Where the tests need the manager to use the communicator class, they can hand it the mock. Later, when implementing the actual communicator class, I can see how it must be used because the interface will already be at least partially defined.

So, back to the test. The manager should ask the communicator for data when it's asked to provide questions on a particular topic. That interaction could look like this (a test in the `QuestionCreationTests` fixture):

```
- (void)testAskingForQuestionsMeansRequestingData {
    MockStackOverflowCommunicator *communicator =
        [[MockStackOverflowCommunicator alloc] init];
    mgr.communicator = communicator;
    Topic *topic = [[Topic alloc] initWithName: @"iPhone"
        tag: @"iphone"];
    [mgr fetchQuestionsOnTopic: topic];
    STAssertTrue([communicator wasAskedToFetchQuestions],
        @"The communicator should need to fetch data.");
}
```

To get this to build, we need to provide a communicator property on the `StackOverflowManager` class:

```
@property (strong) StackOverflowCommunicator *communicator;
```

This means defining the `StackOverflowCommunicator` class interface. At this time, the test and requirements indicate that there should be *some* method called on it, but there is no specification of *what* method. That gives us free rein to define the method as we see fit, especially because we can always change it later:

```
@interface StackOverflowCommunicator : NSObject {

}

- (void)searchForQuestionsWithTag: (NSString *)tag;

@end
```

However, we don't (yet!) need to implement that method on StackOverflow Communicator. Some people reviewing early drafts of the chapter suggested creating an empty implementation of -searchForQuestionsWithTag: here, in order to suppress a compiler warning. That doesn't quite match the "red-green-refactor" scheme. Right now we're concentrating on getting -testAskingForQuestionsMeansRequestingData to pass, and should work on that with extreme prejudice. Tidying up warnings can be left for the refactoring: you could also choose to leave that warning in as a reminder that StackOverflowCommunicator is not yet production ready. That's what warnings are for: They're notices by the compiler that something isn't quite right in your code.

What we *do* need is a mock implementation that provides proof that this method has been called. You may choose to reach for OCMock at this point, but it's very simple to create such a mock from scratch, as an Objective-C class that's added to the BrowseOverflowTests target:

```
@interface MockStackOverflowCommunicator : StackOverflowCommunicator
- (BOOL)wasAskedToFetchQuestions;
@end

@implementation MockStackOverflowCommunicator
{
    BOOL wasAskedToFetchQuestions;
}
- (void)searchForQuestionsWithTag:(NSString *)tag {
    wasAskedToFetchQuestions = YES;
}

- (BOOL)wasAskedToFetchQuestions {
    return wasAskedToFetchQuestions;
}

@end
```

All this implementation does is set a flag when the API method is called. It's not very exciting, and it's not as robust as a mock could be (for example, there's no error if the method is called twice in a test), but it'll do for now. The test will now compile, but it doesn't pass; we didn't implement the -[StackOverflowManager fetchQuestions OnTopic:] method yet. Here's an implementation that, when added to StackOverflowManager.m, passes the test:[2]

```
- (void)fetchQuestionsOnTopic:(Topic *)topic {
    [communicator searchForQuestionsWithTag: [topic tag]];
}
```

There isn't much to the implementation, but we had to write a lot of supporting code to get to this point. That isn't a problem, because a lot of questions were raised—and answered—in writing all that additional code.

Assume for the moment that the StackOverflowCommunicator does its magic (which it will later, when we get around to constructing that class). Two possibilities exist for what happens next:

- The communicator couldn't retrieve information from the Stack Overflow website and tells the manager what went wrong.

- The communicator received some JSON data and sends it back to the manager to make some questions.

Both of these cases must be handled in the application, which means that *both cases must be tested*. A common mistake—not just in TDD, but in any discipline of software engineering—is to only ask about, code and test the "happy path" without specifying or discovering what happens in case of error. Such oversight can lead to software that crashes and burns horribly when presented with unexpected situations—or worse, software that tries to carry on obliviously after an important error has occurred. Even though you're using test-driven development now, a little humility can still go a long way.

Let's start by dealing with the error case. We'll assume that the communicator informs the manager about the error it encountered. The manager should tell its delegate about the problem, but being a Façade, it should report an error at a higher level (that is, "getting the questions you wanted failed," not "looking up a DNS entry failed"). The communication error should still be made available as the underlying error so that if we need error-reporting behavior (for the app's support staff, for example), this error can be seen. The following tests added to the QuestionCreationTests fixture encapsulate those requirements.

```
- (void)testErrorReturnedToDelegateIsNotErrorNotifiedByCommunicator {
    MockStackOverflowManagerDelegate *delegate =
        [[MockStackOverflowManagerDelegate alloc] init];
    mgr.delegate = delegate;
    NSError *underlyingError = [NSError errorWithDomain: @"Test domain"
        code: 0 userInfo: nil];
```

---

2. Don't forget to add the method declaration to StackOverflowManager.h too, so that the method becomes part of the class's API. In general I'll leave this out: Methods on a class that are called from tests are by definition part of that class's interface, so should be defined in the @interface.

```
    [mgr searchingForQuestionsFailedWithError: underlyingError];
    STAssertFalse(underlyingError == [delegate fetchError],
        @"Error should be at the correct level of abstraction");
}


- (void)testErrorReturnedToDelegateDocumentsUnderlyingError {
    MockStackOverflowManagerDelegate *delegate =
        [[MockStackOverflowManagerDelegate alloc] init];
    mgr.delegate = delegate;
    NSError *underlyingError = [NSError errorWithDomain: @"Test domain"
        code: 0 userInfo: nil];
    [mgr searchingForQuestionsFailedWithError: underlyingError];
    STAssertEqualObjects([[[delegate fetchError] userInfo]
        objectForKey: NSUnderlyingErrorKey], underlyingError,
        @"The underlying error should be available to client code");
}
```

It's worth refactoring these tests to move all the common code into a single spot. Before implementing the -searchingForQuestionsFailedWithError: method, notice that the mock delegate needs a -fetchError method to show the test what error it received from the manager. That means that the manager must have some way to signal an error to its delegate, which in turn means a method on the delegate protocol:

```
- (void)fetchingQuestionsOnTopic: (Topic *)topic
                 failedWithError: (NSError *)error;
```

In our mock delegate, the implementation of this method should just squirrel the error away so that the test can later retrieve and examine what the manager object sent.

```
@interface MockStackOverflowManagerDelegate : NSObject
    <StackOverflowManagerDelegate>
@property (strong) NSError *fetchError;
@end


@implementation MockStackOverflowManagerDelegate

@synthesize fetchError;

- (void)fetchingQuestionsOnTopic: (Topic *)topic
                 failedWithError: (NSError *)error {
    self.fetchError = error;
}

@end
```

That's enough to support implementing the method that's being tested, which goes on StackOverflowManager. Notice that the implementation introduces a couple of new constants, which are declared in StackOverflowManager.h like this:

```
extern NSString *StackOverflowManagerError;

enum {
    StackOverflowManagerErrorQuestionSearchCode
};
```

The method implementation and the definition of the string constant both go in `StackOverflowManager.m`.

```
- (void)searchingForQuestionsFailedWithError:(NSError *)error {
    NSDictionary *errorInfo = [NSDictionary dictionaryWithObject: error
        forKey: NSUnderlyingErrorKey];
    NSError *reportableError = [NSError
        errorWithDomain: StackOverflowManagerSearchFailedError
                code: StackOverflowManagerErrorQuestionSearchCode
            userInfo:errorInfo];
    [delegate fetchingQuestionsOnTopic: nil
                failedWithError: reportableError];
}

//...

@end

NSString *StackOverflowManagerError = @"StackOverflowManagerError";
```

Although this method passes its tests, it doesn't seem like the method provides enough utility to complete the API contract. The delegate method includes a 'topic' parameter, explaining which topic the manager couldn't download the content for; but currently, that parameter is set to nil.

Do we need it? Take another look at the description of the app in Chapter 5. "Test-Driven Development of an iOS App." The "landing" view contains a list of topics, but no questions, so although the app needs multiple topics at that point, it probably won't need to fetch questions for any of them. The next view contains a set of questions for one particular topic, so here the app does need the manager to retrieve questions; but there's only one topic involved. It seems that this parameter is extraneous, so remove it to change the delegate method signature in both the interface and implementation to:

```
- (void)fetchingQuestionsFailedWithError: (NSError *)error;
```

It's easy to then change the implementation and the tests to use the updated method signature. Build the project, and then use Xcode's Issue Navigator (the keyboard shortcut is Cmd-4) to find and fix all the compiler warnings and errors.

Okay, so that's the one identified failure case dealt with. The next part of the story is that the communicator retrieves some JSON and sends it to the manager. The manager's job is to pass this JSON to a `QuestionBuilder` object that can create `Question` objects. What we need can be described by this test in the `QuestionCreationTests` fixture:

```
- (void)testQuestionJSONIsPassedToQuestionBuilder {
    FakeQuestionBuilder *builder = [[FakeQuestionBuilder alloc] init];
    mgr.questionBuilder = builder;
    [mgr receivedQuestionsJSON: @"Fake JSON"];
    STAssertEqualObjects(builder.JSON, @"Fake JSON",
        @"Downloaded JSON is sent to the builder");
    mgr.questionBuilder = nil;
}
```

Again, let's take a look at what is needed to make this work. The `FakeQuestion
Builder` is, as the name suggests, the fake version of a `QuestionBuilder`. We don't
have a `QuestionBuilder` class yet, so that class's interface needs to be defined in both
the app and the test case target: It can be a subclass of `NSObject`. We know that it needs
to receive the string from the manager and return question objects it finds by parsing the
string as JSON. Looking at the problem more closely, there's nothing we've done yet that
stops the `QuestionBuilder` from receiving *any* string, which might not be JSON—and
even if it is, might not be usable to create questions. Taking all that together, the
`QuestionBuilder` interface should look like this:

```
- (NSArray *)questionsFromJSON: (NSString *)objectNotation
                        error: (NSError **)error;
```

The fake version—a subclass of `QuestionBuilder` that is defined in the test case target alone— needs to keep a reference to the JSON it receives; we don't (yet) need to
consider the return value or error parameter, so returning `nil` is fine. The header for
`FakeQuestionBuilder` looks like this:

```
#import <Foundation/Foundation.h>
#import "QuestionBuilder.h"

@class Question;

@interface FakeQuestionBuilder : QuestionBuilder
@property (copy) NSString *JSON;
@end
```

This is the implementation of `FakeQuestionBuilder`:

```
#import "FakeQuestionBuilder.h"
#import "Question.h"

@implementation FakeQuestionBuilder

@synthesize JSON;

- (NSArray *)questionsFromJSON: (NSString *)objectNotation
                        error: (NSError **)error {
    self.JSON = objectNotation;
    return nil;
```

```
}
```

```
@end
```

Finally, the `StackOverflowManager` needs to know what `QuestionBuilder` to use, which in the test method is provided as a strong property called `questionBuilder`. Putting all that in place allows us to write this implementation of -[`StackOverflow Manager receivedQuestionsJSON:`].

```
- (void)receivedQuestionsJSON:(NSString *)objectNotation {
    NSArray *questions = [questionBuilder
        questionsFromJSON: objectNotation error: NULL];
}
```

Enough to pass this test, but not enough to be particularly useful. We've already dealt with error reporting for the network communication case; now let's ensure that the manager passes an appropriate error to its delegate if it can't get questions from the `QuestionBuilder`. The first thing to do is to make sure it's explicit that the `Fake QuestionBuilder` will actually return the correct value, and set an error we want. Let's make that controllable from the test fixture:

```
@interface FakeQuestionBuilder : QuestionBuilder {
}
@property (copy) NSString *JSON;
@property (copy) NSArray *arrayToReturn;
@property (copy) NSError *errorToSet;
@end
```

```
@implementation FakeQuestionBuilder
```

```
@synthesize JSON;
@synthesize arrayToReturn;
@synthesize errorToSet;
```

```
- (NSArray *)questionsFromJSON: (NSString *)objectNotation
                        error: (NSError **)error {
    self.JSON = objectNotation;
    return arrayToReturn;
}
```

```
@end
```

Now we write the tests to ensure that when the builder returns nil, the manager tells its delegate about the error. From the application's perspective, this error occurs in the same "get some questions" task that the network error does, so we expect the error to be signaled in the same way. This means we can use the interface for telling the delegate about errors that we built earlier in the chapter. This test goes in `QuestionCreation Tests`; the fixture's instance variables -`setUp` and -`tearDown` methods are also shown to demonstrate how the test is configured.

```
@implementation QuestionCreationTests
{
@private
    StackOverflowManager *mgr;
    MockStackOverflowManagerDelegate *delegate;
    NSError *underlyingError;
}

- (void)setUp {
    mgr = [[StackOverflowManager alloc] init];
    delegate = [[MockStackOverflowManagerDelegate alloc] init];
    mgr.delegate = delegate;
    underlyingError = [NSError errorWithDomain: @"Test domain"
        code: 0 userInfo: nil];
}

- (void)tearDown {
    mgr = nil;
    delegate = nil;
    underlyingError = nil;
}

- (void)testDelegateNotifiedOfErrorWhenQuestionBuilderFails {
    FakeQuestionBuilder *builder = [[FakeQuestionBuilder alloc] init];
    builder.arrayToReturn = nil;
    builder.errorToSet = underlyingError;
    mgr.questionBuilder = builder;
    [mgr receivedQuestionsJSON: @"Fake JSON"];
    STAssertNotNil([[[delegate fetchError] userInfo]
        objectForKey: NSUnderlyingErrorKey],
        @"The delegate should have found out about the error");
    mgr.questionBuilder = nil;
}
```

This requires that we flesh out the implementation of -[StackOverflowManager receivedQuestionsJSON:] to set errors properly.

```
- (void)receivedQuestionsJSON:(NSString *)objectNotation {
    NSError *error = nil;
    NSArray *questions = [questionBuilder
        questionsFromJSON: objectNotation error: &error];
    if (!questions) {
        NSError *reportableError = [NSError
            errorWithDomain: StackOverflowManagerSearchFailedError
                    code: StackOverflowManagerErrorQuestionSearchCode
                userInfo:[NSDictionary dictionaryWithObject: error
                        forKey: NSUnderlyingErrorKey]];
        [delegate fetchingQuestionsFailedWithError: reportableError];
    }
}
```

Oops! I broke something. The new test, `-testDelegateNotifiedOfErrorWhen QuestionBuilderFails`, passes, but now `-testQuestionJSONIsPassedToQuestion Builder` crashes. Let's take a look at the debugger output (look in the Console Navigator—Cmd-7—for the most recent "Test `BrowseOverflowTests`" event):

```
[2259:207] *** Terminating app due to uncaught exception
'NSInvalidArgumentException', reason: '*** -[NSCFDictionary
➥initWithObjects:forKeys:count:]: attempt to insert nil value at objects[0] (key:
➥NSUnderlyingError)'
```

Either the test setup is wrong, and the `StackOverflowManager` class should always receive an error when its question builder returns `nil`, or the code is wrong and should be changed to accept the possibility that it didn't receive an error. I think the latter case is better in this instance. We have one test where the error is important and another where it's unnecessary, so on balance, ignoring a lack of error seems acceptable. That changes the implementation of `-[StackOverflowManager receivedQuestions JSON]`:

```
- (void)receivedQuestionsJSON:(NSString *)objectNotation {
    NSError *error = nil;
    NSArray *questions = [questionBuilder
        questionsFromJSON: objectNotation error: &error];
    if (!questions) {
        NSDictionary *errorInfo = nil;
        if (error) {
            errorInfo = [NSDictionary dictionaryWithObject: error
                forKey: NSUnderlyingErrorKey];
        }
        NSError *reportableError = [NSError
            errorWithDomain: StackOverflowManagerSearchFailedError
                    code: StackOverflowManagerErrorQuestionSearchCode
                userInfo: errorInfo];
        [delegate fetchingQuestionsFailedWithError: reportableError];
    }
}
```

Great—I've fixed the crash, and both tests now pass. Incidentally, this is a good time to refactor both the tests and the code. We have a couple of tests that use the same `FakeQuestionBuilder` instance; that instance could be configured as part of the fixture. Notice that two methods on `StackOverflowManager`, `-receivedQuestionsJSON:` and `-searchingForQuestionsFailedWithError:`—both implement the same code for passing an error to the delegate. This can be pulled out to a private method; I chose to call it `-tellDelegateAboutQuestionSearch Error:`. The classes we've created so far are depicted in Figure 7.2, including the fakes and mocks so that you can see how the tests are supported by these extra classes.

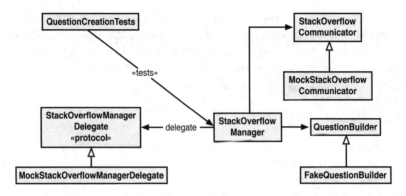

Figure 7.2   Classes created to support the question creation tests.

Testing Private Methods

I have often been asked, "Should I test my private methods?" or the related question "*How should I test my private methods?*" People asking the second question have assumed that the answer to the first is "Yes" and are now looking for a way to expose their classes' private interfaces in their test suites.

My answer relies on observation of a subtle fact: *You already have tested your private methods.* By following the red–green–refactor approach common in test-driven development, you designed your objects' public APIs to do the work those objects need to do. With that work specified by the tests—and the continued execution of the tests assuring you that you haven't broken anything—you are free to organize the internal plumbing of your classes as you see fit.

Your private methods are already tested because all you're doing is refactoring behavior that you already have tests for. You should never end up in a situation where a private method is untested or incompletely tested, because you create them only when you see an opportunity to clean up the implementation of public methods. This ensures that the private methods exist only to support the class's public behavior, and that they must be invoked during testing because they are definitely being called from public methods.

Two things need to happen if the `QuestionBuilder` returns an array of questions:

- The delegate finds out about the questions.
- The manager should *not* tell the delegate that an error occurred.

Let's ensure that both of these things happen, by writing some new tests on the `QuestionCreationTests` fixture.

```
- (void)setUp {
    //...
    Question *question = [[Question alloc] init];
    questionArray = [NSArray arrayWithObject: question];
```

```
}

- (void)tearDown {
    //...
    questionArray = nil;
}


- (void)testDelegateNotToldAboutErrorWhenQuestionsReceived {
    questionBuilder.arrayToReturn = questionArray;
    [mgr receivedQuestionsJSON: @"Fake JSON"];
    STAssertNil([delegate fetchError], @"No error should be received on success");
}


- (void)testDelegateReceivesTheQuestionsDiscoveredByManager {
    questionBuilder.arrayToReturn = questionArray;
    [mgr receivedQuestionsJSON: @"Fake JSON"];
    STAssertEqualObjects([delegate receivedQuestions], questionArray, @"The
➥manager should have sent its questions to the delegate");
}
```

We're already 50% of the way toward success, because one of these two tests passes without making any code changes. The other requires that our fake delegate implementation store the array of questions it receives so the test can ask about it, which in turn needs that the manager inform its delegate about the questions. A new method is needed on the delegate protocol:

```
- (void)didReceiveQuestions: (NSArray *)questions;
```

With these pieces in place, we can extend the StackOverflowManager implementation so that it passes the new test.

```
- (void)receivedQuestionsJSON:(NSString *)objectNotation {
    NSError *error = nil;
    NSArray *questions = [questionBuilder
        questionsFromJSON: objectNotation error: &error];
    if (!questions) {
        [self tellDelegateAboutQuestionSearchError: error];
    }
    else {
        [delegate didReceiveQuestions: questions];
    }
}
```

Did we forget anything? Yes—what happens if the QuestionBuilder returns an empty array? This looks like the success case (an array is returned), but could reasonably be considered an error (no questions are actually provided). In fact, I don't think this is an error. There might really be no questions on a particular topic, and if not, the app would want to know about that. So I'll write a test that shows this should be considered a success case. There aren't any code changes needed, but the test is still useful because it documents that I've considered this case and decided that the StackOverflowManager API works in this particular way.

```
- (void)testEmptyArrayIsPassedToDelegate {
    questionBuilder.arrayToReturn = [NSArray array];
    [mgr receivedQuestionsJSON: @"Fake JSON"];
    STAssertEqualObjects([delegate receivedQuestions], [NSArray array],
        @"Returning an empty array is not an error");
}
```

So now we have the complete workflow from requesting a list of questions on some topic to providing those questions, including handling errors that might occur. However, it still remains to actually fetch the data from the server and construct the questions from the data. Let's solve the latter problem first.

Building Questions from JSON

Having decided how the BrowseOverflow app will retrieve the data describing questions from the Stack Overflow website, we can use that data to create the question objects. It's time to flesh out the implementation of QuestionBuilder and to create a new test fixture called QuestionBuilderTests to describe this implementation. Incidentally, this raises a question about class naming: If we're testing question construction in QuestionBuilderTests, just what was QuestionCreationTests for? It's a valid question; the class names both suggest that they're responsible for the same thing. I'm going to rename QuestionCreationTests to QuestionCreationWorkflowTests, because that class is really testing how the app interacts with the question-creation machinery and isn't about the nuts and bolts of building question objects.

Renaming a class is very simple using Xcode's refactoring capabilities. Select the class name in the interface file, right-click, and choose Rename from the Refactor menu.

The API for QuestionBuilder has already been specified because we needed to know how the class worked to design StackOverflowManager. We can already specify that the string passed to QuestionBuilder will not be nil, because the Stack OverflowManager will have handled any errors that occurred earlier in the process. Also, if the string cannot be parsed as JSON, the QuestionBuilder will return nil and set an error, if the error parameter is non-NULL.

```
@implementation QuestionBuilderTests

- (void)setUp {
    questionBuilder = [[QuestionBuilder alloc] init];
}
```

3. Remember that this unit test is testing the manager unit, not the communicator unit. After we have a complete set of tests and a green bar here, it doesn't mean we're done: We still need to construct the other classes and integrate them.

```
- (void)tearDown {
    questionBuilder = nil;
}


- (void)testThatNilIsNotAnAcceptableParameter {
    STAssertThrows([questionBuilder questionsFromJSON: nil error: NULL],
        @"Lack of data should have been handled elsewhere");
}


- (void)testNilReturnedWhenStringIsNotJSON {
    STAssertNil([questionBuilder questionsFromJSON: @"Not JSON"
                                            error: NULL],
        @"This parameter should not be parsable");
}


- (void)testErrorSetWhenStringIsNotJSON {
    NSError *error = nil;
    [questionBuilder questionsFromJSON:@"Not JSON" error: &error];
    STAssertNotNil(error, @"An error occurred, we should be told");
}


- (void)testPassingNullErrorDoesNotCauseCrash {
    STAssertNoThrow([questionBuilder questionsFromJSON: @"Not JSON"
                                               error: NULL],
        @"Using a NULL error parameter should not be a problem");
}


@end
```

An implementation of the -[QuestionBuilder questionsFromJSON:error:] method that passes these tests is still far from being complete. Notice that the error code and error domain should be defined in the same way as for the StackOverflow Manager's errors, earlier.

```
- (NSArray *)questionsFromJSON:(NSString *)objectNotation
                         error:(NSError **)error {
    NSParameterAssert(objectNotation != nil);
    if (error != NULL) {
        *error = [NSError errorWithDomain: QuestionBuilderErrorDomain
            code: QuestionBuilderInvalidJSONError userInfo: nil];
    }
    return nil;
}
```

It's time to start interpreting the JSON content. To know what we ought to be accepting, we need to look at the Stack Overflow API documentation. The API behavior is specified by example. Although the name of each method and the parameters understood are documentation, we must find out what output to expect by trying the methods out for ourselves. Using the curl command line tool to get http://api.stackoverflow.com/1.1/search?taggcd=iphone&pagesize=20 shows that this data is returned:

```
{
 "total": 2000,
 "page": 1,
 "pagesize": 20,
 "questions": [
  {
   "tags": [
    "iphone",
    "cocoa-touch"
   ],
   "answer_count": 1,
   "favorite_count": 1,
   "question_timeline_url": "/questions/5512861/timeline",
   "question_comments_url": "/questions/5512861/comments",
   "question_answers_url": "/questions/5512861/answers",
   "question_id": 5512861,
   "owner": {
    "user_id": 679808,
    "user_type": "registered",
    "display_name": "vijay singh adhikari",
    "reputation": 141,
    "email_hash": "9c5334a58034d77b048ba9627e169cdd"
   },
   "creation_date": 1301658112,
   "last_edit_date": 1301665259,
   "last_activity_date": 1301665259,
   "up_vote_count": 0,
   "down_vote_count": 0,
   "view_count": 37,
   "score": 0,
   "community_owned": false,
   "title": "Read from uiimageView"
  },
  /* plenty more removed … */
 ]
}
```

The first thing we need to ensure, assuming that the `QuestionBuilder` receives real JSON-formatted data, is that there's an array called "questions" in the returned object.

```
- (void)testRealJSONWithoutQuestionsArrayIsError {
    NSString *jsonString = @"{ \"noquestions\": true }";
    STAssertNil([questionBuilder questionsFromJSON: jsonString
        error: NULL],
        @"No questions to parse in this JSON");
}
```

This test already passes. However, the `QuestionBuilder` only has the error code for "Invalid JSON," which seems inaccurate because the JSON is well-formatted but doesn't contain the necessary information. Let's fix the error that's returned.

```
- (void)testRealJSONWithoutQuestionsReturnsMissingDataError {
    NSString *jsonString = @"{ \"noquestions\": true }";
    NSError *error = nil;
    [questionBuilder questionsFromJSON:jsonString error: &error];
    STAssertEquals([error code], QuestionBuilderMissingDataError,
        @"This case should not be an invalid JSON error");
}
```

Getting this test to pass means that the `QuestionBuilder` must (finally!) actually interpret the JSON it receives. The error code enumeration in `QuestionBuilder.h` must be expanded:

```
enum {
    QuestionBuilderInvalidJSONError,
    QuestionBuilderMissingDataError,
};
```

And now we can build a more complete implementation of `-[QuestionBuilder questionsFromJSON:error:]`.

```
- (NSArray *)questionsFromJSON:(NSString *)objectNotation
                         error:(NSError **)error {
    NSParameterAssert(objectNotation != nil);
    NSData *unicodeNotation = [objectNotation
        dataUsingEncoding: NSUTF8StringEncoding];
    NSError *localError = nil;
    id jsonObject = [NSJSONSerialization
        JSONObjectWithData: unicodeNotation options: 0
        error: &localError];
    NSDictionary *parsedObject = (id)jsonObject;
    if (parsedObject == nil) {
        if (error != NULL) {
            *error = [NSError errorWithDomain:QuestionBuilderErrorDomain
                code: QuestionBuilderInvalidJSONError userInfo: nil];
        }
        return nil;
    }
    NSArray *questions = [parsedObject objectForKey: @"questions"];
    if (questions == nil) {
        if (error != NULL) {
            *error = [NSError errorWithDomain:QuestionBuilderErrorDomain
                code: QuestionBuilderMissingDataError userInfo:nil];
        }
        return nil;
    }
    return nil;
}
```

If the "questions" array is not empty, the builder should create one of the app's Question model objects for each object in the array. The object returned from `-questionsFromJSON:error:` should then be an array, with each member being a Question instance and the same number of those as were objects in the JSON questions list.

We also need to consider some subtleties. The Stack Overflow API documentation says "the API only makes a best effort attempt to fill all applicable fields on returned objects; an application should be able to handle partial returns sensibly." That means our class has to be able to handle the cases where some of the fields are either undefined or set to null in the JSON data. Let's add three tests: First, require that if an array containing one question definition in JSON is passed to the builder, we'll get one question back. Second, ensure that all the fields are set correctly; and third, ensure that an entirely empty question object can be created. We'll assume by induction that if it creates one question correctly, it would create N questions correctly, and that intermediate states of data completeness are okay (though if they aren't valid assumptions, we can always add a test later to demonstrate the problem and prove that we've fixed it).

Where can we get a JSON string that looks like a real Stack Overflow question? Why not from the website itself? In this test I'll use real data: I've pasted in a response from the Stack Overflow API to use in my tests, although I did elide most of the question's body text for brevity. The reasons for pasting it rather than fetching it from the API are to avoid problems with network availability, and to avoid the data changing between runs of the test. This is of paramount importance. We want the tests to fail because the code is buggy, not because the network isn't available.

```
static NSString *questionJSON = @"{"
@"\"total\": 1,"
@"\"page\": 1,"
@"\"pagesize\": 30,"
@"\"questions\": ["
@"{"
@"\"tags\": ["
@"\"iphone\","
@"\"security\","
@"\"keychain\""
@"],"
@"\"answer_count\": 1,"
@"\"accepted_answer_id\": 3231900,"
@"\"favorite_count\": 1,"
@"\"question_timeline_url\": \"/questions/2817980/timeline\","
@"\"question_comments_url\": \"/questions/2817980/comments\","
@"\"question_answers_url\": \"/questions/2817980/answers\","
@"\"question_id\": 2817980,"
@"\"owner\": {"
@"\"user_id\": 23743,"
@"\"user_type\": \"registered\","
```

```
@"\"display_name\": \"Graham Lee\","
@"\"reputation\": 13459,"
@"\"email_hash\": \"563290c0c1b776a315b36e863b388a0c\""
@"},"
@"\"creation_date\": 1273660706,"
@"\"last_activity_date\": 1278965736,"
@"\"up_vote_count\": 2,"
@"\"down_vote_count\": 0,"
@"\"view_count\": 465,"
@"\"score\": 2,"
@"\"community_owned\": false,"
@"\"title\":
    \"Why does Keychain Services return the wrong keychain content?\","
@"\"body\":
    \"<p>I've been trying to use persistent keychain references.</p>\""
@"}"
@"]"
@"}";

- (void)setUp {
    questionBuilder = [[QuestionBuilder alloc] init];
    question = [[questionBuilder questionsFromJSON: questionJSON
                                    error: NULL]
        objectAtIndex: 0];
}

- (void)tearDown {
    questionBuilder = nil;
    question = nil;
}

- (void)testJSONWithOneQuestionReturnsOneQuestionObject {
    NSError *error = nil;
    NSArray *questions = [questionBuilder
        questionsFromJSON: questionJSON error: &error];
    STAssertEquals([questions count], (NSUInteger)1,
        @"The builder should have created a question");
}

- (void)testQuestionCreatedFromJSONHasPropertiesPresentedInJSON {
    STAssertEquals(question.questionID, 2817980,
        @"The question ID should match the data we sent");
    STAssertEquals([question.date timeIntervalSince1970],
        (NSTimeInterval)1273660706,
        @"The date of the question should match the data");
    STAssertEqualObjects(question.title,
      @"Why does Keychain Services return the wrong keychain content?",
      @"Title should match the provided data");
```

```
    STAssertEquals(question.score, 2, @"Score should match the data");
    Person *asker = question.asker;
    STAssertEqualObjects(asker.name, @"Graham Lee",
        @"Looks like I should have asked this question");
    STAssertEqualObjects([asker.avatarURL absoluteString],
        @"http://www.gravatar.com/avatar/563290c0c1b776a315b36e863b388a0c",
        @"The avatar URL should be based on the supplied email hash");
}


- (void)testQuestionCreatedFromEmptyObjectIsStillValidObject {
    NSString *emptyQuestion = @"{ \"questions\": [ {} ] }";
    NSArray *questions = [questionBuilder
        questionsFromJSON: emptyQuestion error: NULL];
    STAssertEquals([questions count], (NSUInteger)1,
        @"QuestionBuilder must handle partial input");
}
```

Notice that in testing the question creation from complete data, I have used multiple assertions in the same test, ensuring that each property is set correctly. I usually try to avoid this style of test, but in this case there wouldn't be much to be gained from splitting the assertions across multiple tests apart from an increased page count. We want to know that the data is consumed correctly in its entirety, so the different assertions all stand together as part of the same test.

Another interesting thing about working with the API is that the search request doesn't return the bodies to the questions. Getting that information (which is surely important) requires making a second request to the server. Should the app do this as part of building the question, or should it retrieve the question's body later? Looking back at the requirements in Chapter 5, it's clear that when the app initially searches for questions, it doesn't need the question bodies; the app just presents a list of question titles and some other information to the user. The question body is not shown until the user drills in by tapping on one of the questions in the list.

That workflow is consistent with holding off from downloading the question body until the user moves to a view where the body will be presented. Therefore, the `Question` class needs to be extended. Each instance should retain its question ID, which can be presented to the service again later to retrieve the body. The `StackOverflow Manager` will need to support that, and the `QuestionBuilder` must be able to add that content to the object.

There are several new tests implemented on different fixtures. First, we'll ensure that the `StackOverflowManager` can handle a request for filling in the question details, by adding these tests to `QuestionCreationTests`.

```
- (void)setUp {
    //...
    questionToFetch = [[Question alloc] init];
    questionToFetch.questionID = 1234;
```

```
    questionArray = [NSArray arrayWithObject: questionToFetch];
    communicator = [[MockStackOverflowCommunicator alloc] init];
    mgr.communicator = communicator;
}

- (void)tearDown {
    //...
    questionToFetch = nil;
    questionArray = nil;
    communicator = nil;
}

- (void)testAskingForQuestionBodyMeansRequestingData {
    [mgr fetchBodyForQuestion: questionToFetch];
    STAssertTrue([communicator wasAskedToFetchBody],
        @"The communicator should need to retrieve data for the"
        @" question body");
}

- (void)testDelegateNotifiedOfFailureToFetchQuestion {
    [mgr fetchingQuestionBodyFailedWithError: underlyingError];
    STAssertNotNil([[[delegate fetchError] userInfo]
        objectForKey: NSUnderlyingErrorKey],
        @"Delegate should have found out about this error");
}

- (void)testManagerPassesRetrievedQuestionBodyToQuestionBuilder {
    [mgr receivedQuestionBodyJSON: @"Fake JSON"];
    STAssertEqualObjects(questionBuilder.JSON, @"Fake JSON",
        @"Successfully-retrieved data should be passed to the builder");
}

- (void)testManagerPassesQuestionItWasSentToQuestionBuilderForFillingIn {
    [mgr fetchBodyForQuestion: questionToFetch];
    [mgr receivedQuestionBodyJSON: @"Fake JSON"];
    STAssertEqualObjects(questionBuilder.questionToFill,
        questionToFetch,
        @"The question should have been passed to the builder");
}
```

Next, require that the `QuestionBuilder` handles the response correctly, filling in the question body when it's valid, and that it contains the required content. These tests belong in `QuestionBuilderTests`.

```
- (void)testBuildingQuestionBodyWithNoDataCannotBeTried {
    STAssertThrows([questionBuilder
        fillInDetailsForQuestion: question fromJSON: nil],
        @"Not receiving data should have been handled earlier");
}
```

```objc
- (void)testBuildingQuestionBodyWithNoQuestionCannotBeTried {
    STAssertThrows([questionBuilder
        fillInDetailsForQuestion: nil fromJSON: questionJSON],
        @"No reason to expect that a nil question is passed");
}


- (void)testNonJSONDataDoesNotCauseABodyToBeAddedToAQuestion {
    [questionBuilder fillInDetailsForQuestion: question
                                     fromJSON: stringIsNotJSON];
    STAssertNil(question.body, @"Body should not have been added");
}


- (void)testJSONWhichDoesNotContainABodyDoesNotCauseBodyToBeAdded {
    [questionBuilder fillInDetailsForQuestion: question
                                     fromJSON: noQuestionsJSONString];
    STAssertNil(question.body, @"There was no body to add");
}


- (void)testBodyContainedInJSONIsAddedToQuestion {
    [questionBuilder fillInDetailsForQuestion: question
                                     fromJSON: questionJSON];
    STAssertEqualObjects(question.body,
        @"<p>I've been trying to use persistent keychain references.</p>",
        @"The correct question body is added");
}
```

Finally, notice that the tests of question creation require that the question have the correct **Person** instance associated with it. Oops! It looks like I forgot to create that property in Chapter 6. Add a test to the **QuestionTests** fixture created in that chapter to ensure that the property exists and works properly.

```objc
- (void)setUp {
    // ...
    asker = [[Person alloc] initWithName: @"Graham Lee"
        avatarLocation:@"http://example.com/avatar.png"];
    question.asker = asker;
}


- (void)testQuestionWasAskedBySomeone {
    STAssertEqualObjects(question.asker, asker,
        @"Question should keep track of who asked it.");
}
```

By now you have seen enough test-driven code implemented to be able to write the code to pass these tests yourself. Consider this your exercise for the chapter—or look at the project in GitHub to see how the code looks, and at the very similar code for the **AnswerBuilder** class. Because it turns out that both **QuestionBuilder** and

`AnswerBuilder` need to define `Person` instances—describing people who asked or answered questions—I also refactored `QuestionBuilder`'s `Person`-creation code out into a separate `PersonBuilder` class.

Now the app can take JSON data in the format provided by the StackOverflow API and use it to construct question objects suitable for display to the user. There's just one step left before we move on to the display side, and that's downloading the content from the network. This is the subject of the next chapter.

8

Networking Code

The code in BrowseOverflow can parse data received from the Stack Overflow website and use it to build model objects that will be used in the app. The problem of fetching the data from the website in the first place still remains. In this chapter you'll see how to build that code, and how to deal with the problem of talking to the outside world in a test-driven fashion.

On the face of it, the problem we have to deal with next in BrowseOverflow seems intractable: looking back to Chapter 3, "How to Write a Unit Test," you'll remember that unit tests are supposed to be fast, repeatable, and reliable. How do you achieve those properties when dealing with network code? So many issues can affect the performance and reliability of a network connection: the local hardware configuration, the wires, routers, switches, and computers that make up the network, errors in the numerous protocols used to find and talk to a server—the list goes on. How can we take all those into account in our tests?

The simple answer is that we won't take these into account. In fact, we want to remove any reliance on the network from our test code. Removing the network from networking code? How will we do that? To answer that question, let's look at the design of Apple's Cocoa API for fetching network content: NSURLConnection.

NSURLConnection Class Design

To initiate a network operation using NSURLConnection, you create a new connection instance with an NSURLRequest that encapsulates the URL you want to fetch content from, in addition to some properties such as how the retrieved content should be cached.

NSURLConnection manages choosing a protocol handler based on the URL's protocol (http:// or ftp://), fetching content and dealing with errors. Whenever something novel occurs—such as new data being received or the protocol needing authentication to proceed—the NSURLConnection informs its delegate, which is the application's interface to the facility. This organization is outlined in Figure 8.1.

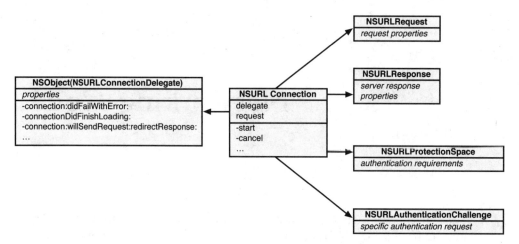

Figure 8.1   The separation of concerns between NSURLConnection
and its delegate.

The delegate pattern is used throughout the Cocoa APIs; indeed, you've already encountered it in the BrowseOverflow app because the StackOverflowManager class uses a delegate to communicate with the app. The advantage of the delegate class is that it separates the business of interacting with a subsystem from the performance of that subsystem's duties. The delegate just needs to know when interesting things happen, and be able to express the application's needs if a decision ever needs to be made.

For networking code, this means that as long as the delegate does the correct thing when it receives a callback, it doesn't matter whether that callback comes from an NSURLConnection *or a test harness.* The test cases can set up "fake" networking scenarios and investigate how the application code responds; if that works properly, we can be reasonably confident that it will work when interacting with a real network connection. The unit tests don't need to talk to a network; they can pretend to be the network. We'll use the NSURLConnectionDelegate methods to implement StackOverflow Communicator's dealings with the network and the Stack Overflow web service.

StackOverflowCommunicator Implementation

Most of the application's interface to StackOverflowCommunicator has already been defined when we designed the StackOverflowManager to use the communicator class. What's left is to fill in the defined methods, ensuring that they create connections to appropriate URLs. In addition, we will make the communicator a delegate of NSURLConnection, so we must be certain that the delegate methods are implemented and working correctly. Let's start with creating the connections. The first step in getting this working is to ensure that the communicator tries to download content from the correct URLs. We'll need a new test fixture, StackOverflowCommunicatorTests.

```objc
- (void)testSearchingForQuestionsOnTopicCallsTopicAPI {
    StackOverflowCommunicator *communicator =
        [[StackOverflowCommunicator alloc] init];
    [communicator searchForQuestionsWithTag: @"ios"];
    STAssertEqualObjects([[communicator URLToFetch] absoluteString],
        @"http://api.stackoverflow.com/1.1/search?tagged=ios&pagesize=20",
        @"Use the search API to find questions with a particular tag");
}
```

This requires a point in the communicator's workflow where the test can sense what URL it's trying to access. The communicator itself will need to keep track of the URL it's using:

```objc
@interface StackOverflowCommunicator : NSObject {
@protected
    NSURL *fetchingURL;
}

- (void)searchForQuestionsWithTag: (NSString *)tag;
- (void)downloadInformationForQuestionWithID: (NSInteger)identifier;
- (void)downloadAnswersToQuestionWithID: (NSInteger)identifier;
- (void)fetchBodyForQuestion: (NSInteger)questionID;

@end
```

But the ability to inspect that URL is needed only in tests; it's not naturally a part of the class's API. Define a subclass of `StackOverflowCommunicator` that offers this ability. This subclass will be used only in the unit test's target, not in the app.

```objc
@interface InspectableStackOverflowCommunicator :
    StackOverflowCommunicator
- (NSURL *)URLToFetch;

@end


@implementation InspectableStackOverflowCommunicator

- (NSURL *)URLToFetch {
    return fetchingURL;
}

@end
```

This pattern of defining a subclass with the introspection capabilities needed to support testing helps to keep the test code separate from the production code. The subclass is defined only in the test target, and its superclass (the production class) only needs to contain application code. If you don't like the idea of creating a subclass just to add a getter for an otherwise private instance variable, an alternative exists. Key-Value Coding will let you find the value of an instance variable even if no accessor methods are defined for it, so you could use [StackOverflowCommunicator valueForKey: @"fetchingURL"] in the test case instead of creating this subclass. However, I find that the pattern shown here is more explicit in documenting that the variable is only being retrieved to support the tests.

Now the test can be refactored to use an instance of this inspectable subclass.

```
- (void)testSearchingForQuestionsOnTopicCallsTopicAPI {
    InspectableStackOverflowCommunicator *communicator =
        [[InspectableStackOverflowCommunicator alloc] init];
    [communicator searchForQuestionsWithTag: @"ios"];
    STAssertEqualObjects([[communicator URLToFetch] absoluteString],
        @"http://api.stackoverflow.com/1.1/search?tagged=ios&pagesize=20",
        @"Use the search API to find questions with a particular tag");
}
```

That gives us enough supporting material to work on the code to implement this behavior.

```
@implementation StackOverflowCommunicator

- (void)fetchContentAtURL:(NSURL *)url {
    fetchingURL = url;
}


- (void)searchForQuestionsWithTag:(NSString *)tag {
    [self fetchContentAtURL: [NSURL URLWithString:
        [NSString stringWithFormat:
        @"http://api.stackoverflow.com/1.1/search?tagged=%@&pagesize=20",
        tag]]];
}

@end
```

The tests for initiating calls to fill in question and answer details will look very similar.

```
- (void)setUp {
    communicator = [[InspectableStackOverflowCommunicator alloc] init];
}

- (void)tearDown {
    communicator = nil;
}

- (void)testFillingInQuestionBodyCallsQuestionAPI {
    [communicator downloadInformationForQuestionWithID: 12345];
    STAssertEqualObjects([[communicator URLToFetch] absoluteString],
        @"http://api.stackoverflow.com/1.1/questions/12345?body=true",
        @"Use the question API to get the body for a question");
}
```

```
- (void)testFetchingAnswersToQuestionCallsQuestionAPI {
    [communicator downloadAnswersToQuestionWithID: 12345];
    STAssertEqualObjects([[communicator URLToFetch] absoluteString],
  @"http://api.stackoverflow.com/1.1/questions/12345/answers?body=true",
      @"Use the question API to get answers on a given question");
}
```

With those tests passing, we know that the communicator is talking to the correct API methods. It would be possible to have the methods on `StackOverflowCommunicator` return hard-coded URLs pasted from the test cases as things currently stand. If you want to be certain that the methods are doing the correct thing, you could create extra tests that exercise the same code with different tag strings and question identifiers. Personally, I trust myself enough not to "cheat" at writing code (but not enough to assume I get the code correct[1] even when I'm not cheating; hence the baby steps and unit tests).

The next thing that needs to happen is that the communicator must create an `NSURLConnection` object that will download the networked content. First, the test:

```
- (void)testSearchingForQuestionsCreatesURLConnection {
    [communicator searchForQuestionsWithTag: @"ios"];
    STAssertNotNil([communicator currentURLConnection],
        @"There should be a URL connection in-flight now.");
    [communicator cancelAndDiscardURLConnection];
}
```

It looks like we'll add two methods on the `InspectableStackOverflow Communicator` class: the first to find out what `NSURLConnection` the object has created, and the second to throw it away to help the test clean up after itself. (In particular, the documentation for `NSURLConnection` says that it retains its delegate; that connection will need to be removed.)

```
- (NSURLConnection *)currentURLConnection {
    return fetchingConnection;
}
```

```
- (void)cancelAndDiscardURLConnection {
    [fetchingConnection cancel];
    fetchingConnection = nil;
}
```

This turns out not to be so true. When I came to implement the code for this test, I decided that the communicator would also need to throw away any in-progress connection if it needs to start a new one. The test for that looks like this:

1. Guessing or assuming that code is correct often fails when considering edge cases. Where the question ID is of type `NSInteger`, does the code work across its entire signed 32-bit range? On Mac OS X, `NSInteger` can be a 64-bit type; will the code work in these cases, too?

```
- (void)testStartingNewSearchThrowsOutOldConnection {
    [communicator searchForQuestionsWithTag: @"ios"];
    NSURLConnection *firstConnection =
        [communicator currentURLConnection];
    [communicator searchForQuestionsWithTag: @"cocoa"];
    STAssertFalse([[communicator currentURLConnection]
        isEqual: firstConnection],
        @"The communicator needs to replace its URL connection"
        @" to start a new one");
    [communicator cancelAndDiscardURLConnection];
}
```

When I came to make both of these tests pass, this is the method I came up with on the real `StackOverflowCommunicator` class (that is, this implementation is not specific to the inspectable subclass).

```
- (void)fetchContentAtURL:(NSURL *)url {
    fetchingURL = url;

    NSURLRequest *request = [NSURLRequest requestWithURL: fetchingURL];

    [fetchingConnection cancel];
    fetchingConnection = [NSURLConnection connectionWithRequest: request
                                                       delegate: self];

}
```

It looks like the real `StackOverflowCommunicator` can internally make use of the `-cancelAndDiscardURLConnection` method, so I'm going to remove it from the `InspectableStackOverflowCommunicator` and put it on the production class. That can easily be done in Xcode by selecting the method in `InspectableStackOverflow Communicator.m` and choosing the Move Up refactoring from Xcode's Edit, Refactor menu.

The tests in place now demonstrate that a `NSURLConnection` instance gets created when searching for tagged questions. Whether you use knowledge of the class design to declare the other cases of retrieving question content and answers covered (because all cases use `-fetchContentAtURL:`) is up to you. To save a few rainforests, I'll leave them out here, although you can see them in the sample code at github.

What happens next is that control is handed over to `NSURLConnection`, which will call back into `StackOverflowCommunicator` at various points defined in the documentation.[2] Not all of the delegate methods will be needed in this code. Here are the requirements:

- When a response is received, if it has HTTP status 200 (OK) the communicator should prepare to receive data from the connection.

---

2. Apple's class reference for `NSURLConnection` is currently at http://developer.apple.com/ library/ios/#documentation/Cocoa/Reference/Foundation/Classes/NSURLConnection_ Class/Reference/Reference.html.

- If a response is received that has an HTTP error status but is not a redirect, the communicator should send an error to the `StackOverflowManager`. Additionally, it should cancel the connection.

- When the connection receives new data, the communicator should append it to the data it has received so far.

- If the connection fails with an error, the manager should be notified of the error, using whichever method was defined in Chapter 7 for that purpose. The communicator can discard any data fetched before the error occurred.

- If the connection succeeds, the data received should be communicated to the manager using the appropriate `StackOverflowManager` API. The communicator can then discard its local copy of the data.

There are two design issues to solve before proceeding. One is how to let the communicator object know about its manager. Because the manager itself has a delegate, and the communicator is a delegate of its `NSURLConnection`, it seems appropriate to make the manager a delegate of the communicator so there is a single pattern used throughout the interaction.

The second design problem to solve is how to decide which of the manager's methods to signal when success or failure occur. Because of the way the beginning of the `NSURLConnection` interaction was designed, all three requests for different types of data funnel into the same method for initiating a connection. This is desirable; the work done in each case is very similar, so it would be a waste to have three versions of the code. We will, however, need a way for the communicator class to keep track of what it's supposed to be doing so it can choose the correct manager methods to invoke on completion.

My preferred solution here is to use blocks. The three "entry points" into `StackOverflowCommunicator`—that is, the three methods that `StackOverflow Manager` can call—can each create two blocks, containing the code to run on success or failure of the URL connection. The actual connection delegate code can then be general purpose and invoke the blocks at appropriate times to get the correct logic executed.

With the goal of working toward this design, it's time to start writing the tests. When I wrote the first of these tests, I wanted to cancel the network connection after setting up the original method and before simulating connection delegate events. The reason for doing this was to avoid any chance that the URL connection might get scheduled on a run loop and run to completion while the tests were running. I realized I'd also have to do that in every subsequent test of the connection delegate callbacks. Therefore, I broke out the creation of the `NSURLConnection` in -`fetchContentAtURL:` into a separate helper method, and created a new tests-only subclass `NonNetworkedStackOverflow Communicator` that doesn't actually create the `NSURLConnection` instance.

As the components of the class fell into place as the test coverage grew, it became clear that the method signature needed changing, so in the following code you'll see references to -`fetchContentAtURL:completionHandler:errorHandler:`. The first things to test were the interfaces between the URL connection delegate code and the rest of the logic. That means success and failure conditions should each send appropriate messages to the communicator's own delegate.

A slight wrinkle in defining the error-handling is related to the way in which NSURLConnection processes its responses. If it gets a body of data from the URL in question, then *even if that body describes an error* at the protocol level, NSURLConnection believes it has succeeded. You need to investigate whether the response you receive represents an error such as HTTP status 404 and handle it appropriately. The tests appropriate to fetching questions on a topic are shown here; the others are very similar.

```
- (void)setUp {
    communicator = [[InspectableStackOverflowCommunicator alloc] init];
    nnCommunicator = [[NonNetworkedStackOverflowCommunicator alloc]
        init];
    manager = [[MockStackOverflowManager alloc] init];
    nnCommunicator.delegate = manager;
    fourOhFourResponse = [[FakeURLResponse alloc]
        initWithStatusCode: 404];
    receivedData = [@"Result" dataUsingEncoding: NSUTF8StringEncoding];
}


- (void)tearDown {
    [communicator cancelAndDiscardURLConnection];
    communicator = nil;
    nnCommunicator = nil;
    manager = nil;
    fourOhFourResponse = nil;
    receivedData = nil;
}


- (void)testReceivingResponseDiscardsExistingData {
    nnCommunicator.receivedData = [@"Hello"
        dataUsingEncoding: NSUTF8StringEncoding];
    [nnCommunicator searchForQuestionsWithTag: @"ios"];
    [nnCommunicator connection: nil didReceiveResponse: nil];
    STAssertEquals([nnCommunicator.receivedData length], (NSUInteger)0,
        @"Data should have been discarded");
}


- (void)testReceivingResponseWith404StatusPassesErrorToDelegate {
    [nnCommunicator searchForQuestionsWithTag: @"ios"];
    [nnCommunicator connection: nil didReceiveResponse:
        (NSURLResponse *)fourOhFourResponse];
    STAssertEquals([manager topicFailureErrorCode], 404,
        @"Fetch failure was passed through to delegate");
}


- (void)testNoErrorReceivedOn200Status {
```

```
        FakeURLResponse *twoHundredResponse =
            [[FakeURLResponse alloc] initWithStatusCode: 200];
        [nnCommunicator searchForQuestionsWithTag: @"ios"];
        [nnCommunicator connection: nil didReceiveResponse:
            (NSURLResponse *)twoHundredResponse];
        STAssertFalse([manager topicFailureErrorCode] == 200,
            @"No need for error on 200 response");
}


- (void)testConnectionFailingPassesErrorToDelegate {
        [nnCommunicator searchForQuestionsWithTag: @"ios"];
        NSError *error = [NSError errorWithDomain: @"Fake domain"
            code: 12345 userInfo: nil];
        [nnCommunicator connection: nil didFailWithError: error];
        STAssertEquals([manager topicFailureErrorCode], 12345,
            @"Failure to connect should get passed to the delegate");
}


- (void)testSuccessfulQuestionSearchPassesDataToDelegate {
        [nnCommunicator searchForQuestionsWithTag: @"ios"];
        [nnCommunicator setReceivedData: receivedData];
        [nnCommunicator connectionDidFinishLoading: nil];
        STAssertEqualObjects([manager topicSearchString], @"Result",
            @"The delegate should have received data on success");
}
```

All those tests provide enough information to guide the implementation of some of the `StackOverflowCommunicator` delegate methods. Before looking at the code, it's useful to see the class layout in Figure 8.2 to appreciate how the design of this part of the app has evolved in response to trying to test it. This will also explain some of the new classes that appear in the preceding testing code.

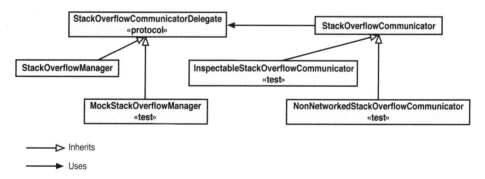

Figure 8.2   The classes created so far to implement and assist testing of the `StackOverflowCommunicator` networking code.

It may seem counterproductive to have created three new test classes (four, if you count the FakeURLResponse class) and separated one class's interface out into a protocol just to fill in a few details of an existing class, but it's a common way of working. The benefits are that we now have two (production) classes that interact only across an abstract interface—the StackOverflowCommunicatorDelegate protocol—and that can each be replaced by other implementations without affecting each other. The benefit we've seen in relation to functional testing is that either class can be substituted for one entirely under the control of the test developer. This substitution can be employed in other aspects of testing. For example, in performance testing the application, the entire networking component could be replaced with a simulation that delivers data (and errors) at a predictable rate to the rest of the app. An integration test could retrieve known data from a local web server to avoid problems connecting across the Internet to stackoverflow.com.

You should be careful about how you divide functionality between test harness code and production code. If you end up writing a test that's only exercising harness code, you either put code in the harness that ought to be in the app, or you made your fake objects so hard to understand that you need to test them. Either way, you have a problem that needs addressing, because you have a test that isn't telling you anything about how your app behaves.

Back to the code: Here's the expanded interface for the StackOverflow Communicator class, along with the newly implemented methods. Again, only the topic-searching code is shown for brevity; the question body and answer list fetching code just differs in the completion and error-handling blocks.

```
#import <Foundation/Foundation.h>
#import "StackOverflowCommunicatorDelegate.h"

@interface StackOverflowCommunicator : NSObject {
@protected
    NSURL *fetchingURL;
    NSURLConnection *fetchingConnection;
    NSMutableData *receivedData;
@private
    id <StackOverflowCommunicatorDelegate> delegate;
    void (^errorHandler)(NSError *);
    void (^successHandler)(NSString *);
}

@property (assign) id <StackOverflowCommunicatorDelegate> delegate;

- (void)searchForQuestionsWithTag: (NSString *)tag;
- (void)downloadInformationForQuestionWithID: (NSInteger)identifier;
- (void)downloadAnswersToQuestionWithID: (NSInteger)identifier;

- (void)cancelAndDiscardURLConnection;
@end
```

```objc
extern NSString *StackOverflowCommunicatorErrorDomain;

@implementation StackOverflowCommunicator

@synthesize delegate;

- (void)launchConnectionForRequest: (NSURLRequest *)request  {
  [self cancelAndDiscardURLConnection];
    fetchingConnection = [NSURLConnection connectionWithRequest: request
                                                        delegate: self];

}
- (void)fetchContentAtURL:(NSURL *)url
            errorHandler:(void (^)(NSError *))errorBlock
          successHandler:(void (^)(NSString *))successBlock {
    fetchingURL = url;
    errorHandler = [errorBlock copy];
    successHandler = [successBlock copy];
    NSURLRequest *request = [NSURLRequest requestWithURL: fetchingURL];

    [self launchConnectionForRequest: request];


}


- (void)searchForQuestionsWithTag:(NSString *)tag {
    [self fetchContentAtURL: [NSURL URLWithString:
                                [NSString stringWithFormat:
        @"http://api.stackoverflow.com/1.1/search?tagged=%@&pagesize=20",
        tag]]
                errorHandler: ^(NSError *error) {
                    [delegate searchingForQuestionsFailedWithError:
                        error];
                }
              successHandler: ^(NSString *objectNotation) {
                  [delegate receivedQuestionsJSON: objectNotation];
              }];
}

- (void)connection:(NSURLConnection *)connection
didReceiveResponse:(NSURLResponse *)response {
    receivedData = nil;
    NSHTTPURLResponse *httpResponse = (NSHTTPURLResponse *)response;
    if ([httpResponse statusCode] != 200) {
        NSError *error = [NSError
            errorWithDomain: StackOverflowCommunicatorErrorDomain
                       code: [httpResponse statusCode]
                   userInfo: nil];
        errorHandler(error);
        [self cancelAndDiscardURLConnection];
```

```
    }
    else {
        receivedData = [[NSMutableData alloc] init];
    }
}

- (void)connection:(NSURLConnection *)connection
  didFailWithError:(NSError *)error {
    receivedData = nil;
    fetchingConnection = nil;
    fetchingURL = nil;
    errorHandler(error);
}


- (void)connectionDidFinishLoading:(NSURLConnection *)connection {
    fetchingConnection = nil;
    fetchingURL = nil;
    NSString *receivedText = [[NSString alloc]
        initWithData: receivedData

        encoding: NSUTF8StringEncoding];
    receivedData = nil;
    successHandler(receivedText);
}


- (void)dealloc {
    [fetchingConnection cancel];
}

@end

NSString *StackOverflowCommunicatorErrorDomain =
    @"StackOverflowCommunicatorErrorDomain";
```

There's just one remaining part left to this class. When data is received by the communicator class, it should append that data to the portion of the response it has already gathered. The test for that looks like this:

```
- (void)testAdditionalDataAppendedToDownload {
    [nnCommunicator setReceivedData: receivedData];
    NSData *extraData = [@" appended" dataUsingEncoding: NSUTF8StringEncoding];
    [nnCommunicator connection: nil didReceiveData: extraData];
    NSString *combinedString = [[NSString alloc]
        initWithData: [nnCommunicator receivedData]
        encoding: NSUTF8StringEncoding];
    STAssertEqualObjects(combinedString, @"Result appended",
        @"Received data should be appended to the downloaded data");
}
```

It requires adding this method to `StackOverflowCommunicator`:

```
- (void)connection:(NSURLConnection *)connection
   didReceiveData:(NSData *)data {
   [receivedData appendData: data];
}
```

Conclusion

Over the preceding few pages, we've grown a network-handling class for the BrowseOverflow app, using tests to guide the design and implementation. By adopting the delegate pattern and creating suitable fake object classes to act as a test harness for the production code, we've managed to build and test this network handler without connecting to the network at all.

Even though interacting with the network is complicated, error prone, and nondeterministic, we've still managed to meet the expectation that the project's unit tests should be repeatable, reliable, and fast. At this point the project's unit test suite still takes under 0.1s to execute on any Mac I care to try it on, which is more than fast enough that I can run the tests every time I build without being slowed down in my work.

Now that we have all the code necessary to fetch data from the website and model it inside the app, the remaining task is to present this data to the users and allow them to interact with it. The next chapter will describe building the view controllers necessary to give users of BrowseOverflow something to look at.

9

View Controllers

The BrowseOverflow app now has a very stable base, because all the model and "business logic" code has been grown using tests. Many people attempting to adopt app-wide unit testing practices of any form—including TDD—get despondent when moving "higher up" in the app toward the controller and view layers. How can code that is supposed to interact with a user be subjected to automated testing? That is exactly what you'll find out in this chapter as we build up the view controllers and associated objects.

Class Organization

Each of the views shown and described in Chapter 5, "Test-Driven Development of an iOS App," is basically the same: There's a table, whether it's a table of topic names, of question titles or the question body and answers. Navigating through the app provides a "master-detail" representation, where tapping on an item at one level provides more information about that item. Therefore, there's really only one view to support: a table view with a data source to represent the information being displayed and a delegate to respond to taps from the user, preparing the next level of table view if appropriate.

If there's only one view in the app, then only one view controller is needed. A problem frequently occurring in iOS apps is having a different view controller and XIB for every level in an app, even though they're all presenting data in very similar ways. The end result of this is a lot of repeated code throughout the app, with the application's behavior being very tightly coupled to the data presentation.

The principle culprit for this repetition of code is the use of Apple's `UITableViewController` class. By putting the view management and data preparation into the same object, this class makes it harder to write code that can be reused in different contexts: You might find that you need to show the same data but provide different behavior, or show different data in a similar context. `UITableViewController` makes it difficult to do either. It is what object-oriented programmers refer to as a "God class": a class that has absorbed all the functionality in an app and is responsible for everything.

With this goal of reusability in mind, we'll aim for the solution shown in Figure 9.1. There's a single `UIViewController` subclass called `BrowseOverflowViewController`, which holds a reference to a table view data source object (that is, a custom class that implements the `UITableViewDataSource` protocol) and delegate object (a custom implementation of `UITableViewDelegate`). There will be a different data source and delegate at each level of the application, and it's through these objects that the custom app behavior and information presentation will be provided. The `BrowseOverflowViewController` will also have a reference to a `UITableView` instance because it's responsible for setting up the view and, therefore, will hook up the data source and delegate to the table view.

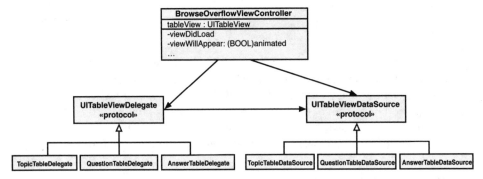

Figure 9.1   Class diagram for the view controllers in the BrowseOverflow app.

The View Controller Class

With just one view controller in the whole application, after we've implemented this one class we have most of the app's presentation done, right? Actually, this will probably turn out not to be true. The design shown in Figure 9.1 means that most of the data preparation (that is, translating the model objects' properties into elements of the view) will be done by the various `UITableViewDataSource` implementations.

First we need to create the class. Apple supplies a template for a `UIViewController` subclass that allows us to avoid having to write some of the code from scratch. Use Xcode's File, New, New File menu item to bring up the file template chooser, and select UIViewController subclass. Click Next, and click Next again (leaving the class as a subclass of UIViewController, not targeted for iPad, and with a XIB for user interface). Finally, name the file `BrowseOverflowViewController.m` and add it to both the app and test case targets. Put the file in the project's group for application files, so that it does not get lost among the test fixture files.

The first few tests are simple: We want the view controller to have strong properties to track the other objects that will help to prepare the view—in other words, the table view, its data source and delegate. Here's the implementation of a new test case fixture called `BrowseOverflowViewControllerTests` that checks for these details. Just to provide some variation from the similar tests in Chapter 6, "The Data Model"—and showing again that TDD does not constrain developers to any one choice of implementation—these tests use the property introspection capabilities of the Objective-C runtime to find out whether the properties exist.

The Objective-C Runtime

The resolution of methods, properties, and other features of objects and classes in the Objective-C language is performed at runtime by a library of C functions. In this respect, Objective-C differs from other compiled object-oriented languages like C++ and Java, which do all that work in the compiler.

An advantage of Objective-C's dynamic approach is that the runtime functions are available to application (and test) code, providing a very powerful collection of introspection capabilities as well as the capability for an application to modify a class at runtime. The introspection facility is useful in testing whether a class implements some expected method, which, in addition to supporting unit tests, also makes it easy for applications to target multiple versions of an operating system, framework, or library. If the app discovers at runtime that some feature is missing, it can avoid using that feature.

The Objective-C Runtime library also provides other features, such as the associated storage facility that is used later in this chapter. Apple's documentation on the library can be found here: http://developer.apple.com/library/ios/#documentation/Cocoa/Conceptual/ObjCRuntimeGuide/Introduction/Introduction.html#//apple_ref/doc/uid/TP40008048-CH1-SW1.

```
#import "BrowseOverflowViewControllerTests.h"
#import "BrowseOverflowViewController.h"

@implementation BrowseOverflowViewControllerTests
{
    BrowseOverflowViewController *viewController;
}

- (void)setUp {
    viewController = [[BrowseOverflowViewController alloc] init];
}

- (void)tearDown {
    viewController = nil;
}

- (void)testViewControllerHasATableViewProperty {
    objc_property_t tableViewProperty =
        class_getProperty([viewController class], "tableView");
    STAssertTrue(tableViewProperty != NULL,
        @"BrowseOverflowViewController needs a table view");
}
```

```
- (void)testViewControllerHasADataSourceProperty {
    objc_property_t dataSourceProperty =
        class_getProperty([viewController class], "dataSource");
    STAssertTrue(dataSourceProperty != NULL,
        @"View Controller needs a data source");
}

- (void)testViewControllerHasATableViewDelegateProperty {
    objc_property_t delegateProperty =
        class_getProperty([viewController class], "tableViewDelegate");
    STAssertTrue(delegateProperty != NULL,
        @"View Controller needs a table view delegate");
}
@end
```

The tests require synthesized properties on the `BrowseOverflowViewController` class, defined like this in the interface:

```
#import <UIKit/UIKit.h>

@interface BrowseOverflowViewController : UIViewController

@property (strong) UITableView *tableView;
@property (strong) id <UITableViewDataSource> dataSource;
@property (strong) id <UITableViewDelegate> tableViewDelegate;

@end
```

The implementation is similarly simple:

```
@implementation BrowseOverflowViewController

@synthesize tableView;
@synthesize dataSource;
@synthesize tableViewDelegate;

@end
```

The view controller's primary responsibility will be to ensure that the table view is connected to its data source and delegate, so that the table has something to do. This needs to be done after the view is loaded (otherwise the table view won't be there to connect); it seems that -viewDidLoad would be a good place to expect this to be done. Before we go overboard on creating more fake objects, it would be good to try writing the test using a real `UITableView`. Here are two new tests on `BrowseOverflowViewControllerTests`, along with the changes in the fixture:

```objc
@implementation BrowseOverflowViewControllerTests
{
    BrowseOverflowViewController *viewController;
    UITableView *tableView;
}

- (void)setUp {
    viewController = [[BrowseOverflowViewController alloc] init];
    tableView = [[UITableView alloc] init];
    viewController.tableView = tableView;
}

- (void)tearDown {
    viewController = nil;
    tableView = nil;
}

- (void)testViewControllerConnectsDataSourceInViewDidLoad {
    id <UITableViewDataSource> dataSource =
        [[EmptyTableViewDataSource alloc] init];
    viewController.dataSource = dataSource;
    [viewController viewDidLoad];
    STAssertEqualObjects([tableView dataSource], dataSource,
    @"View controller should have set the table view's data source");
}

- (void)testViewControllerConnectsDelegateInViewDidLoad {
    id <UITableViewDelegate> delegate =
        [[EmptyTableViewDelegate alloc] init];
    viewController.tableViewDelegate = delegate;
    [viewController viewDidLoad];
    STAssertEqualObjects([tableView delegate], delegate,    @"View
controller should have set the table view's delegate");

}

@end
```

We'll need to provide implementations of the data source and delegate protocols, but hopefully we'll be able to reuse those later. The protocol implementations can both be do-nothing classes that just conform to the required protocols. In the case of the data source protocol, two required methods will need implementing, but placeholder implementations will be fine because we don't have any indication of what those methods would do yet. Those empty classes are both shown next. Although these classes are not SenTestCase subclasses, they are for the moment only being used to support the tests, so you can group them with the test fixtures in Xcode's project navigator.

EmptyTableViewDataSource.h

```
#import <UIKit/UIKit.h>

@interface EmptyTableViewDataSource : NSObject <UITableViewDataSource>

@end
```

EmptyTableViewDataSource.m

```
#import "EmptyTableViewDataSource.h"

@implementation EmptyTableViewDataSource

- (NSInteger)tableView:(UITableView *)tableView
    numberOfRowsInSection:(NSInteger)section {
    return 0;
}

- (UITableViewCell *)tableView:(UITableView *)tableView
    cellForRowAtIndexPath:(NSIndexPath *)indexPath {
    return nil;
}

@end
```

EmptyTableViewDelegate.h

```
#import <UIKit/UIKit.h>

@interface EmptyTableViewDelegate : NSObject <UITableViewDelegate>

@end
```

EmptyTableViewDelegate.m

```
#import "EmptyTableViewDelegate.h"

@implementation EmptyTableViewDelegate

@end
```

After all that, the implementation of - [BrowseOverflowViewController view DidLoad] is almost anticlimactically brief. The template code provided by Apple already calls through to the superclass's implementation of the method. The changes added to make the preceding tests pass are shown in bold next.

```
- (void)viewDidLoad
{
    [super viewDidLoad];
    self.tableView.delegate = self.tableViewDelegate;
    self.tableView.dataSource = self.dataSource;
}
```

Now that we have the table view configured with a data source and delegate, we should give it some data to display. Let's start at the beginning of the app, with the list of topics.

TopicTableDataSource and TopicTableDelegate

The first view a user sees should be a list of topics so that the user can choose one to look at recent questions on that topic. Reviewing the model objects we created in Chapter 6, you can see that although Topics can hold Questions, and Questions can have Answers, nothing contains a Topic. If all we need is a list of topics, the topic data source just needs to hold a NSArray of Topic instances.

We already have an empty data source that we're not using—well, for nothing other than to *be* a data source, anyway—so let's add the array to that. First, we'll change its name: It's going to stop being an EmptyTableViewDataSource and start being a TopicTableDataSource. This is easily done with Xcode's refactoring capabilities: Right-click the EmptyTableViewDataSource's name in its interface file, choose Refactor, Rename, and type TopicTableDataSource. Xcode should rename the class and its source files and also make changes to the BrowseOverflowViewControllerTests fixture to use the new name. It's worth running the tests again to make sure all that worked. After it did, add the TopicTableDataSource class to the app target; it's just become production code.

Let's ensure that we can provide an array of topics to the data source, by creating a new test in a new test fixture, TopicTableDataSourceTests.

```
#import "TopicTableDataSourceTests.h"
#import "TopicTableDataSource.h"
#import "Topic.h"

@implementation TopicTableDataSourceTests

- (void)testTopicDataSourceCanReceiveAListOfTopics {
    TopicTableDataSource *dataSource =
        [[TopicTableDataSource alloc] init];
    Topic *sampleTopic = [[Topic alloc] initWithName: @"iPhone"
                                                  tag: @"iphone"];
    NSArray *topicsList = [NSArray arrayWithObject: sampleTopic];
    STAssertNoThrow([dataSource setTopics: topicsList],
```

```
        @"The data source needs a list of topics");
}

@end
```

Notice that there's no need—certainly not at the moment, anyway—to implement a getter for this property. An instance variable and a setter method in `TopicTableDataSource` will work:

```
- (void)setTopics: (NSArray *)newTopics {
    topics = newTopics;
}
```

Now that the object has a list of topics, it should prepare those topics for display in a table view. One of the things a table view needs to know is how many rows to display, which should be the number of `Topic` instances the data source has. Unless you tell it otherwise, a table view has a single section (section 0), so it will ask only how many rows there are in section 0. I'll add a couple of different tests to `TopicTableDataSource` to enforce some generality in the method. Here is how the whole fixture looks after refactoring the existing code: Because the `-setUp` method and one of the tests depends on `-[TopicTableDataSource setTopics:]` working, I decided it was OK to remove the test for that method's existence. It wouldn't be a problem to have left it, and some people do: It's still available via git's history[1] should I need it in the future.

```
#import "TopicTableDataSourceTests.h"
#import "TopicTableDataSource.h"
#import "Topic.h"

@implementation TopicTableDataSourceTests
{
    TopicTableDataSource *dataSource;
    NSArray *topicsList;
}

- (void)setUp {
    dataSource = [[TopicTableDataSource alloc] init];
    Topic *sampleTopic = [[Topic alloc] initWithName: @"iPhone"
                                                  tag: @"iphone"];
    topicsList = [NSArray arrayWithObject: sampleTopic];
    [dataSource setTopics: topicsList];
}

- (void)tearDown {
    dataSource = nil;
```

---

1. And it seems someone wrote a book about it anyway.

```
    topicsList = nil;
}


- (void)testOneTableRowForOneTopic {
    STAssertEquals((NSInteger)[topicsList count],
        [dataSource tableView: nil numberOfRowsInSection: 0],
        @"As there's one topic, there should be one row in the table");
}


- (void)testTwoTableRowsForTwoTopics {
    Topic *topic1 = [[Topic alloc] initWithName: @"Mac OS X"
                                            tag: @"macosx"];
    Topic *topic2 = [[Topic alloc] initWithName: @"Cocoa"
                                            tag: @"cocoa"];
    NSArray *twoTopicsList = [NSArray arrayWithObjects:
        topic1, topic2, nil];
    [dataSource setTopics: twoTopicsList];
    STAssertEquals((NSInteger)[twoTopicsList count],
        [dataSource tableView: nil numberOfRowsInSection: 0],
        @"There should be two rows in the table for two topics");
}


@end
```

That seems like a good set of tests, except that because I believe the table view "will ask only how many rows there are in section 0," I should make that requirement explicit. If it turns out to be wrong later, I want to find out in the noisiest way possible. This test requires the data source to fail if asked for section 1. A table with more than one section would ask for section 1 in addition to other sections.

```
- (void)testOneSectionInTheTableView {
    STAssertThrows([dataSource tableView: nil
                    numberOfRowsInSection: 1],
        @"Data source doesn't allow asking about additional sections");
}
```

The implementation of `-[TopicTableDataSource tableView:numberOfRowsInSection:]` that passes all of these tests is shown next.

```
- (NSInteger)tableView:(UITableView *)tableView
  numberOfRowsInSection:(NSInteger)section {
    NSParameterAssert(section == 0);
    return [topics count];
}
```

The other thing that a table view data source needs to do is to prepare cells for the table view to display. For every `Topic` in the list, there should be a cell. Conversely, the data source shouldn't prepare cells for any row in the table for which a `Topic` doesn't exist: This isn't expected to happen. Where there is a `Topic`, the text label in the cell should be the title of the Topic. This set of requirements can—you've guessed it—be expressed as a collection of unit tests on the TopicTableDataSourceTests fixture.

```
- (void)testDataSourceCellCreationExpectsOneSection {
    NSIndexPath *secondSection = [NSIndexPath indexPathForRow: 0
                                                    inSection: 1];
    STAssertThrows([dataSource tableView: nil
                       cellForRowAtIndexPath: secondSection],
        @"Data source will not prepare cells for unexpected sections");
}


- (void)testDataSourceCellCreationWillNotCreateMoreRowsThanItHasTopics
{
    NSIndexPath *afterLastTopic =
        [NSIndexPath indexPathForRow: [topicsList count] inSection: 0];
    STAssertThrows([dataSource tableView: nil
                       cellForRowAtIndexPath: afterLastTopic],
        @"Data source will not prepare more cells than there are topics");
}


- (void)testCellCreatedByDataSourceContainsTopicTitleAsTextLabel {
    NSIndexPath *firstTopic = [NSIndexPath indexPathForRow: 0
                                                 inSection: 0];
    UITableViewCell *firstCell = [dataSource tableView: nil
                              cellForRowAtIndexPath: firstTopic];
    NSString *cellTitle = firstCell.textLabel.text;
    STAssertEqualObjects(@"iPhone", cellTitle,
        @"Cell's title should be equal to the topic's title");
}
```

We immediately hit a problem when we try to satisfy these requirements in application code. The initializer for UITableViewCell looks like this:

```
- (id)initWithStyle:(UITableViewCellStyle)style
    reuseIdentifier:(NSString *)reuseIdentifier;
```

There's nothing in the app's requirements to tell us what value these style and reuseIdentifier parameters should take. That's because they're not really customer requirements; the reuse identifier is just a contract between the table view and its data source to allow the table view to recycle previously created cells. The customers and users probably don't care what we do with this value. They might care if the application runs out of memory through creating too many cells, but performance testing is outside the remit of unit testing. You can do anything here, from allowing the code to use any reuse identifier to enforcing a value through a test as an internal requirement on the code.

Similarly, users might have an opinion on what the table view cells *look* like, but it doesn't matter so much what cell style we use to get there. Unit tests on view code are a tricky subject. Most of the details of an app's presentation won't be in code anyway; they'll be in graphics assets and XIB files. If customers don't like the graphics, you just change them. It shouldn't be too contentious then to leave presentation details *in code* untested: flexibility being more important than (what are ultimately subjective) opinions of correctness.[2]

All of this means that our requirements are indeed complete, and that it's time to implement -[TopicTableDataSource tableView:cellForRowAtIndexPath:].

```
- (UITableViewCell *)tableView:(UITableView *)tableView
➥cellForRowAtIndexPath:(NSIndexPath *)indexPath {
    NSParameterAssert([indexPath section] == 0);
    NSParameterAssert([indexPath row] < [topics count]);
    UITableViewCell *topicCell =
        [[UITableViewCell alloc] initWithStyle:
        UITableViewCellStyleDefault reuseIdentifier: @"Topic"];
    topicCell.textLabel.text =
        [[topics objectAtIndex: [indexPath row]] name];
    return topicCell;
}
```

Knowing something about the use of UITableView, it would be standard practice to allow the table view to dequeue cells for reuse by the data source. We can't predict how or when the table view will do this, and making sure that the table view and data source work together well is the responsibility of an integration test, not a unit test; remember that unit testing is only one of many testing tools at our disposal. But we can ensure that our tests still pass when we change the implementation of -[TopicTableDataSource tableView:cellForRowAtIndexPath:].

```
NSString *topicCellReuseIdentifier = @"Topic";

- (UITableViewCell *)tableView:(UITableView *)tableView
➥cellForRowAtIndexPath:(NSIndexPath *)indexPath {
    NSParameterAssert([indexPath section] == 0);
    NSParameterAssert([indexPath row] < [topics count]);
    UITableViewCell *topicCell =[tableView
        dequeueReusableCellWithIdentifier: topicCellReuseIdentifier];
    if (!topicCell) {
        topicCell = [[UITableViewCell alloc]
            initWithStyle: UITableViewCellStyleDefault
          reuseIdentifier: topicCellReuseIdentifier];
    }
    topicCell.textLabel.text =
        [[topics objectAtIndex: [indexPath row]] name];
    return topicCell;
}
```

2. This is about presentation, not about the functional behavior of drawing to a view. If some view code is supposed to display certain data and doesn't, or draws only an arc segment where it's supposed to draw a complete circle, those are bugs: bugs that can be expressed as tests. But testing whether the interface that the code and other assets create is liked, or usable, must be left to other means.

Indeed, the tests do still pass.

With the user able to see a list of topics, selecting any of those topics should take the user to the list of questions in that topic. Selection is handled in the table view's delegate, specifically these methods:

```
- (NSIndexPath *)tableView:(UITableView *)tableView
    willSelectRowAtIndexPath:(NSIndexPath *)indexPath;
- (void)tableView:(UITableView *)tableView
    didSelectRowAtIndexPath:(NSIndexPath *)indexPath;
```

The first method is used to veto or change the user's selection of a table view row, which doesn't seem to fit what we need to do. We need to find out when the user has selected a topic so that the app can present the question list: That's a job for ...didSelectRow.... As with the data source class, we can co-opt the existing empty delegate class by refactoring it to be named `TopicTableDelegate`.

It doesn't seem like a good idea for the delegate to actually prepare the next view controller: That would mix the responsibilities of a table view delegate with view management. A better design is to have the delegate notify the view controller about the selected `Topic`, so that the view controller can interact with its navigation controller to push the next view controller into place. That means the delegate instance needs to have a reference to the data source object. It would be appropriate to set that up while the table view is being configured. Here is the `BrowseOverflowViewControllerTests` fixture after adding that requirement; unchanged test methods are not shown here.

```
@implementation BrowseOverflowViewControllerTests
{
    BrowseOverflowViewController *viewController;
    UITableView *tableView;
    id <UITableViewDataSource> dataSource;
    TopicTableDelegate *delegate;
}

- (void)setUp {
    viewController = [[BrowseOverflowViewController alloc] init];
    tableView = [[UITableView alloc] init];
    viewController.tableView = tableView;
    dataSource = [[TopicTableDataSource alloc] init];
    delegate = [[TopicTableDelegate alloc] init];
    viewController.dataSource = dataSource;
    viewController.tableViewDelegate = delegate;
}

- (void)tearDown {
    viewController = nil;
    tableView = nil;
    dataSource = nil;
}
```

```
- (void)testViewControllerConnectsDataSourceInViewDidLoad {
    [viewController viewDidLoad];
    STAssertEqualObjects([tableView dataSource], dataSource,
    @"View controller should have set the table view's data source");
}

- (void)testViewControllerConnectsDelegateInViewDidLoad {
    [viewController viewDidLoad];
    STAssertEqualObjects([tableView delegate], delegate,
    @"View controller should have set the table view's delegate");
}

- (void)testViewControllerConnectsDataSourceToDelegate {
    [viewController viewDidLoad];
    STAssertEqualObjects(delegate.tableDataSource, dataSource,
    @"The view controller should tell the table view delegate about
    its data source");
}

@end
```

To get the new -testViewControllerConnectsDataSourceToDelegate test to compile requires a new property on the TopicTableDelegate class.

```
#import <UIKit/UIKit.h>

@class TopicTableDataSource;

@interface TopicTableDelegate : NSObject <UITableViewDelegate>

@property (strong) TopicTableDataSource *tableDataSource;

@end
```

The implementation just needs the corresponding @synthesize directive. Now we are in a position to add the code to BrowseOverflowViewController to make this happen. Initially this seems like a simple, one-line addition to -viewDidLoad is all we need:

```
    self.tableViewDelegate.tableDataSource = self.dataSource;
```

Unfortunately, that's not so. The tableViewDelegate property is currently of type id <UITableViewDelegate>, and that type doesn't have a tableDataSource property. We need to change the type of tableViewDelegate to TopicTableDelegate. However, this might stop the BrowseOverflowViewController from being a general class that works for each view in the app, as originally planned. For the moment we'll make this change anyway, and press on with implementing the delegate behavior. We can evaluate whether to use this class in a more general context when we come to build the code for the questions table.

Change the type of the `tableViewDelegate` property, and you'll find you also need to change the type of the `BrowseOverflowViewController`'s `dataSource` property to `TopicTableDataSource`. After you've made both of those changes, the preceding line can be added to `-[BrowseOverflowViewController viewDidLoad]`. Now the tests pass again.

On to the delegate's behavior. It should find out which `Topic` object was represented by the tapped cell and create a notification to pass to the view controller, telling to it push a new view controller for questions in that `Topic`. The first part of what we'll need is still on the data source: a method to report the `Topic` instance that's represented by a particular table view cell. Cell locations are identified by index paths, so we're really asking for the `Topic` at a particular index path, expressed here as a test on `TopicTableDataSourceTests`.

```
- (void)testDataSourceIndicatesWhichTopicIsRepresentedForAnIndexPath {
    NSIndexPath *firstRow = [NSIndexPath indexPathForRow: 0
                                              inSection: 0];
    Topic *firstTopic = [dataSource topicForIndexPath: firstRow];
    STAssertEqualObjects(firstTopic.tag, @"iphone",
        @"The iPhone Topic is at row 0");
}
```

This implementation on `TopicTableDataSource` will be sufficient. The method should also be declared in the class's interface. Notice that I've been able to refactor some of the table view preparation code to use the new method: These changes are also shown.

```
- (Topic *)topicForIndexPath:(NSIndexPath *)indexPath {
    return [topics objectAtIndex: [indexPath row]];
}


- (UITableViewCell *)tableView:(UITableView *)tableView
        cellForRowAtIndexPath:(NSIndexPath *)indexPath {
    NSParameterAssert([indexPath section] == 0);
    NSParameterAssert([indexPath row] < [topics count]);
    UITableViewCell *topicCell = [tableView
        dequeueReusableCellWithIdentifier: topicCellReuseIdentifier];
    if (!topicCell) {
        topicCell = [[UITableViewCell alloc]
            initWithStyle: UITableViewCellStyleDefault
          reuseIdentifier: topicCellReuseIdentifier];
    }
    topicCell.textLabel.text =
        [[self topicForIndexPath: indexPath] name];
    return topicCell;
}
```

Now we have the infrastructure to build `-[TopicTableDelegate tableView: didSelectRowAtIndexPath:]`. Remember that we require it to post a notification, with the selected Topic instance as the notification's object. We immediately run into a problem: Notifications are normally posted to the -[NSNotificationCenter defaultCenter] singleton, but that object offers no way to investigate its state. How can we tell that the notification was posted?

One obvious way is to use the fact that if the object under test posts a notification, we can receive that notification in the test code. This means using a real, live NSNotificationCenter: The trade-off against creating a fake notification center is that the real notification center might introduce complications that stop tests being reliably repeatable, or make them very slow. On the other hand, it takes time to build a fake class.

NSNotificationCenter is not too complicated. It just keeps track of what invocations to call on what objects when a notification is posted. It doesn't even do any asynchronous work. It will be easiest to create the test using a real object: If it turns out to be problematic, we can rebuild the test. Here is a new fixture, TopicTableDelegateTests, making use of the NSNotificationCenter.

```
#import "TopicTableDelegateTests.h"
#import "TopicTableDelegate.h"
#import "TopicTableDataSource.h"
#import "Topic.h"

@implementation TopicTableDelegateTests
{
    NSNotification *receivedNotification;
    TopicTableDataSource *dataSource;
    TopicTableDelegate *delegate;
    Topic *iPhoneTopic;
}

- (void)setUp {
    delegate = [[TopicTableDelegate alloc] init];
    dataSource = [[TopicTableDataSource alloc] init];
    iPhoneTopic = [[Topic alloc] initWithName: @"iPhone"
                                          tag: @"iphone"];
    [dataSource setTopics: [NSArray arrayWithObject: iPhoneTopic]];
    delegate.tableDataSource = dataSource;
    [[NSNotificationCenter defaultCenter]
        addObserver: self
           selector: @selector(didReceiveNotification:)
               name: TopicTableDidSelectTopicNotification
             object: nil];
}

- (void)tearDown {
    receivedNotification = nil;
    dataSource = nil;
```

```
    delegate = nil;
    iPhoneTopic = nil;
    [[NSNotificationCenter defaultCenter] removeObserver: self];
}


- (void)didReceiveNotification: (NSNotification *)note {
    receivedNotification = note;
}


- (void)testDelegatePostsNotificationOnSelectionShowingWhichTopicWasSelected {
    NSIndexPath *selection = [NSIndexPath indexPathForRow: 0
                                                inSection: 0];
    [delegate tableView: nil didSelectRowAtIndexPath: selection];
    STAssertEqualObjects([receivedNotification name],
        @"TopicTableDidSelectTopicNotification",
        @"The delegate should notify that a topic was selected");
    STAssertEqualObjects([receivedNotification object],
        iPhoneTopic,
        @"The notification should indicate which topic was selected");
}


@end
```

It's very important to remove the test fixture as an observer in -tearDown. Failure to do so would mean the notification center keeping a stale reference to the fixture instance after OCUnit is finished with it, which might lead to a crash in a later test.

With that infrastructure in place, the -[TopicTableDelegate tableView: didSelectRowAtIndexPath:] method can look like this. The TopicTableDidSelectTopicNotification constant should be defined in TopicTableDelegate.m, and exposed via an extern declaration in the header.

```
- (void)tableView:(UITableView *)tableView
        didSelectRowAtIndexPath:(NSIndexPath *)indexPath {
    NSNotification *note =
        [NSNotification notificationWithName:
            TopicTableDidSelectTopicNotification
            object: [tableDataSource topicForIndexPath: indexPath]];
    [[NSNotificationCenter defaultCenter] postNotification: note];
}
```

This allows the test to pass, so we're at the green stage in red—green—refactor. Actually, refactoring seems like a good idea: We had to go through a lot of changes to make the BrowseOverflowViewController's instance variable types more specific, just to get this table view delegate class to work. After we got there, we found that the object needs to ask the data source for some internal data to do its thing. Perhaps it was overly aggressive to make the delegate and data source different objects. It would be good to combine these objects, removing the public access to the data source's internal details and, hopefully, cleaning up some of the mess we made in the view controller.[3]

The first step is to remove the -tableView:didSelectRowAtIndexPath: method from the TopicTableDelegate class and put it onto the TopicTableDataSource class. But wait: What we *actually* want to do is to demonstrate that the TopicTableDataSource class can exhibit the same selection behavior that we previously implemented on TopicTableDelegate. We should write a test. In fact, we can change the way TopicTableDelegateTests works so that it tests the data source. Here is that fixture again: Most of the changes are removed lines, and the test sends a delegate message to the data source instead of the (removed) delegate object.

```
#import "TopicTableDelegateTests.h"
#import "TopicTableDataSource.h"
#import "Topic.h"

@implementation TopicTableDelegateTests
{
    NSNotification *receivedNotification;
    TopicTableDataSource *dataSource;
    Topic *iPhoneTopic;
}

- (void)setUp {
    dataSource = [[TopicTableDataSource alloc] init];
    iPhoneTopic = [[Topic alloc] initWithName: @"iPhone"
                                          tag: @"iphone"];
    [dataSource setTopics: [NSArray arrayWithObject: iPhoneTopic]];
    [[NSNotificationCenter defaultCenter]
        addObserver: self
           selector: @selector(didReceiveNotification:)
               name: TopicTableDidSelectTopicNotification
             object: nil];
}

- (void)tearDown {
    receivedNotification = nil;
    dataSource = nil;
    iPhoneTopic = nil;
    [[NSNotificationCenter defaultCenter] removeObserver: self];
}
```

3. If you followed along making all the changes in this section, I apologize now, and offer as consolation that you can look forward to following along with all the refactoring. This kind of change is quite common in test-driven development, but will ultimately be for the best. We've tried something out, found that we can make it work, and then also discovered a more satisfactory way of doing the same thing. Two for the price of one, if you will.

```
- (void)didReceiveNotification: (NSNotification *)note {
    receivedNotification = note;
}


- (void)testDelegatePostsNotificationOnSelectionShowingWhichTopicWasSelected {
    NSIndexPath *selection = [NSIndexPath indexPathForRow: 0
                                                inSection: 0];
    [dataSource tableView: nil didSelectRowAtIndexPath: selection];
    STAssertEqualObjects([receivedNotification name],
        @"TopicTableDidSelectTopicNotification",
        @"The delegate should notify that a topic was selected");
    STAssertEqualObjects([receivedNotification object],
        iPhoneTopic,
        @"The notification should indicate which topic was selected");
}

@end
```

We find that the test no longer builds. The data source object doesn't respond to the method being tested, and the compiler can no longer find the definition of the notification name constant. The implementations on `TopicTableDelegate` ought to work—let's remove them from that class and migrate them over to `TopicTableDataSource` (literally a cut-and-paste job). We should add `UITableViewDelegate` to the list of protocols `TopicTableDataSource` conforms to. Here are the complete interface and implementation with changes highlighted.

TopicTableDataSource.h

```
#import <UIKit/UIKit.h>

@class Topic;

@interface TopicTableDataSource : NSObject <UITableViewDataSource,
        UITableViewDelegate>

- (void)setTopics: (NSArray *)newTopics;
- (Topic *)topicForIndexPath: (NSIndexPath *)indexPath;

@end

extern NSString *TopicTableDidSelectTopicNotification;
```

TopicTableDataSource.m

```
#import "TopicTableDataSource.h"
#import "Topic.h"
```

```objc
NSString *topicCellReuseIdentifier = @"Topic";

@implementation TopicTableDataSource
{
    NSArray *topics;
}

- (void)setTopics: (NSArray *)newTopics {
    topics = newTopics;
}

- (NSInteger)tableView:(UITableView *)tableView
 numberOfRowsInSection:(NSInteger)section {
    NSParameterAssert(section == 0);
    return [topics count];
}

- (Topic *)topicForIndexPath:(NSIndexPath *)indexPath {
    return [topics objectAtIndex: [indexPath row]];
}

- (UITableViewCell *)tableView:(UITableView *)tableView
         cellForRowAtIndexPath:(NSIndexPath *)indexPath {
    NSParameterAssert([indexPath section] == 0);
    NSParameterAssert([indexPath row] < [topics count]);
    UITableViewCell *topicCell = [tableView
        dequeueReusableCellWithIdentifier: topicCellReuseIdentifier];
    if (!topicCell) {
        topicCell = [[UITableViewCell alloc]
            initWithStyle: UITableViewCellStyleDefault
          reuseIdentifier: topicCellReuseIdentifier];
    }
    topicCell.textLabel.text =
        [[self topicForIndexPath: indexPath] name];
    return topicCell;
}

- (void)tableView:(UITableView *)tableView
    didSelectRowAtIndexPath:(NSIndexPath *)indexPath {
    NSNotification *note = [NSNotification
        notificationWithName: TopicTableDidSelectTopicNotification
                      object: [self topicForIndexPath: indexPath]];
    [[NSNotificationCenter defaultCenter] postNotification: note];
}

@end

NSString *TopicTableDidSelectTopicNotification =
    @"TopicTableDidSelectTopicNotification";
```

When I run the tests now, everything works, but there's a warning in `BrowseOverflowViewControllerTests` relating to a type conversion using the `TopicTableDataSource` class in an instance variable. We need to clean up that fixture and indeed, the `BrowseOverflowViewController` class itself. Most of what we're doing is removing code or just changing types; there won't be any sample code to show, so just follow along with the discussion for the next couple of paragraphs. We'll take a look at the final state of the classes at the end.

The first thing to notice is that because the `TopicTableDelegate` no longer does anything, there's no need for the view controller to have an instance, nor for it to pass the instance to a table view. It should instead pass the `TopicTableDataSource` instance as the table's delegate. This means that `-[BrowseOverflowViewControllerTests testViewControllerHasATableViewDelegateProperty]` and `-testView ControllerConnectsDataSourceToDelegate` are no longer necessary and can be removed.

Furthermore, the `-testViewControllerConnectsDelegateInViewDidLoad` test should ensure that the table view's delegate is connected to the view controller's data source property. The data source is now fulfilling both roles. Having made this change, we find that the test fixture isn't using its `delegate` instance variable at all, so it can be removed along with references in `-setUp` and `-tearDown`. Also, the type of the `dataSource` instance variable can be changed to `id <UITableViewDataSource, UITableViewDelegate>` to reflect that variable's dual role.

Now we find that a test starts failing again: `BrowseOverflowViewController` still passes its delegate property to the table view, instead of using the data source as the delegate. That line needs changing in `-viewDidLoad` to use the data source for both purposes.

That makes the test pass, but there's now untested code. `BrowseOverflowView Controller` still has a delegate property and, indeed, passes it a data source in `-viewDidLoad`. None of this is required anymore, so we can remove all the definitions and uses of the delegate property. Finally, because the view controller no longer needs to know about custom methods on the data source object, we can return to using the generic `id <UITableViewDataSource, UITableViewDelegate>` type to refer to that property.

However, it's not quite final. Notice that the `TopicTableDelegate` class is no longer used nor tested at all; it's entirely redundant. You can convince yourself of this by doing a projectwide search in Xcode. A more incontrovertible demonstration is to remove that class completely and run the tests again. The suite still builds and passes.

For reference, here are the files affected by that refactoring work (the ones that remain, anyway). As an aside, because the `TopicTableDataSource` no longer needs to tell any external objects about which `Topic` is at which index path, you can remove `-[TopicTableDataSourceTests testDataSourceIndicatesWhichTopicIs RepresentedForAnIndexPath]`. The method `-[TopicTableDataSource topicForIndexPath:]` is still used internally, so don't delete it. You could move the declaration out of the header file and into a class continuation if you wanted to "tidy up" the interface, though. Remember, even though you remove that test, the method is still effectively being tested because it's used elsewhere in the class.

BrowseOverflowViewControllerTests.m

```objc
#import "BrowseOverflowViewControllerTests.h"
#import "BrowseOverflowViewController.h"
#import "TopicTableDataSource.h"

@implementation BrowseOverflowViewControllerTests
{
    BrowseOverflowViewController *viewController;
    UITableView *tableView;
    id <UITableViewDataSource, UITableViewDelegate> dataSource;
}

- (void)setUp {
    viewController = [[BrowseOverflowViewController alloc] init];
    tableView = [[UITableView alloc] init];
    viewController.tableView = tableView;
    dataSource = [[TopicTableDataSource alloc] init];
    viewController.dataSource = dataSource;
}

- (void)tearDown {
    viewController = nil;
    tableView = nil;
    dataSource = nil;
}

- (void)testViewControllerHasATableViewProperty {
    objc_property_t tableViewProperty =
        class_getProperty([viewController class], "tableView");
    STAssertTrue(tableViewProperty != NULL,
        @"BrowseOverflowViewController needs a table view");
}

- (void)testViewControllerHasADataSourceProperty {
    objc_property_t dataSourceProperty =
        class_getProperty([viewController class], "dataSource");
    STAssertTrue(dataSourceProperty != NULL,
        @"View Controller needs a data source");
}

- (void)testViewControllerConnectsDataSourceInViewDidLoad {
    [viewController viewDidLoad];
```

```
        STAssertEqualObjects([tableView dataSource], dataSource,
            @"View controller should have set the table view's data source");
}


- (void)testViewControllerConnectsDelegateInViewDidLoad {
    [viewController viewDidLoad];
    STAssertEqualObjects([tableView delegate], dataSource,
        @"View controller should have set the table view's delegate");
}

@end
```

BrowseOverflowViewController.h

```
#import <UIKit/UIKit.h>

@interface BrowseOverflowViewController : UIViewController

@property (strong) UITableView *tableView;
@property (strong) id <UITableViewDataSource, UITableViewDelegate>
    dataSource;

@end
```

BrowseOverflowViewController.m

```
#import "BrowseOverflowViewController.h"
#import "TopicTableDataSource.h"

@implementation BrowseOverflowViewController

@synthesize tableView;
@synthesize dataSource;

- (void)viewDidLoad
{
    [super viewDidLoad];
    self.tableView.delegate = self.dataSource;
    self.tableView.dataSource = self.dataSource;
}

@end
```

This seems like a much better situation. The view controller is again independent of the details of the table data source. A class that needed to know too much about the insides of another has been merged, creating a single well-encapsulated class with a clear responsibility. And the tests still run. To complete the story of the topics table, we need to create the questions table, and present it on the screen.

Telling the View Controller to Create a New View Controller

The view controller should create a new view controller that is set up to display questions in the selected topic. The first thing we need it to do is register for the notification sent by the data source. We only want for the view controller to push a new view while its own view is active. In other words, a view controller shouldn't push the next view while it's lying dormant in the background, because that will allow the view hierarchy to get out of sync.

This can be arranged by registering for the notification in `- [BrowseOverflowView Controller viewDidAppear:]` and removing that notification in `- [BrowseOver flowViewController viewWillDisappear:]`, so that the view controller will receive the notification only while its view is active. Let's write tests to require these methods to perform the correct registration and deregistration. These tests will require an interesting situation that we haven't yet come across: test code implemented on the class under test, rather than in a fake object or test fixture. We need a method that the view controller executes in response to the notification, that we can use to discover when the class has received the notification.

It would be poor design to implement that method on the `BrowseOverflowView Controller` class, which is supposed to be production code, not test-supporting code. Objective-C offers us a way to keep the separation between test code and production code while still adding a method onto the required class: using categories. We can create a category whose code is stored in the test fixture, but that adds additional methods to `BrowseOverflowViewController`. Here is the category, along with the tests implemented on `BrowseOverflowViewControllerTests`. Both of these parts live in the `BrowseOverflowViewControllerTests.m` implementation file.

```
static const char *notificationKey =
"BrowseOverflowViewControllerTestsAssociatedNotificationKey";
@implementation BrowseOverflowViewController (TestNotificationDelivery)

- (void)userDidSelectTopicNotification: (NSNotification *)note {
    objc_setAssociatedObject(self, notificationKey, note,
        OBJC_ASSOCIATION_RETAIN);
}

@end


@implementation BrowseOverflowViewControllerTests

- (void)setUp {
    //...
    objc_removeAssociatedObjects(viewController);
}
```

```objc
- (void)tearDown {
    objc_removeAssociatedObjects(viewController);
    //...
}

//...
- (void)testDefaultStateOfViewControllerDoesNotReceiveNotifications {
    [[NSNotificationCenter defaultCenter]
     postNotificationName: TopicTableDidSelectTopicNotification
     object: nil
     userInfo: nil];
    STAssertNil(objc_getAssociatedObject(viewController,
        notificationKey),
        @"Notification should not be received before -viewDidAppear:");
}

- (void)testViewControllerReceivesTableSelectionNotificationAfterViewDidAppear {
    [viewController viewDidAppear: NO];
    [[NSNotificationCenter defaultCenter]
     postNotificationName: TopicTableDidSelectTopicNotification
     object: nil
     userInfo: nil];
    STAssertNotNil(objc_getAssociatedObject(viewController,
        notificationKey),
        @"After -viewDidAppear: the view controller should handle"
        @"selection notifications");
}

- (void)testViewControllerDoesNotReceiveTableSelectNotificationAfterViewWill
➥Disappear {
    [viewController viewDidAppear: NO];
    [viewController viewWillDisappear: NO];
    [[NSNotificationCenter defaultCenter]
     postNotificationName: TopicTableDidSelectTopicNotification
     object: nil
     userInfo: nil];
    STAssertNil(objc_getAssociatedObject(viewController,
        notificationKey),
        @"After -viewWillDisappear: is called, the view controller"
        @"should no longer respond to topic selection notifications");
}

@end
```

The category method uses Objective-C's associated storage facility to record the notification received by a BrowseOverflowViewController object. The tests set up the associated storage, configure the view controller instance, and then post a notification. If the class is adding and removing itself as an observer as required, the associated object should be set only when the notification is received after calling -viewDidAppear: but before calling -viewWillDisappear: and not at any other time.

Two of these tests—which ensure that the view controller doesn't receive the notifications at different points in its life cycle—already pass, because the view controller currently doesn't receive any notifications at all. This can be quickly remedied by adding the following methods to BrowseOverflowViewController.

```
- (void)viewDidAppear:(BOOL)animated {
    [[NSNotificationCenter defaultCenter]
    addObserver: self
    selector: @selector(userDidSelectTopicNotification:)
    name: TopicTableDidSelectTopicNotification
    object: nil];
}

- (void)viewWillDisappear:(BOOL)animated {
    [[NSNotificationCenter defaultCenter]
    removeObserver: self
    name: TopicTableDidSelectTopicNotification
    object: nil];
}
```

However, this cannot be considered a complete implementation of those methods. Apple's class documentation for UIViewController[4] says, for each of these methods, "If you override this method, you must call super at some point in your implementation." We must require this of our own methods, but how?

To check whether an object being tested calls a method previously, we have been providing fake implementations of those methods that record whether they are called, and the parameters if applicable. You can't make a class extend one class in the app and a different class in the test fixture, so the only way we could insert sensing code to check for calls to super would be if we could replace the real methods on UIViewController with our sensing methods. Luckily, the Objective-C runtime allows us to do exactly that: replace one method on a class with another. Initially, this requires adding our sensing methods to a category on UIViewController; again I've chosen to add this short category to BrowseOverflowViewControllerTests.m because it (currently) only supports tests in that fixture.

```
static const char *viewDidAppearKey =
    "BrowseOverflowViewControllerTestsViewDidAppearKey";
static const char *viewWillDisappearKey =
    "BrowseOverflowViewControllerTestsViewWillDisappearKey";
```

4. http://developer.apple.com/library/ios/#documentation/uikit/reference/UIViewController_Class/Reference/Reference.html

```
@implementation UIViewController (TestSuperclassCalled)

- (void)browseOverflowViewControllerTests_viewDidAppear: (BOOL)animated
{
    NSNumber *parameter = [NSNumber numberWithBool: animated];
    objc_setAssociatedObject(self, viewDidAppearKey, parameter,
        OBJC_ASSOCIATION_RETAIN);
}

- (void)browseOverflowViewControllerTests_viewWillDisappear:
    (BOOL)animated {
    NSNumber *parameter = [NSNumber numberWithBool: animated];
    objc_setAssociatedObject(self, viewWillDisappearKey, parameter,
        OBJC_ASSOCIATION_RETAIN);
}

@end
```

In -[BrowseOverflowViewControllerTests setUp], the fixture should swap the real implementations for the fake ones. This arranges that when, for example, a -viewDidAppear: message is sent to a UIViewController instance, the implementation of -browseOverflowViewControllerTests_viewDidAppear: will be run instead. Similarly, the -tearDown method swaps the implementations back to their original positions. Because we'll need to swap methods four times (once each for two methods in -setUp, and again in -tearDown) I'll create a class method on the test fixture to do the actual swapping.

```
@implementation BrowseOverflowViewControllerTests
{
    //...
    SEL realViewDidAppear, testViewDidAppear;
    SEL realViewWillDisappear, testViewWillDisappear;
}

+ (void)swapInstanceMethodsForClass: (Class) cls selector: (SEL)sel1
    andSelector: (SEL)sel2 {
    Method method1 = class_getInstanceMethod(cls, sel1);
    Method method2 = class_getInstanceMethod(cls, sel2);
    method_exchangeImplementations(method1, method2);
}

- (void)setUp {
    //...
    realViewDidAppear = @selector(viewDidAppear:);
    testViewDidAppear =
        @selector(browseOverflowViewControllerTests_viewDidAppear:);
    [BrowseOverflowViewControllerTests
        swapInstanceMethodsForClass: [UIViewController class]
```

```
                              selector: realViewDidAppear
                           andSelector: testViewDidAppear];

    realViewWillDisappear = @selector(viewWillDisappear:);
    testViewWillDisappear =
      @selector(browseOverflowViewControllerTests_viewWillDisappear:);
    [BrowseOverflowViewControllerTests
        swapInstanceMethodsForClass: [UIViewController class]
                           selector: realViewWillDisappear
                        andSelector: testViewWillDisappear];
}

- (void)tearDown {
    //...
    [BrowseOverflowViewControllerTests
        swapInstanceMethodsForClass: [UIViewController class]
                           selector: realViewDidAppear
                        andSelector: testViewDidAppear];
    [BrowseOverflowViewControllerTests
        swapInstanceMethodsForClass: [UIViewController class]
                           selector: realViewWillDisappear
                        andSelector: testViewWillDisappear];
}
```

This approach is not without its limitations. Interesting things could happen with the tests if the framework tries to run multiple tests in parallel. This could cause the test versions of the methods to be swapped back for the Apple-supplied implementations while tests are running, meaning that results are not reliably reported. OCUnit does not currently offer the capability to execute tests concurrently, but you should bear this in mind if future versions of the framework add that capability. Nevertheless, the technique allows us to test that the super implementation of the methods is called.

```
- (void)testViewControllerCallsSuperViewDidAppear {
    [viewController viewDidAppear: NO];
    STAssertNotNil(objc_getAssociatedObject(viewController,
        viewDidAppearKey),
        @"-viewDidAppear: should call through to superclass"
        @"implementation");
}

- (void)testViewControllerCallsSuperViewWillDisappear {
    [viewController viewWillDisappear: NO];
    STAssertNotNil(objc_getAssociatedObject(viewController,
        viewWillDisappearKey),
        @"-viewWillDisappear: should call through to superclass"
        @"implementation");
}
```

Neither of the methods currently invokes the superclass implementation, but that can be fixed: Add the appropriate calls to super in -[BrowseOverflowViewController viewDidAppear:] and -[BrowseOverflowViewController viewWillDisappear:].[5]

Now let's build the code that will be executed when the user selects a topic, the code that will pass the selected topic to a newly created view controller. The first thing to notice is that we're already (ab)using the BrowseOverflowViewController's reaction to the topic selection notification to investigate when the notification is received, whereas we now need to use it to supply production behavior. Again, the method-exchanging approach used previously will help to have it both ways: We'll provide an (initially empty) implementation of -[BrowseOverflowViewController userDidSelectTopicNotification] in the production class, rename the method in the test support category, and ensure that the tests that need the support version exchange the methods correctly. The changes to the category and test fixture in BrowseOverflowViewControllerTests.m are shown here. Notice that in this case, only the tests that require the altered behavior from the category swap the method implementations. It is not done in -setUp, so that tests requiring the default behavior can function.

```
@implementation BrowseOverflowViewController (TestNotificationDelivery)

- (void)browseOverflowControllerTests_userDidSelectTopicNotification:
    (NSNotification *)note {
    objc_setAssociatedObject(self, notificationKey, note,
        OBJC_ASSOCIATION_RETAIN);
}

@end

//...

@implementation BrowseOverflowViewControllerTests
{
    BrowseOverflowViewController *viewController;
    UITableView *tableView;
    id <UITableViewDataSource, UITableViewDelegate> dataSource;
    SEL realViewDidAppear, testViewDidAppear;
    SEL realViewWillDisappear, testViewWillDisappear;
    SEL realUserDidSelectTopic, testUserDidSelectTopic;
}
```

5. One of this chapter's technical reviewers made the valid point that all the contortions gone through previously to test this delegation to the superclass in a test demonstrate one thing: that a unit test might not be the best place to express this requirement. This sort of thing is something the static analyzer could easily detect; however, when I tried that it didn't report a problem.

```
- (void)setUp {
    viewController = [[BrowseOverflowViewController alloc] init];
    tableView = [[UITableView alloc] init];
    viewController.tableView = tableView;
    dataSource = [[TopicTableDataSource alloc] init];
    viewController.dataSource = dataSource;
    objc_removeAssociatedObjects(viewController);

    realViewDidAppear = @selector(viewDidAppear:);
    testViewDidAppear =
        @selector(browseOverflowViewControllerTests_viewDidAppear:);
    [BrowseOverflowViewControllerTests
        swapInstanceMethodsForClass: [UIViewController class]
                    selector: realViewDidAppear
                 andSelector: testViewDidAppear];

    realViewWillDisappear = @selector(viewWillDisappear:);
    testViewWillDisappear =
      @selector(browseOverflowViewControllerTests_viewWillDisappear:);
    [BrowseOverflowViewControllerTests
        swapInstanceMethodsForClass: [UIViewController class]
                    selector: realViewWillDisappear
                 andSelector: testViewWillDisappear];

    realUserDidSelectTopic = @selector(userDidSelectTopicNotification:);
    testUserDidSelectTopic =
@selector(browseOverflowControllerTests_userDidSelectTopicNotification:)
;}
//...


- (void)testDefaultStateOfViewControllerDoesNotReceiveNotifications {
    [BrowseOverflowViewControllerTests
        swapInstanceMethodsForClass:
            [BrowseOverflowViewController class]
                        selector: realUserDidSelectTopic
                     andSelector: testUserDidSelectTopic];
    [[NSNotificationCenter defaultCenter]
    postNotificationName: TopicTableDidSelectTopicNotification
    object: nil
    userInfo: nil];
    STAssertNil(objc_getAssociatedObject(viewController,
        notificationKey),
        @"Notification should not be received before
➥-viewDidAppear:");
    [BrowseOverflowViewControllerTests
        swapInstanceMethodsForClass:
            [BrowseOverflowViewController class]
                        selector: realUserDidSelectTopic
                     andSelector: testUserDidSelectTopic];
}
```

```
- (void)testViewControllerReceivesTableSelectionNotificationAfterViewDidAppear {
    [BrowseOverflowViewControllerTests
        swapInstanceMethodsForClass:
            [BrowseOverflowViewController class]
                    selector: realUserDidSelectTopic
                    andSelector: testUserDidSelectTopic];
    [viewController viewDidAppear: NO];
    [[NSNotificationCenter defaultCenter]
     postNotificationName: TopicTableDidSelectTopicNotification
     object: nil
     userInfo: nil];
    STAssertNotNil(objc_getAssociatedObject(viewController,
        notificationKey),
        @"After -viewDidAppear: the view controller should handle"
        @" selection notifications");
    [BrowseOverflowViewControllerTests
        swapInstanceMethodsForClass:
            [BrowseOverflowViewController class]
                    selector: realUserDidSelectTopic
                    andSelector: testUserDidSelectTopic];
}

- (void)testViewControllerDoesNotReceiveTableSelectNotificationAfterViewWill
  Disappear {
    [BrowseOverflowViewControllerTests
        swapInstanceMethodsForClass:
            [BrowseOverflowViewController class]
                    selector: realUserDidSelectTopic
                    andSelector: testUserDidSelectTopic];
    [viewController viewDidAppear: NO];
    [viewController viewWillDisappear: NO];
    [[NSNotificationCenter defaultCenter]
     postNotificationName: TopicTableDidSelectTopicNotification
     object: nil
     userInfo: nil];
    STAssertNil(objc_getAssociatedObject(viewController,
        notificationKey),
        @"After -viewWillDisappear: is called, the view controller"
        @" should no longer respond to topic selection notifications");
    [BrowseOverflowViewControllerTests
        swapInstanceMethodsForClass:
            [BrowseOverflowViewController class]
                    selector: realUserDidSelectTopic
                    andSelector: testUserDidSelectTopic];
}
@end
```

That little bit of refactoring allows us to write tests of the behavior of the object when it does receive a new notification. The main feature of this behavior is that the view controller should push another view controller onto the navigation stack. Should the view controller find out about its `UINavigationController` instance via its existing `navigationController` property, or should we have the application's code pass a navigation controller to the class via a property that we define? The second approach seems redundant; Apple has already arranged that a view controller is told where its navigation controller is, so there's no need to reinvent that particular wheel.

It seems we might be able to use the `UINavigationController` in a test without modification or resorting to fakes. The controller has a `topViewController` property that returns the view controller at the top of the navigation stack. With any luck, we should be able to see that pushing our new view controller changes the `topViewController` property. Initially, let's change `-[BrowseOverflowView` `ControllerTests setUp]` to put the view controller under test into a `UINavigationController`. We need to make sure that doing so doesn't break any of the existing behavior.

```
@implementation BrowseOverflowViewControllerTests
{
    //...
    UINavigationController *navController;
}

- (void)setUp {
    //...
    navController = [[UINavigationController alloc]
        initWithRootViewController: viewController];
}

- (void)tearDown {
    //...
    navController = nil;
}

//tests...
@end
```

When we run the tests again, we find that they still all pass; putting the `BrowseOverflowViewController` inside a `UINavigationController` doesn't break anything. Let's press on. As a result of running `-userDidSelectTopicNotification:` the `topViewController` of the navigation controller should be a new instance of `BrowseOverflowViewController`.

```
- (void)testSelectingTopicPushesNewViewController {
    [viewController userDidSelectTopicNotification: nil];
    UIViewController *currentTopVC = navController.topViewController;
    STAssertFalse([currentTopVC isEqual: viewController],
```

```
        @"New view controller should be pushed onto the stack");
    STAssertTrue([currentTopVC isKindOfClass:
    [BrowseOverflowViewController class]],
        @"New view controller should be a BrowseOverflowViewController");
}
```

New code must be added to the `BrowseOverflowViewController`'s implementa-tion of `-userDidSelectTopicNotification:` to make this happen (note: This is the method in `BrowseOverflowViewController.m`, not the category method in the test fixture).

```
- (void)userDidSelectTopicNotification: (NSNotification *)note {
    BrowseOverflowViewController *nextViewController =
        [[BrowseOverflowViewController alloc] init];
    [[self navigationController] pushViewController: nextViewController
                                          animated: YES];
}
```

But the new view controller doesn't have a table data source. That's not correct. We need a data source for the question list associated with the selected topic. The topic should be the object referenced in the notification, which we could configure the data source with.

```
- (void)testNewViewControllerHasAQuestionListDataSourceForTheSelectedTopic {
    Topic *iPhoneTopic = [[Topic alloc] initWithName: @"iPhone"
                                                 tag: @"iphone"];
    NSNotification *iPhoneTopicSelectedNotification =
        [NSNotification notificationWithName:
            TopicTableDidSelectTopicNotification
        object: iPhoneTopic];
    [viewController userDidSelectTopicNotification:
        iPhoneTopicSelectedNotification];
    BrowseOverflowViewController *nextViewController =
        (BrowseOverflowViewController *)navController.topViewController;
    STAssertTrue([nextViewController.dataSource
        isKindOfClass: [QuestionListTableDataSource class]],
        @"Selecting a topic should push a list of questions");
    STAssertEqualObjects([(QuestionListTableDataSource *)
      nextViewController.dataSource topic], iPhoneTopic,
      @"The questions to display should come from the selected topic");
}
```

This test gives us the first clues we need to implement the next part of the app: the data source for a list of questions in one topic.

The Question List Data Source

Before getting at all involved with new functionality on this object, we need to make the final test from the previous section pass. That requires a new app class, called `QuestionListTableDataSource`, with a `topic` property that is set to a `Topic` instance. Because it's being used as the `dataSource` property of the

`BrowseOverflowViewController`, we know that it needs to conform to the table view delegate and data source protocols. That means providing implementations of a couple of required methods in the data source protocol, which again we'll fill in later.

QuestionListTableDataSource.h

```
#import <Foundation/Foundation.h>

@class Topic;
@interface QuestionListTableDataSource : NSObject
    <UITableViewDataSource, UITableViewDelegate>

@property (strong) Topic *topic;

@end
```

QuestionListTableDataSource.m

```
#import "QuestionListTableDataSource.h"

@implementation QuestionListTableDataSource

@synthesize topic;

- (NSInteger)tableView:(UITableView *)tableView
   numberOfRowsInSection:(NSInteger)section {
     return 0;
}

- (UITableViewCell *)tableView:(UITableView *)tableView
         cellForRowAtIndexPath:(NSIndexPath *)indexPath {
     return nil;
}

@end
```

Then we should create and configure one of these in `-[BrowseOverflowView Controller userDidSelectTopicNotification:]`.

```
- (void)userDidSelectTopicNotification: (NSNotification *)note {
     Topic * selectedTopic = (Topic *)[note object];
     BrowseOverflowViewController *nextViewController =
         [[BrowseOverflowViewController alloc] init];
     QuestionListTableDataSource *questionsDataSource =
         [[QuestionListTableDataSource alloc] init];
     questionsDataSource.topic = selectedTopic;
     nextViewController.dataSource = questionsDataSource;
     [[self navigationController] pushViewController: nextViewController
         animated: YES];
}
```

The actual business of displaying questions is fairly similar to the business of configuring cells for the Topic table view, so these tests will look similar. The key difference is that there are more details of the question to display—the title, score, asker's name and avatar—and by default, table view cells do not have the capability to display this many separate details. An easy way to configure a cell to show multiple different properties of the question is to define a custom cell subclass with the subviews appropriate for those properties. So the tests we write for the UITableViewDataSource methods—tests on a new fixture, QuestionListTableDataSourceTests—will require that those properties exist.

```
@implementation QuestionListTableDataSourceTests
{
    QuestionListTableDataSource *dataSource;
    Topic *iPhoneTopic;
    NSIndexPath *firstCell;
    Question *question1, *question2;
    Person *asker1;
}

- (void)setUp {
    dataSource = [[QuestionListTableDataSource alloc] init];
    iPhoneTopic = [[Topic alloc] initWithName: @"iPhone"
                                          tag: @"iphone"];
    dataSource.topic = iPhoneTopic;
    firstCell = [NSIndexPath indexPathForRow: 0 inSection: 0];
    question1 = [[Question alloc] init];
    question1.title = @"Question One";
    question1.score = 2;
    question2 = [[Question alloc] init];
    question2.title = @"Question Two";

    asker1 = [[Person alloc] initWithName: @"Graham Lee"
            avatarLocation:
  @"http://www.gravatar.com/avatar/563290c0c1b776a315b36e863b388a0c"];
    question1.asker = asker1;
}

- (void)tearDown {
    dataSource = nil;
    iPhoneTopic = nil;
    firstCell = nil;
    question1 = nil;
    question2 = nil;
    asker1 = nil;
}
```

```
- (void)testTopicWithNoQuestionsLeadsToOneRowInTheTable {
    STAssertEquals([dataSource tableView: nil numberOfRowsInSection: 0],
        (NSInteger)1,
        @"The table view needs a 'no data yet' placeholder cell");
}


- (void)testTopicWithQuestionsResultsInOneRowPerQuestionInTheTable {
    [iPhoneTopic addQuestion: question1];
    [iPhoneTopic addQuestion: question2];
    STAssertEquals([dataSource tableView: nil numberOfRowsInSection: 0],
        (NSInteger)2,
        @"Two questions in the topic means two rows in the table");
}


- (void)testContentOfPlaceholderCell {
    UITableViewCell *placeholderCell = [dataSource tableView: nil
        cellForRowAtIndexPath: firstCell];
    STAssertEqualObjects(placeholderCell.textLabel.text,
        @"There was a problem connecting to the network.",
        @"The placeholder cell ought to display a placeholder message");
}


- (void)testPlaceholderCellNotReturnedWhenQuestionsExist {
    [iPhoneTopic addQuestion: question1];
    UITableViewCell *cell = [dataSource tableView: nil
        cellForRowAtIndexPath: firstCell];
    STAssertFalse([cell.textLabel.text isEqualToString:
        @"There was a problem connecting to the network."],
        @"Placeholder should only be shown when there's no content");
}


- (void)testCellPropertiesAreTheSameAsTheQuestion {
    [iPhoneTopic addQuestion: question1];
    QuestionSummaryCell *cell =
        (QuestionSummaryCell *)[dataSource tableView: nil
        cellForRowAtIndexPath: firstCell];
    STAssertEqualObjects(cell.titleLabel.text,
        @"Question One",
        @"Question cells display the question's title");
    STAssertEqualObjects(cell.scoreLabel.text, @"2",
        @"Question cells display the question's score");
    STAssertEqualObjects(cell.nameLabel.text, @"Graham Lee",
        @"Question cells display the asker's name");
}
```

There are two distinct situations this data source needs to take into account, because it's displaying data that will come from the network. It's possible that a slow or unavailable network means the topic won't have any question data available at the time the table is displayed, in which case the table should show a placeholder describing the problem. That is why this fixture tests that there's still one row in the table view even when there aren't any questions in the topic—the placeholder cell should still exist.

Getting these tests to pass requires extending our trivial implementation of QuestionListTableDataSource:

QuestionListTableDataSource.h

```objc
#import <Foundation/Foundation.h>

@class Topic;
@class QuestionSummaryCell;
@class AvatarStore;

@interface QuestionListTableDataSource : NSObject
    <UITableViewDataSource, UITableViewDelegate>

@property (strong) Topic *topic;
@property (weak) IBOutlet QuestionSummaryCell *summaryCell;

@end
```

QuestionListTableDataSource.m

```objc
@implementation QuestionListTableDataSource

@synthesize topic;
@synthesize summaryCell;

- (NSInteger)tableView:(UITableView *)aTableView
 numberOfRowsInSection:(NSInteger)section {
    return [[topic recentQuestions] count] ?: 1;
}

- (UITableViewCell *)tableView:(UITableView *)aTableView
        cellForRowAtIndexPath:(NSIndexPath *)indexPath {
    UITableViewCell *cell = nil;
    if ([topic.recentQuestions count]) {
        Question *question = [topic.recentQuestions
            objectAtIndex: indexPath.row];
        summaryCell = [tableView
            dequeueReusableCellWithIdentifier: @"question"];
        if (!summaryCell) {
            [[NSBundle bundleForClass: [self class]]
                loadNibNamed: @"QuestionSummaryCell"
                       owner: self
                     options: nil];
        }
        summaryCell.titleLabel.text = question.title;
        summaryCell.scoreLabel.text =
```

```
            [NSString stringWithFormat: @"%d", question.score];
        summaryCell.nameLabel.text = question.asker.name;

        cell = summaryCell;
        summaryCell = nil;
    }
    else {
        cell = [tableView dequeueReusableCellWithIdentifier:
            @"placeholder"];
        if (!cell) {
            cell = [[UITableViewCell alloc]
                initWithStyle: UITableViewCellStyleDefault
              reuseIdentifier: @"placeholder"];
        }
        cell.textLabel.text =
            @"There was a problem connecting to the network.";
    }
    return cell;
}

@end
```

That doesn't yet get us to passing tests. The test calls for `QuestionListTableData` `Source` to use a special `UITableViewCell` subclass called `QuestionSummaryCell`. It's quite easy to define this class.

QuestionSummaryCell.h

```
#import <UIKit/UIKit.h>

@interface QuestionSummaryCell : UITableViewCell

@property (strong) IBOutlet UILabel *titleLabel;
@property (strong) IBOutlet UILabel *scoreLabel;
@property (strong) IBOutlet UILabel *nameLabel;

@end
```

QuestionSummaryCell.m

```
#import "QuestionSummaryCell.h"

@implementation QuestionSummaryCell

@synthesize titleLabel;
@synthesize scoreLabel;
@synthesize nameLabel;

@end
```

Even now we're not in a position to get the tests to pass. Why not? The various properties on the `QuestionSummaryCell` need initialization for the test to work. In the production code, it would be useful to use a XIB file, so that display properties such as the subview's positions, fonts, sizes, and so on are easily configurable without having to change the code. It would be possible to create a collection of view objects in the test fixture to pass in to the cell during tests. Then we would have to arrange for this collection of objects to be used by the `-tableView:cellForRowAtIndexPath:` method in a test, but the objects from the XIB in the app. That's some complexity to add to a method just so that it can be used in a test.

Is there a problem with using the XIB in both the app and the test? It makes the code simpler, although it does mean that problems in the XIB file might manifest as unit test failures, leading us to spend time tracking bugs in the code that don't really exist. It's a trade-off, to be sure, but in this case I think it's worthwhile.

Create a new empty XIB file, calling it "QuestionSummaryCell.xib". Lay out a `UITableViewCell` instance, with the labels required to display the various properties. Change the cell's class to `QuestionSummaryCell`, and connect the labels to the cell's outlets in the header file as shown in Figure 9.2. Outlets are connected by holding the Ctrl key and dragging from the label in the XIB to the declaration of the outlet property in the header file.

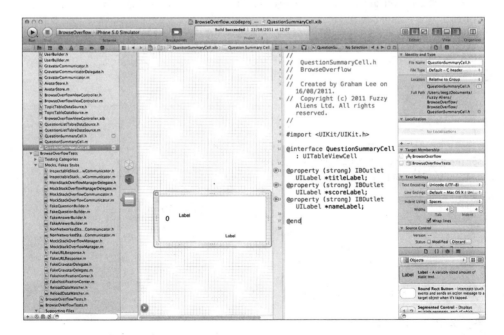

Figure 9.2   Layout of views in `QuestionSummaryCell.xib`, and connections to the cell's properties.

Finally, change the class of the "File's Owner" to QuestionListTableDataSource, and connect the cell to that class's summaryCell outlet. Now the tests written for the cell creation previously can pass, because the XIB file allows the test (and app) to generate cells configurable in the way required by the tests.

This isn't a complete implementation of the table view's data source methods. We still need to display avatar images of the person who asked each question. Here are the additions to the QuestionListTableDataSourceTests fixture:[6]

```
@implementation QuestionListTableDataSourceTests
{
  //...
    AvatarStore *store;
    NSNotification *receivedNotification;
}


- (void)didReceiveNotification: (NSNotification *)note {
    receivedNotification = note;
}


- (void)setUp {
  //...
    store = [[AvatarStore alloc] init];
}


- (void)tearDown {
    // ...
    store = nil;
    receivedNotification = nil;
}


//...


- (void)testCellGetsImageFromAvatarStore {
    dataSource.avatarStore = store;
    NSURL *imageURL = [[NSBundle bundleForClass: [self class]]
        URLForResource: @"Graham_Lee"
        withExtension: @"jpg"];
    NSData *imageData = [NSData dataWithContentsOfURL: imageURL];
    [store setData: imageData forLocation:
  @"http://www.gravatar.com/avatar/563290c0c1b776a315b36e863b388a0c"];
    [iPhoneTopic addQuestion: question1];
    QuestionSummaryCell *cell =
        (QuestionSummaryCell *) [dataSource tableView: nil
```

6. The AvatarStore class can be found in the book's sample code project at GitHub. It's responsible for fetching avatar images from the gravatar.com website and notifying the app when new images are available. Because it's mainly doing network tasks, building this part of the app is very similar to constructing the StackOverflowManager and StackOverflowCommunicator seen earlier in the project.

```
                                cellForRowAtIndexPath: firstCell];
    STAssertNotNil(cell.avatarView.image,
        @"The avatar store should supply the avatar images");
}


- (void)testQuestionListRegistersForAvatarNotifications {
    FakeNotificationCenter *center =
        [[FakeNotificationCenter alloc] init];
    dataSource.notificationCenter = (NSNotificationCenter *)center;
    [dataSource registerForUpdatesToAvatarStore: store];
    STAssertTrue([center hasObject: dataSource
        forNotification: AvatarStoreDidUpdateContentNotification],
  @"The data source should know when new images have been downloaded");
}


- (void)testQuestionListStopsRegisteringForAvatarNotifications {
    FakeNotificationCenter *center =
        [[FakeNotificationCenter alloc] init];
    dataSource.notificationCenter = (NSNotificationCenter *)center;
    [dataSource registerForUpdatesToAvatarStore: store];
    [dataSource removeObservationOfUpdatesToAvatarStore: store];
    STAssertFalse([center hasObject: dataSource
        forNotification: AvatarStoreDidUpdateContentNotification],
        @"The data source should no longer listen to avatar store"
        @" notifications");
}


- (void)testQuestionListCausesTableReloadOnAvatarNotification {
    ReloadDataWatcher *fakeTableView = [[ReloadDataWatcher alloc] init];
    dataSource.tableView = (UITableView *)fakeTableView;
    [dataSource avatarStoreDidUpdateContent: nil];
    STAssertTrue([fakeTableView didReceiveReloadData],
        @"Data source should get the table view to reload when new data"
        @" is available");
}

@end
```

The data source will attempt to populate a `UIImageView` in the cell using data from the `AvatarStore`. Because you can only create a `UIImage` with data that really is an image, I've added a (rather handsome) sample image to the project that can be used in the test target. Either use this image or provide your own. Because the `AvatarStore` might not have received the image data from the remote server when the table view is drawn, the `AvatarStore` will post notifications when it gets new content. The data source must listen for these notifications and tell the table to reload its data—meaning that it needs a reference to the table view. Here is the new state of the `Question ListTableDataSource` class, with changes highlighted:

QuestionListTableDataSource.h

```objc
#import <Foundation/Foundation.h>

@class Topic;
@class QuestionSummaryCell;
@class AvatarStore;

@interface QuestionListTableDataSource : NSObject
    <UITableViewDataSource, UITableViewDelegate>

@property (strong) Topic *topic;
@property (weak) IBOutlet QuestionSummaryCell *summaryCell;
@property (strong) AvatarStore *avatarStore;
@property (weak) UITableView *tableView;
@property (strong) NSNotificationCenter *notificationCenter;

- (void)registerForUpdatesToAvatarStore: (AvatarStore *)store;
- (void)removeObservationOfUpdatesToAvatarStore: (AvatarStore *)store;
- (void)avatarStoreDidUpdateContent: (NSNotification *)notification;

@end
```

QuestionListTableDataSource.m

```objc
#import "QuestionListTableDataSource.h"
#import "QuestionSummaryCell.h"
#import "Topic.h"
#import "Question.h"
#import "Person.h"
#import "AvatarStore.h"

@implementation QuestionListTableDataSource

@synthesize topic;
@synthesize summaryCell;
@synthesize avatarStore;
@synthesize tableView;
@synthesize notificationCenter;

- (NSInteger)tableView:(UITableView *)aTableView
 numberOfRowsInSection:(NSInteger)section {
    return [[topic recentQuestions] count] ?: 1;
}
```

```
- (UITableViewCell *)tableView:(UITableView *)aTableView
        cellForRowAtIndexPath:(NSIndexPath *)indexPath {
    UITableViewCell *cell = nil;
    if ([topic.recentQuestions count]) {
        Question *question = [topic.recentQuestions
            objectAtIndex: indexPath.row];
        summaryCell = [tableView dequeueReusableCellWithIdentifier:
            @"question"];
        if (!summaryCell) {
            [[NSBundle bundleForClass: [self class]]
                        loadNibNamed: @"QuestionSummaryCell"
                              owner: self
                            options: nil];
        }
        summaryCell.titleLabel.text = question.title;
        summaryCell.scoreLabel.text =
            [NSString stringWithFormat: @"%d", question.score];
        summaryCell.nameLabel.text = question.asker.name;

        NSData *avatarData = [avatarStore dataForURL:
          question.asker.avatarURL];
        if (avatarData) {
          summaryCell.avatarView.image = [UIImage imageWithData:
              avatarData];
        }
        cell = summaryCell;
        summaryCell = nil;
    }
    else {
        cell = [tableView dequeueReusableCellWithIdentifier:
            @"placeholder"];
        if (!cell) {
            cell = [[UITableViewCell alloc]
                initWithStyle: UITableViewCellStyleDefault
                reuseIdentifier: @"placeholder"];
        }
        cell.textLabel.text =
            @"There was a problem connecting to the network.";
    }
    return cell;
}


- (void)registerForUpdatesToAvatarStore:(AvatarStore *)store {
    [notificationCenter addObserver: self
        selector: @selector(avatarStoreDidUpdateContent:)
            name: AvatarStoreDidUpdateContentNotification
          object: store];
}
```

```
- (void)removeObservationOfUpdatesToAvatarStore: (AvatarStore *)store {
    [notificationCenter removeObserver: self
        name: AvatarStoreDidUpdateContentNotification
      object: store];
}


- (void)avatarStoreDidUpdateContent:(NSNotification *)notification {
    [tableView reloadData];
}
```

@end

The link from a data source to its table view will be set up in -[BrowseOverflow
ViewController viewDidLoad], so the test to ensure that it happens goes in
BrowseOverflowViewControllerTests.

```
- (void)testViewControllerConnectsTableViewBacklinkInViewDidLoad {
    QuestionListTableDataSource *questionDataSource =
        [[QuestionListTableDataSource alloc] init];
    viewController.dataSource = questionDataSource;
    [viewController viewDidLoad];
    STAssertEqualObjects(questionDataSource.tableView,
        tableView,
        @"Back-link to table view should be set in data source");
}
```

To avoid breaking anything, the view controller should set this property only when
the dataSource object defines the property. (Remember, TopicTableDataSource
objects don't have a link back to their table view.)

```
- (void)viewDidLoad
{
    [super viewDidLoad];
    self.tableView.delegate = self.dataSource;
    self.tableView.dataSource = self.dataSource;
    objc_property_t tableViewProperty =
        class_getProperty([dataSource class], "tableView");
    if (tableViewProperty) {
        [dataSource setValue: tableView forKey: @"tableView"];
    }
}
```

The final step is to add the UIImageView to the XIB and connect it to the outlet
defined previously on the QuestionSummaryCell. The XIB should end up looking like
Figure 9.3.

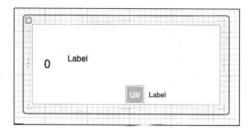

Figure 9.3   Layout of views in `QuestionSummaryCell.xib`,
with the image view added.

Where Next

From here on out, the behavior looks similar to that you've already seen throughout this chapter. Selection of a question from the list is handled in a way very similar to that for selecting a topic; after a question is selected, another view controller is pushed, this time displaying the question content and any answers that have been provided. You could decide to implement this code yourself as an exercise—remember to write tests first!—or grab the sample code from GitHub and see how I did it.

With the view controllers and table data sources in place, all the components of the app are in place, and the one remaining task is to ensure that they are all properly connected. This will be the topic of the next chapter, after which we should have a complete and working app.

10

Putting It All Together

We've created all the parts of the app now—a data model along with the behavior needed to update the model from the Internet; classes to present the data in views; and controllers to take care of the application's workflow. What we haven't done yet is put these classes together to make a complete, functioning application. Hopefully, the work we've put into designing these classes to be used and to work in isolation means it won't be too hard to construct the app.

Completing the Application's Workflow

The finishing touch is to make sure that the classes we've created are instantiated and configured correctly to support the application workflow. They all work in isolation, but can we integrate them into an app? I certainly hope so; but if any problems appear, we should create tests to ensure that we fix them.

It makes sense to start from the beginning—the first view in the app is the list of topics, so the application should make sure that the list exists and that the view controller is ready to display the list for the user. The entry point for the application is in the app delegate's -application:didFinishLaunchingWithOptions: method, so the work to configure and display the first view should occur there. Testing that method should be done in a fixture for the app delegate; that doesn't exist, so we should create BrowseOverflowAppDelegateTests first.

The sample app delegate creates a navigation controller and configures it as the window's root view controller. Here's the template code:

```
- (BOOL)application:(UIApplication *)application
    didFinishLaunchingWithOptions:(NSDictionary *)launchOptions
{
    // Override point for customization after application launch.
    // Add the navigation controller's view to the window and display.
    self.window.rootViewController = self.navigationController;
    [self.window makeKeyAndVisible];
    return YES;
}
```

I'm happy to believe that Apple's engineers know how to write iOS apps, but because I'll be making changes to this method, I want to ensure that I don't break any of their sterling work. Therefore I'll begin by encapsulating the current behavior as testable requirements on the method.

BrowseOverflowAppDelegateTests.h

```
#import <SenTestingKit/SenTestingKit.h>

@interface BrowseOverflowAppDelegateTests : SenTestCase

@end
```

BrowseOverflowAppDelegateTests.m

```
#import "BrowseOverflowAppDelegateTests.h"

#import <UIKit/UIKit.h>
#import "BrowseOverflowAppDelegate.h"

@implementation BrowseOverflowAppDelegateTests {
    UIWindow *window;
    UINavigationController *navigationController;
    BrowseOverflowAppDelegate *appDelegate;
}

- (void)setUp {
    window = [[UIWindow alloc] init];
    navigationController = [[UINavigationController alloc] init];
    appDelegate = [[BrowseOverflowAppDelegate alloc] init];
    appDelegate.window = window;
    appDelegate.navigationController = navigationController;
}

- (void)tearDown {
    window = nil;
    navigationController = nil;
    appDelegate = nil;
}

- (void)testWindowIsKeyAfterApplicationLaunch {
    [appDelegate application: nil didFinishLaunchingWithOptions: nil];
    STAssertTrue(window.keyWindow,
        @"App delegate's window should be key");
}

- (void)testWindowHasRootNavigationControllerAfterApplicationLaunch {
    [appDelegate application: nil didFinishLaunchingWithOptions: nil];
```

```
        STAssertEqualObjects(window.rootViewController,
            navigationController,
            @"App delegate's navigation controller should be the root VC");
}


- (void)testAppDidFinishLaunchingReturnsYES {
    STAssertTrue([appDelegate application: nil
        didFinishLaunchingWithOptions: nil],
        @"Method should return YES");
}

@end
```

These tests pass without issue because they were reverse-engineered from the code.[1] What we get here is notification if any changes made to this method break the existing behavior. Incidentally, the fact that these tests are motivated by existing code rather than by design is clear in the form of the tests. For example, we have a test called "testAppDidFinishLaunchingReturnsYES"—it doesn't express what the intention behind returning YES is, or what it means to return YES, just that this is what we expect to happen.

Now that we know what will happen if we break anything, we can get on with expressing the application's behavior. The app should start by showing a list of topics, and we've already arranged that a BrowseOverflowViewController using a TopicTableDataSource can do that. So a reasonable set of requirements would be that after the app launches, the root navigation controller's top view controller should be a BrowseOverflowViewController, and that it has a TopicTableDataSource configured as its data source object. Because the app's launch behavior is determined by the app delegate, these tests both belong on BrowseOverflowAppDelegateTests.

```
- (void)testNavigationControllerShowsABrowseOverflowViewController {
    [appDelegate application: nil didFinishLaunchingWithOptions: nil];
    id visibleViewController =
        appDelegate.navigationController.topViewController;
    STAssertTrue([visibleViewController isKindOfClass:
        [BrowseOverflowViewController class]],
        @"Views in this app are supplied by BrowseOverflowViewControllers");
}


- (void)testFirstViewControllerHasATopicTableDataSource {
    [appDelegate application: nil didFinishLaunchingWithOptions: nil];
    BrowseOverflowViewController *viewController =
        (BrowseOverflowViewController *)
         appDelegate.navigationController.topViewController;
    STAssertTrue([viewController.dataSource isKindOfClass:
        [TopicTableDataSource class]],
```

---

1. In fact you might find that you need to add the BrowseOverflowAppDelegate.m source file to the test bundle target's "Compile Sources" build phase to get the test to compile successfully, if Xcode hasn't already done that for you.

```
            @"First view should display a list of topics");
}
```

These tests will fail because there currently isn't a top view controller in the navigation controller's stack. The -application:didFinishLaunchingWithOptions: method should supply the correct objects.

```
- (BOOL)application:(UIApplication *)application
    didFinishLaunchingWithOptions:(NSDictionary *)launchOptions
{
    BrowseOverflowViewController *firstViewController =
        [[BrowseOverflowViewController alloc] initWithNibName: nil
        bundle: nil];
    TopicTableDataSource *dataSource =
        [[TopicTableDataSource alloc] init];
    firstViewController.dataSource = dataSource;
    self.navigationController.viewControllers =
        [NSArray arrayWithObject: firstViewController];
    self.window.rootViewController = self.navigationController;
    [self.window makeKeyAndVisible];
    return YES;
}
```

That's the view controller, but what content should it display? It's best to leave that flexible; although the list of topics shown in the app will need to be distributed as part of the app, there's no "correct" value, and it could change as new topics get used on the website, or whoever is marketing BrowseOverflow wants to promote different terms. We won't require a specific value for the contents of the list, but we will make sure the app starts with a non-zero-length list of topics to display.

```
- (void)testTopicListIsNotEmptyOnAppLaunch {
    [appDelegate application: nil didFinishLaunchingWithOptions: nil];
    id <UITableViewDataSource> dataSource =
      [(BrowseOverflowViewController *)[appDelegate.navigationController
      topViewController] dataSource];
    STAssertFalse([dataSource tableView: nil
                  numberOfRowsInSection: 0] == 0,
        @"There should be some rows to display");
}
```

There are many ways to get this list into the data source. For now, a method on the app delegate that constructs the array in code will be sufficient.

```
- (NSArray *)topics {
    NSString *tags[] = { @"iphone", @"cocoa-touch", @"uikit",
        @"objective-c", @"xcode" };
    NSString *names[] = { @"iPhone", @"Cocoa Touch", @"UIKit",
        @"Objective-C", @"Xcode" };
    NSMutableArray *topicList = [NSMutableArray array];
    for (NSInteger i = 0; i < 5; i++) {
        Topic *thisTopic = [[Topic alloc] initWithName: names[i]
                                                   tag: tags[i]];
```

```
        [topicList addObject: thisTopic];
    }
    return [topicList copy];
}

- (BOOL)application:(UIApplication *)application
didFinishLaunchingWithOptions:(NSDictionary *)launchOptions
{
    BrowseOverflowViewController *firstViewController =
[[BrowseOverflowViewController alloc] initWithNibName: nil bundle: nil];
    TopicTableDataSource *dataSource = [[TopicTableDataSource alloc]
        init];
    [dataSource setTopics: [self topics]];
    firstViewController.dataSource = dataSource;
    self.navigationController.viewControllers =
        [NSArray arrayWithObject: firstViewController];
    self.window.rootViewController = self.navigationController;
    [self.window makeKeyAndVisible];
    return YES;
}
```

This should be everything needed to get the first view onto the screen, so it's time to take a look at how the application behaves. Run the application by pressing Command-R, or by clicking the Run button on the left of Xcode's toolbar. You'll be greeted by the disappointing sight of Figure 10.1.

Figure 10.1   Current state of the BrowseOverflow application.

That's unexpected. When this happened, I went back to the tests and reexamined whether my expectations were being met: Does the application definitely configure the correct view controller? The `BrowseOverflowAppDelegateTests` fixture ensures that this is the case. Does the view controller configure the table view's data source? Yes, that's required in `BrowseOverflowViewControllerTests`. Does the view controller put a `UITableView` onto the screen? That's not controlled by code, so there's no test for it; it's in the XIB. Inspecting `BrowseOverflowViewController.xib` shows that there isn't a table view in it. Put a `UITableView` into the interface, and connect it to the `tableView` property on the class to end up with a situation shown in Figure 10.2.

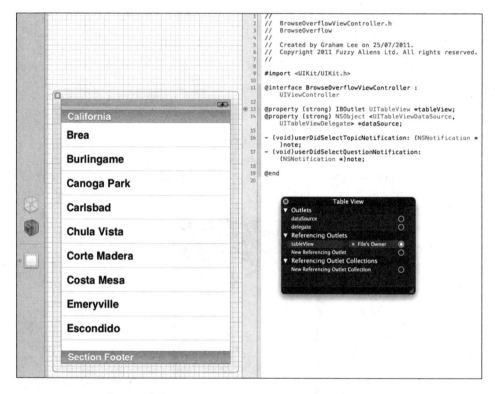

Figure 10.2   Configuring a table view in Interface Builder.

This mistake serves to reiterate a point I made in Chapter 1, "About Software Testing and Unit Testing": that test-driven code is not guaranteed to result in a working app. It reduces the risk associated with bugs in the code, but in this case a bug in the data means that the app did not function correctly. Unit testing is a useful tool but is not the only tool in the box. Anyway, with that issue fixed, let's check whether the app does something useful now. Run it again, to see the more pleasant sight that is Figure 10.3.

Figure 10.3   The Topic table view displayed by the running app.

It's satisfying to finally see the app doing something useful, having spent so many chapters on writing code. Let's capitalize on this result by getting the next view—the table of questions for a particular topic—to follow on. This will be a little more complex than the topic table was, because the app needs to (asynchronously) fetch content from the network and display that content when it loads. We've written code for that, in the StackOverflowManager and its connected classes. So far, that code hasn't been integrated into the app workflow at all.

The StackOverflowManager was designed to take a delegate it would inform when important events occur. Because there's a one-one relationship between the manager object and its delegate, it makes sense for each class that needs to use StackOverflowManager's features to have its own instance. There are a lot of components to configure—the StackOverflowManager uses a StackOverflowCommunicator and all the various ...Builder classes—and it makes sense to do this in a single place to reduce code duplication. Some developers would look for a Dependency Injection or Inversion of Control framework.

That level of configurability is useful when there are multiple implementations of a class and an expectation that changing between implementations (particularly after the app is in the field) is a common occurrence, but that is not true in this case. We can create an object that is responsible for creating and vending configured instances of the necessary classes. Notice that because this is all we need, the principle of YAGNI (Ya Ain't Gonna Need It) leads us to avoid doing anything more complicated—not just out of principle, but because then we would need to write a load of tests and application code for functionality the app won't make use of. This configuration will be represented by a new class, called `BrowseOverflowObjectConfiguration`, with a new test fixture, `BrowseOverflowObjectConfigurationTests`. The test fixture is shown here.

```
#import "BrowseOverflowObjectConfigurationTests.h"
#import "BrowseOverflowObjectConfiguration.h"
#import "StackOverflowManager.h"

#import <UIKit/UIKit.h>

@implementation BrowseOverflowObjectConfigurationTests

- (void)testConfigurationOfCreatedStackOverflowManager {
    BrowseOverflowObjectConfiguration *configuration =
        [[BrowseOverflowObjectConfiguration alloc] init];
    StackOverflowManager *manager =
        [configuration stackOverflowManager];
    STAssertNotNil(manager, @"The StackOverflowManager should
➥exist");
    STAssertNotNil(manager.communicator,
        @"Manager should have a StackOverflowCommunicator");
    STAssertNotNil(manager.questionBuilder,
        @"Manager should have a question builder");
    STAssertNotNil(manager.answerBuilder,
        @"Manager should have an answer builder");
    STAssertEqualObjects(manager.communicator.delegate, manager,
        @"The manager is the communicator's delegate");
}

@end
```

The implementation of the class, `BrowseOverflowObjectConfiguration`, is shown next.

BrowseOverflowObjectConfiguration.h

```
#import <Foundation/Foundation.h>

@class StackOverflowManager;

@interface BrowseOverflowObjectConfiguration : NSObject

- (StackOverflowManager *)stackOverflowManager;

@end
```

BrowseOverflowObjectConfiguration.m

```objc
#import "BrowseOverflowObjectConfiguration.h"
#import "StackOverflowManager.h"
#import "StackOverflowCommunicator.h"
#import "QuestionBuilder.h"
#import "AnswerBuilder.h"

@implementation BrowseOverflowObjectConfiguration

- (StackOverflowManager *)stackOverflowManager {
    StackOverflowManager *manager = [[StackOverflowManager alloc] init];
    manager.communicator = [[StackOverflowCommunicator alloc] init];
    manager.communicator.delegate = manager;
    manager.questionBuilder = [[QuestionBuilder alloc] init];
    manager.answerBuilder = [[AnswerBuilder alloc] init];
    return manager;
}

@end
```

Because this object represents application-level configuration, it makes sense for the class to be instantiated once, in the application delegate, and passed to the view controllers, which can make use of the `StackOverflowManager` instances it creates as they need them. That requirement can be specified as a test in the `BrowseOverflowApp DelegateTests` fixture.

```objc
- (void)testFirstViewControllerHasAnObjectConfiguration {
    [appDelegate application: nil didFinishLaunchingWithOptions: nil];
    BrowseOverflowViewController *topicViewController =
      (BrowseOverflowViewController *)[appDelegate.navigationController
      topViewController];
    STAssertNotNil(topicViewController.objectConfiguration,
  @"The view controller should have an object configuration instance");
}
```

This requires a simple property declaration and synthesis on the `BrowseOverflow ViewController` class, and the following addition to `-[BrowseOverflowAppDelegate application:didFinishLaunchingWithOptions:]`.

```objc
- (BOOL)application:(UIApplication *)application
    didFinishLaunchingWithOptions:(NSDictionary *)launchOptions
{
    BrowseOverflowViewController *firstViewController =
        [[BrowseOverflowViewController alloc] initWithNibName: nil
                                                       bundle: nil];
    firstViewController.objectConfiguration =
        [[BrowseOverflowObjectConfiguration alloc] init];
```

```
TopicTableDataSource *dataSource =
    [[TopicTableDataSource alloc] init];
[dataSource setTopics: [self topics]];
firstViewController.dataSource = dataSource;
self.navigationController.viewControllers =
    [NSArray arrayWithObject: firstViewController];
self.window.rootViewController = self.navigationController;
[self.window makeKeyAndVisible];
return YES;
}
```

That addresses the topic list view controller, but it's the question list and question detail views that will need to make use of `StackOverflowManager` objects. Therefore, the view controller should, when creating new view controllers to push onto the navigation stack, pass the object configuration instance through to the new controllers. This test belongs on the `BrowseOverflowViewControllerTests` fixture.

```
- (void)testSelectingTopicNotificationPassesObjectConfigurationToNewViewController
➥{
    BrowseOverflowObjectConfiguration *objectConfiguration =
        [[BrowseOverflowObjectConfiguration alloc] init];
    viewController.objectConfiguration = objectConfiguration;
    [viewController userDidSelectTopicNotification: nil];
    BrowseOverflowViewController *newTopVC =
        (BrowseOverflowViewController *)navController.topViewController;
    STAssertEqualObjects(newTopVC.objectConfiguration,
        objectConfiguration,
        @"The object configuration should be passed through to the"
        @" new view controller");
}
```

One line must be added to `-[BrowseOverflowViewControlleruserDid SelectTopicNotification:]`.

```
nextViewController.objectConfiguration = self.objectConfiguration;
```

The test and code change required to support the same behavior on question selection is very similar—the view controller showing the question's details needs to be able to create a `StackOverflowManager`, so it should receive the `BrowseOverflowObject Configuration` instance, too.

Now that the view controllers have the capability to download content from Stack Overflow, they should actually do so. Taking the question list view as an example, we want to start downloading data before the view appears, to improve the chance that the data is ready to display when the table is shown to the user, or shortly after. The view controller's `-viewWillAppear:` method is an appropriate point in the view controller's life cycle to do this work.

As ever, the test shouldn't actually connect to the network. Because the view controller gets its `StackOverflowManager` configured by the `BrowseOverflowObject Configuration` class, we have an opportunity to change the object it receives by changing the behavior of the object configuration instance it uses. A subclass of BrowseOverflowObjectConfiguration can support unit tests by allowing the test fixture to decide what object the view controller will use.

TestObjectConfiguration.h

```
#import "BrowseOverflowObjectConfiguration.h"

@interface TestObjectConfiguration : BrowseOverflowObjectConfiguration

@property (strong) id objectToReturn;

@end
```

TestObjectConfiguration.m

```
#import "TestObjectConfiguration.h"

@implementation TestObjectConfiguration

@synthesize objectToReturn;

- (StackOverflowManager *)stackOverflowManager {
    return (StackOverflowManager *)self.objectToReturn;
}

@end
```

Now a test on BrowseOverflowViewControllerTests can use this object to set up a test that determines whether the view controller asks the manager to fetch a list of questions to populate a QuestionListTableDataSource.

```
- (void)testViewWillAppearOnQuestionListInitiatesLoadingOfQuestions {
    TestObjectConfiguration *configuration =
        [[TestObjectConfiguration alloc] init];
    MockStackOverflowManager *manager =
        [[MockStackOverflowManager alloc] init];
    configuration.objectToReturn = manager;
    viewController.objectConfiguration = configuration;
    viewController.dataSource =
        [[QuestionListTableDataSource alloc] init];
    [viewController viewWillAppear: YES];
    STAssertTrue([manager didFetchQuestions],
        @"View controller should have arranged for question content"
        @" to be downloaded");
}
```

The `MockStackOverflowManager` manager currently supports only testing the `StackOverflowCommunicator` delegate API, but we need to extend it to detect whether the "external" API requests from the app are being called. A simple flag to report whether the `-fetchQuestionsOnTopic:` message was sent will support the preceding test.

MockStackOverflowManager.h

```
@class Topic;

@interface MockStackOverflowManager : NSObject
    <StackOverflowCommunicatorDelegate> {
    // ...
    BOOL wasAskedToFetchQuestions;
}
// ...

- (BOOL)didFetchQuestions;
- (void)fetchQuestionsOnTopic: (Topic *)topic;
@end
```

MockStackOverflowManager.m

```
#import "MockStackOverflowManager.h"
#import "Topic.h"

@implementation MockStackOverflowManager
// ...
- (BOOL)didFetchQuestions {
    return wasAskedToFetchQuestions;
}

- (void)fetchQuestionsOnTopic:(Topic *)topic {
    wasAskedToFetchQuestions = YES;
}
@end
```

Now the app code can be implemented, in `-[BrowseOverflowViewController viewWillAppear:]`. It only makes sense for the question list to be fetched when the table is going to display a list of questions, so the code incorporates that condition. Don't forget to write additional tests to ensure that the question list isn't requested at other times (and that the question details are loaded when required).

```
- (void)viewWillAppear:(BOOL)animated {
    [super viewWillAppear: animated];
    self.manager = [objectConfiguration stackOverflowManager];
    if ([self.dataSource isKindOfClass:
        [QuestionListTableDataSource class]]) {
        Topic *selectedTopic =
```

```
        [(QuestionListTableDataSource *)self.dataSource topic];
    [self.manager fetchQuestionsOnTopic: selectedTopic];
  }
}
```

That covers loading the data, but what about using it? After the stack overflow manager has downloaded the content and prepared the model objects, it will use its delegate protocol to signal to the view controller that the data is ready, or that there was an error in the process. We therefore require that when the `StackOverflowManager` instance is created, the view controller is set as its delegate and that the `BrowseOverflowView Controller` class conforms to the delegate protocol. This pair of tests belongs on the `BrowseOverflowViewControllerTests` fixture.

```
- (void)testViewControllerConformsToStackOverflowManagerDelegateProtocol {
    STAssertTrue([viewController conformsToProtocol:
        @protocol(StackOverflowManagerDelegate)],
        @"View controllers need to be StackOverflowManagerDelegates");
}
```

```
-
(void)testViewControllerConfiguredAsStackOverflowManagerDelegateOnManagerCreation
➡{
    [viewController viewWillAppear: YES];
    STAssertEqualObjects(viewController.manager.delegate,
        viewController,
        @"View controller sets itself as the manager's delegate");
}
```

The first test can easily be made to pass by changing the declaration of `Browse OverflowViewController` to:

```
@interface BrowseOverflowViewController : UIViewController
    <StackOverflowManagerDelegate>
```

This introduces a number of warnings, because the protocol requires a number of methods to be implemented on the conforming class. We don't know what those methods need to do yet, so we provide empty method bodies.

A single line added to `-[BrowseOverflowController viewWillAppear:]` is sufficient to get the other test passing.

```
- (void)viewWillAppear:(BOOL)animated {
    [super viewWillAppear: animated];
    self.manager = [objectConfiguration stackOverflowManager];
    self.manager.delegate = self;
    // ...
}
```

However, making this test pass comes at the cost of earlier tests failing. Where we've used the `MockStackOverflowManager` instance to examine how the view controller uses its manager, that object doesn't have a delegate property, so the view controller is sending it messages it doesn't implement. It should be easy enough to add a property of type id to the `MockStackOverflowManager` class to suppress these errors without changing the behavior of the tests.

Now let's think about the requirements of those protocol methods. When the view controller receives notification from the `StackOverflowManager` that some questions have been downloaded, it should add those questions to its data source (which is, presumably, a `QuestionListTableDataSource`) and tell the table view to reload its data. Remember, although the `StackOverflowManager`'s helpers download and create a list of `Question` objects, they do not then add the questions to the selected `Topic`. On `BrowseOverflowViewControllerTests`:

```
- (void)testDownloadedQuestionsAreAddedToTopic {
    QuestionListTableDataSource *topicDataSource =
        [[QuestionListTableDataSource alloc] init];
    viewController.dataSource = topicDataSource;
    Topic *topic = [[Topic alloc] initWithName: @"iPhone"
                                           tag: @"iphone"];
    topicDataSource.topic = topic;
    Question *question1 = [[Question alloc] init];
    [viewController didReceiveQuestions:
        [NSArray arrayWithObject: question1]];
    STAssertEqualObjects([topic.recentQuestions lastObject], question1,
        @"Question was added to the topic");
}


- (void)testTableViewReloadedWhenQuestionsReceived {
    QuestionListTableDataSource *topicDataSource =
        [[QuestionListTableDataSource alloc] init];
    viewController.dataSource = topicDataSource;
    ReloadDataWatcher *watcher = [[ReloadDataWatcher alloc] init];
    viewController.tableView = (UITableView *)watcher;
    [viewController didReceiveQuestions: [NSArray array]];
    STAssertTrue([watcher didReceiveReloadData],
        @"Table view was reloaded after fetching new data");
}
```

Notice that the `topicDataSource` object is used in both tests; that's a good opportunity for refactoring. The `ReloadDataWatcher` class was introduced in the previous chapter to support testing the avatar-loading code.

An implementation of `-[BrowseOverflowViewControllerdidReceive` `Questions:]` that passes the preceding two tests looks like this:

```
- (void)didReceiveQuestions:(NSArray *)questions {
    Topic *topic =
        ((QuestionListTableDataSource *)self.dataSource).topic;
    for (Question *thisQuestion in questions) {
        [topic addQuestion: thisQuestion];
    }
    [tableView reloadData];
}
```

This brings up the question: What do we do when there was an error downloading the questions? There's no need to add any questions to the topic—we don't have any to add—and the app shouldn't remove any it has already downloaded, because the user may want to review those questions even when no more can be retrieved. Therefore, there won't be any change to the app's data regarding the currently viewed topic, so there's no need to reload the table.

The app could present the error to the user, but because it's likely to be due to something out of the user's hands (stackoverflow.com being down or unreachable is the most likely culprit), there would be little for the user to do. It seems that doing nothing at all is appropriate, so that the `-[BrowseOverflowViewControllerfetchingQuestions FailedWithError:]` method can be left empty.[2]

As before in this chapter, the code required to handle the `QuestionDetail DataSource` case (dealing with received answers and the question's body) is similar to the code we've just added, so it is left out. Have a go at implementing it yourself, or look at the project on GitHub.

Displaying User Avatars

The final missing piece of the puzzle is to give the question list and detail data source classes avatar stores, so they can display images for the people who ask and answer questions on Stack Overflow. As with the `StackOverflowManager`, `AvatarStore` instances have some specific configuration requirements—they must be passed a notification center to use—so it makes sense to set them up in the `BrowseOverflow ObjectConfiguration` class. Additionally, because the store is a cache, it seems sensible to use the same instance for each data source. That doesn't mean making the `AvatarStore` a singleton; instead, the configuration class should know to return the same object every time it's asked.

> ### Singletons or Single Instances?
>
> This difference between "there can only ever be one of these objects" and "this application needs only one instance of this class" is a subtle one, but making the wrong choice can lead to problems maintaining and developing the app. As you've already seen when using the `NSNotificationCenter` class, testing code that uses Singleton classes is tricky and requires special tricks. Because testing is a special example of reusing a class in a different context, the general conclusion is that reusing code that relies on the Singleton pattern is difficult.
>
> So when should a class be a Singleton, and when should we just arrange for there to be only one instance of a non-Singleton class? When there is genuinely a reason why more than one instance of a class cannot work in any context, Singleton may be a useful pattern. In any other case, it's unnecessary and can work against you. If the same object is

---

2. Because the method doesn't need to do anything, you may consider making the method optional in the protocol declaration and requiring that StackOverflowManager test for its existence before invoking it.

being used in multiple contexts, a possibility exists that concurrency problems will be exhibited, even if those contexts are functionally unrelated.

Consider the example of UIKit's `UIApplication` class. Instances of `UIApplication` represent the state of this process's app. Any process can only ever be a part of one application, so there's a reason why enforcing that only one instance of `UIApplication` can exist in each process.

Most developers do not implement the Singleton pattern for their app delegate classes, despite the fact that each app has only a single Instance of the class. Are they wrong to work this way? Probably not; the important property of the app delegate is that there should be one instance per `UIApplication` instance. This means that there happens to be a single app delegate per process—because `UIApplication` is a Singleton—not that the app delegate must by necessity be a Singleton.

The tests that require `BrowseOverflowObjectConfiguration` to return a configured instance of `AvatarStore`—and the same instance on every invocation—go in the `BrowseOverflowObjectConfigurationTests` fixture.

```
@implementation BrowseOverflowObjectConfigurationTests
{
    BrowseOverflowObjectConfiguration *configuration;
}

- (void)setUp {
    configuration = [[BrowseOverflowObjectConfiguration alloc] init];
}

- (void)tearDown {
    configuration = nil;
}

- (void)testConfigurationOfCreatedAvatarStore {
    AvatarStore *store = [configuration avatarStore];
    STAssertEqualObjects([store notificationCenter],
        [NSNotificationCenter defaultCenter],
        @"Configured AvatarStore posts notifications to"
        @" the default center");
}

- (void)testSameAvatarStoreAlwaysReturned {
    AvatarStore *store1 = [configuration avatarStore];
    AvatarStore *store2 = [configuration avatarStore];
    STAssertEqualObjects(store1, store2,
        @"The same store should always be used");
}

@end
```

We can't currently see what notification center the `AvatarStore` object will use. Previously, I created an `AvatarStore+TestingExtensions` category[3] to provide extra visibility into the class, and we can add a method there to see its notification center. (Don't forget to import the category header into the test fixture.)

```
- (NSNotificationCenter *)notificationCenter {
    return notificationCenter;
}
```

It's easy to get the first test to pass, by creating a method on `BrowseOverflow ObjectConfiguration` that returns a correctly configured instance of `AvatarStore`.

```
- (AvatarStore *)avatarStore {
    AvatarStore *avatarStore = [[AvatarStore alloc] init];
    [avatarStore useNotificationCenter:
        [NSNotificationCenter defaultCenter]];
    return avatarStore;
}
```

This implementation doesn't satisfy the second requirement, that the object returned must always be the same instance of `AvatarStore`. We can arrange that using the Grand Central Dispatch library.

```
- (AvatarStore *)avatarStore {
    static AvatarStore *avatarStore = nil;
    static dispatch_once_t onceToken;
    dispatch_once(&onceToken, ^{
        avatarStore = [[AvatarStore alloc] init];
        [avatarStore useNotificationCenter:
            [NSNotificationCenter defaultCenter]];
    });
    return avatarStore;
}
```

In this version of the method, the `onceToken` variable is used as an indication to `dispatch_once()` whether or not the block that creates the `AvatarStore` instance has already been executed. If not, it creates a new instance; otherwise, it skips that code and returns the previously created object. In this way the class itself is not required to be a Singleton, but the configuration object can ensure it only ever hands out one object, no matter how many times an avatar store is requested.

Now the view controller should pass a configured avatar store to each data source that needs one. This needs to be done before the view appears, and it seems sensible to put this code into the `-viewWillAppear:` method because that's where the view controller does the rest of its configuration of its data source objects. So, in `Browse OverflowViewControllerTests`, write a new test that requires the data sources to

---

3. If you haven't already done so, you can get this file by cloning the GitHub project at
   https://github.com/iamleeg/BrowseOverflow.

have an avatar store object after - [BrowseOverflowViewController viewWillAppear:] is called.

```
- (void)testQuestionListViewIsGivenAnAvatarStore {
    QuestionListTableDataSource *listDataSource =
        [[QuestionListTableDataSource alloc] init];
    viewController.dataSource = listDataSource;
    [viewController viewWillAppear: YES];
    STAssertNotNil(listDataSource.avatarStore,
        @"The avatarStore property should be configured in"
        @" -viewWillAppear:");
}
```

Again, implementing this test reveals a problem elsewhere in the app. Now that the list view is configured with an avatar store, it's calling out to that store for images whenever it's asked to prepare a table view cell. This is causing an exception to be thrown in the test suite:

```
2011-11-22 07:42:21.671 BrowseOverflow[582:fb03] *** Terminating app due to
➥uncaught exception 'NSInvalidArgumentException', reason: '-[__NSCFDictionary
➥setObject:forKey:]: attempt to insert nil key'
```

The call stack shows that this is happening in the - [AvatarStore dataForURL:] method. The method is reproduced next, with the crashing line shown in bold:

```
- (NSData *)dataForURL:(NSURL *)url {
    NSData *avatarData = [dataCache objectForKey: [url absoluteString]];
    if (!avatarData) {
        GravatarCommunicator *communicator =
            [[GravatarCommunicator alloc] init];
        [communicators setObject: communicator
                          forKey: [url absoluteString]];
        communicator.delegate = self;
        [communicator fetchDataForURL: url];
    }
    return avatarData;
}
```

The problem is that the URL being given to the store is nil, and the code can't cope with that. It's tempting to go back to the test that's calling this code and fill in the model objects to avoid this crash. In this case, that is not the right approach: The app should be more robust about handling unexpected inputs. Instead of changing all the places where the AvatarStore is invoked with a nil URL, I'm going to require that it handle that case gracefully, with a new test on AvatarStoreTests.

```
- (void)testNilDataReturnedWhenNilURLPassed {
    STAssertNil([store dataForURL: nil],
                @"Don't return data when passed a nil URL");
}
```

The changes to the `AvatarStore` class are straightforward:

```
- (NSData *)dataForURL:(NSURL *)url {
    if (url == nil) {
        return nil;
    }
    // ...
```

Finishing Off and Tidying Up

That's nearly everything, but we need to tie up a few loose ends before we can call the app complete. Well, some of them seem more like "glaring mistakes" than "loose ends," but we'll come to that later.

To start with, the `QuestionListTableDataSource` needs to know which notification center instance to use when the user selects a question in the list, and the `BrowseOverflowViewController` doesn't currently tell it. It should, and we can require that with a test on `BrowseOverflowViewControllerTests`:

```
- (void)testViewControllerHooksUpQuestionListNotificationCenterInViewDidAppear {
    QuestionListTableDataSource *questionDataSource =
        [[QuestionListTableDataSource alloc] init];
    viewController.dataSource = questionDataSource;
    [viewController viewDidAppear: YES];
    STAssertEqualObjects(questionDataSource.notificationCenter,
        [NSNotificationCenter defaultCenter], @"");
}
```

The addition to `-[BrowseOverflowViewController viewDidAppear:]` is very simple.

```
    if ([self.dataSource isKindOfClass:
        [QuestionListTableDataSource class]]) {
        ((QuestionListTableDataSource *)dataSource).notificationCenter =
            [NSNotificationCenter defaultCenter];
    }
```

Unfortunately, when I added this test and code to the test suite, I found that an unrelated test started to fail. If you're unlucky[4] you'll have found this, too, but catching this failure seems dependent on a race condition. In `-[QuestionDetailDataSource testAnswererPropertiesInAnswerCell]`, an assertion failure in `-[AnswerBuilder addAnswersToQuestion:fromJSON:error:]` is occurring: the question parameter should never be `nil` but for some reason, in this test, it is.

What's really weird about that is that the `-testAnswererPropertiesInAnswerCell` method doesn't use an `AnswerBuilder` instance. What it *does* use, on the other hand, is the run loop; this is one of the tests that spins the run loop for a short time to

---

4. Or, if you value learning from mistakes above an easy life, "if you're lucky."

let a `UIWebView` load its content. Because the view controller is now hooking up a notification center to the `QuestionListTableDataSource`, notifications that were previously getting lost by being sent to nil are now being caught, and handled when this test runs the run loop. In other words, there's always been a problem, but unfortunately we've only just started detecting it.

To find where the code was going wrong, I had to perform that task seldom relied on by test-driven developers: I used the debugger. Specifically, I added a breakpoint on `-addAnswersToQuestion:fromJSON:error:` with a condition of `question==nil`. I found that `-[BrowseOverflowViewControllerTeststestDefaultStateOfView ControllerDoesNotReceiveQuestionSelectionNotification]` is using `nil` as the argument for a notification that will eventually make its way into a parameter of the method:

```
- (void)testDefaultStateOfViewControllerDoesNotReceiveTopicSelectionNotifications
{
    [BrowseOverflowViewControllerTests
        swapInstanceMethodsForClass: [BrowseOverflowViewController class]
                       selector: realUserDidSelectTopic
                    andSelector: testUserDidSelectTopic];
    [[NSNotificationCenter defaultCenter]
     postNotificationName: TopicTableDidSelectTopicNotification
     object: nil
     userInfo: nil];
    STAssertNil(objc_getAssociatedObject(viewController,
        notificationKey),
          @"Notification should not be received before -viewDidAppear:");
    [BrowseOverflowViewControllerTests swapInstanceMethodsForClass:
        [BrowseOverflowViewController class]
        selector: realUserDidSelectTopic
     andSelector: testUserDidSelectTopic];
}
```

To reiterate, this has never been acceptable, but I've been getting away with it until now. The solution is to `alloc` and `init` a `Question` instance and use it in this test.

```
- (void)testDefaultStateOfViewControllerDoesNotReceiveTopicSelectionNotifications
{
    Question *question = [[Question alloc] init];
    [BrowseOverflowViewControllerTests
        swapInstanceMethodsForClass: [BrowseOverflowViewController class]
                       selector: realUserDidSelectTopic
                    andSelector: testUserDidSelectTopic];
    [[NSNotificationCenter defaultCenter]
     postNotificationName: TopicTableDidSelectTopicNotification
     object: question
     userInfo: nil];
```

```
STAssertNil(objc_getAssociatedObject(viewController,
    notificationKey),
    @"Notification should not be received before -viewDidAppear:");
[BrowseOverflowViewControllerTests
    swapInstanceMethodsForClass: [BrowseOverflowViewController class]
                    selector: realUserDidSelectTopic
                 andSelector: testUserDidSelectTopic];
}
```

Now the app works completely, but it's not very beautiful. In fact, it's downright ugly. Figures 10.4 and 10.5 demonstrate what's going wrong, in the question list and question detail views, respectively.

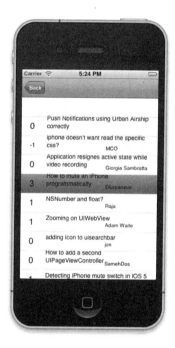

Figure 10.4   BrowseOverflow's question list view.

Figure 10.5   BrowseOverflow showing the detail of a question,
and the answers.

The most obvious problem is that the content from each row is overlapping the adjacent rows. The cause is that the table view isn't being told how much space to leave for each row, so it is using its default value, even though we've added custom rows of a different size.

Some programmers would say at this point that "views cannot be unit tested" and would switch to writing untested code at this point, but I think this is too soon. Writing unit tests for some aspects of view code can be a Sisyphean task. Aesthetic requirements are more variable than logical requirements, and don't have the same binary "works/doesn't work" property that is the cornerstone of unit testing. Demonstrating that a particular pixel on the screen should be a particular shade of red is something you can write the test for, but when your graphical designer decides that a different shade of red should be used, or some text overlaps that pixel, your test starts failing.

In this case, we can clearly define a requirement on the view in a way that has a yes/no answer and that is a measure of "correctness" rather than whimsy: The height of a row in the table view should be larger than the height of the content of that row. Simple to express, obvious whether it's satisfied or not—something we can write a test for.

A table view gets the height for each row from its delegate, so the code that configures the height of the question list cells belongs in QuestionListTableDataSource. Therefore the test belongs in QuestionListTableDataSourceTests:

```
- (void)testHeightOfAQuestionRowIsAtLeastTheSameAsTheHeightOfTheCell {
    [iPhoneTopic addQuestion: question1];
    UITableViewCell *cell = [dataSource tableView: nil
                            cellForRowAtIndexPath: firstCell];
    NSInteger height = [dataSource tableView: nil
                        heightForRowAtIndexPath: firstCell];
    STAssertTrue(height >= cell.frame.size.height,
        @"Give the table enough space to draw the view.");
}
```

There is no implementation of that method yet. For a first passing implementation of the code, I'll look in the `QuestionSummaryCell.xib` file to see how big the row should be and return that number.

```
- (CGFloat)tableView:(UITableView *)tableView
    heightForRowAtIndexPath:(NSIndexPath *)indexPath {
    return 132.0f;
}
```

A similar method must be implemented on the `QuestionDetailDataSource` class to set the heights of the question body and answer cells in the other table.

The rows in the table are now the correct height, which makes it easy to see that a problem exists in the question detail view, as demonstrated in Figure 10.6. The question body is not being displayed correctly in the top row.

Figure 10.6   The question detail is missing the most important part: the question that was asked.

The problem is that the `StackOverflowManager` doesn't tell its delegate when this content is downloaded, so the view controller does not know that the view needs updating. A new test on `QuestionCreationWorkflowTests` should require that the manager tell its delegate about the event.

```
- (void)testManagerNotifiesDelegateWhenQuestionBodyIsReceived {
    [mgr fetchBodyForQuestion: questionToFetch];
    [mgr receivedQuestionBodyJSON: @"Fake JSON"];
    STAssertEqualObjects(delegate.bodyQuestion, questionToFetch,
        @"Update delegate when question body filled");
}
```

This needs a new method in the `StackOverflowManagerDelegate` protocol that the manager can call when the question body is filled in.

```
- (void)bodyReceivedForQuestion: (Question *)question;
```

To see this method being called, the `MockStackOverflowManagerDelegate` should implement it, along with a method to test whether it received the delegate method.

MockStackOverflowManagerDelegate.h

```
@interface MockStackOverflowManagerDelegate : NSObject
    <StackOverflowManagerDelegate>
// ...
@property (strong) Question *bodyQuestion;

@end
```

MockStackOverflowManagerDelegate.m

```
// ...
@synthesize bodyQuestion;

- (void)bodyReceivedForQuestion:(Question *)question {
    self.bodyQuestion = question;
}
// ...
```

This test will not pass until the manager calls the delegate method, so `-[StackOverflowManager receivedQuestionBodyJSON:]` needs updating.

```
- (void)receivedQuestionBodyJSON:(NSString *)objectNotation {
    [questionBuilder fillInDetailsForQuestion: self.questionToFill
                                     fromJSON: objectNotation];
    [delegate bodyReceivedForQuestion: self.questionToFill];
    self.questionToFill = nil;
}
```

The `BrowseOverflowViewControllerTests` fixture should require that when the view controller receives that delegate callback, it tells the table to update.

```
- (void)testTableReloadedWhenQuestionBodyReceived {
    QuestionDetailDataSource *detailDataSource =
        [[QuestionDetailDataSource alloc] init];
    viewController.dataSource = detailDataSource;
    ReloadDataWatcher *watcher = [[ReloadDataWatcher alloc] init];
    viewController.tableView = (UITableView *)watcher;
    [viewController bodyReceivedForQuestion: nil];
    STAssertTrue([watcher didReceiveReloadData],
        @"Table reloaded when question body received");
}
```

Finally, the delegate method should be implemented on `BrowseOverflowView Controller` so that this test passes.

```
- (void)bodyReceivedForQuestion:(Question *)question {
    [tableView reloadData];
}
```

This doesn't appear to address the problem. `StackOverflowCommunicator` was only designed to deal with one "in-flight" network connection at a time, but the view controller is asking for both the question body and its answers together. As a simple workaround, change the `QuestionCreationWorkflowTests` fixture to require that the `StackOverflowManager` ask a second communicator instance to fetch the question body.

```
@implementation QuestionCreationWorkflowTests
{
@private
    StackOverflowManager *mgr;
    MockStackOverflowManagerDelegate *delegate;
    FakeQuestionBuilder *questionBuilder;
    MockStackOverflowCommunicator *communicator;
    MockStackOverflowCommunicator *bodyCommunicator;
    Question *questionToFetch;
    NSError *underlyingError;
    NSArray *questionArray;
}

- (void)setUp {
    mgr = [[StackOverflowManager alloc] init];
    delegate = [[MockStackOverflowManagerDelegate alloc] init];
    mgr.delegate = delegate;
    underlyingError = [NSError errorWithDomain: @"Test domain"
                                          code: 0
                                      userInfo: nil];
    questionBuilder = [[FakeQuestionBuilder alloc] init];
```

```
    questionBuilder.arrayToReturn = nil;
    mgr.questionBuilder = questionBuilder;
    questionToFetch = [[Question alloc] init];
    questionToFetch.questionID = 1234;
    questionArray = [NSArray arrayWithObject: questionToFetch];
    communicator = [[MockStackOverflowCommunicator alloc] init];
    mgr.communicator = communicator;
    bodyCommunicator = [[MockStackOverflowCommunicator alloc] init];
    mgr.bodyCommunicator = bodyCommunicator;
}

- (void)tearDown {
    mgr = nil;
    delegate = nil;
    questionBuilder = nil;
    questionToFetch = nil;
    questionArray = nil;
    communicator = nil;
    bodyCommunicator = nil;
    underlyingError = nil;
}

// ...

- (void)testAskingForQuestionBodyMeansRequestingData {
    [mgr fetchBodyForQuestion: questionToFetch];
    STAssertTrue([bodyCommunicator wasAskedToFetchBody],
        @"The communicator should need to retrieve data for"
        @" the question body");
}

// ...
```

The bodyCommunicator property must be declared and synthesized on Stack OverflowManager. To pass this test, the manager should use the new property.

```
- (void)fetchBodyForQuestion: (Question *)question {
    self.questionToFill = question;
    [bodyCommunicator downloadInformationForQuestionWithID:
        question.questionID];
}
```

The BrowseOverflowObjectConfiguration class is required to fill in this property in a test on the BrowseOverflowObjectConfigurationTests suite.

```
- (void)testConfigurationOfCreatedStackOverflowManager {
    StackOverflowManager *manager = [configuration
        stackOverflowManager];
    STAssertNotNil(manager, @"The StackOverflowManager should exist");
```

```
    STAssertNotNil(manager.communicator,
        @"Manager should have a StackOverflowCommunicator");
    STAssertNotNil(manager.bodyCommunicator,
        @"Manager needs a second StackOverflowCommunicator");
    STAssertNotNil(manager.questionBuilder,
        @"Manager should have a question builder");
    STAssertNotNil(manager.answerBuilder,
        @"Manager should have an answer builder");
    STAssertEqualObjects(manager.communicator.delegate, manager,
        @"The manager is the communicator's delegate");
    STAssertEqualObjects(manager.bodyCommunicator.delegate, manager,
        @"The manager is the delegate of the body communicator");
}
```

Change the implementation of the object configuration class to pass this test.

```
- (StackOverflowManager *)stackOverflowManager {
    StackOverflowManager *manager = [[StackOverflowManager alloc] init];
    manager.communicator = [[StackOverflowCommunicator alloc] init];
    manager.communicator.delegate = manager;
    manager.bodyCommunicator = [[StackOverflowCommunicator alloc] init];
    manager.bodyCommunicator.delegate = manager;
    manager.questionBuilder = [[QuestionBuilder alloc] init];
    manager.answerBuilder = [[AnswerBuilder alloc] init];
    return manager;
}
```

Again we find the assertion failure where the answer builder is being asked to add answers to a nil question. This time, there are two reasons. The first is because the StackOverflowManager is using an internal instance variable, questionToFill, to track where the body and the answers are stored, and when either succeeds this variable is set to nil, which will break when the other success or failure method is called. That this variable is used for filling in the question body is an internal detail of the class, so it can be refactored (to use a different instance variable) without affecting the tests. Assuming a new Question property, questionNeedingBody, the following methods on StackOverflowManager can be changed:

```
- (void)fetchBodyForQuestion: (Question *)question {
    self.questionNeedingBody = question;
    [bodyCommunicator downloadInformationForQuestionWithID:
        question.questionID];
}
```

```
- (void)receivedQuestionBodyJSON:(NSString *)objectNotation {
    [questionBuilder fillInDetailsForQuestion: self.questionNeedingBody
                                     fromJSON: objectNotation];
    [delegate bodyReceivedForQuestion: self.questionNeedingBody];
    self.questionNeedingBody = nil;
}
```

```
- (void)fetchingQuestionBodyFailedWithError:(NSError *)error {
    NSDictionary *errorInfo = nil;
    if (error) {
        errorInfo = [NSDictionary dictionaryWithObject: error
            forKey: NSUnderlyingErrorKey];
    }
    NSError *reportableError = [NSError
        errorWithDomain: StackOverflowManagerError
                code: StackOverflowManagerErrorQuestionBodyFetchCode
            userInfo:errorInfo];
    [delegate fetchingQuestionBodyFailedWithError: reportableError];
    self.questionNeedingBody = nil;
}
```

The second problem before we can move on is that the app can call - [Question Builder fillInDetailsForQuestion:fromJSON:] with JSON that contains no questions, but the app will still try to extract a question from the (empty) array contained in that JSON. Because this is data from the server that could potentially be broken in this way in the running app, this should not crash the app. We require in QuestionBuilderTests that data with an empty questions array should be accepted.

```
- (void)testEmptyQuestionsArrayDoesNotCrash {
    STAssertNoThrow([questionBuilder fillInDetailsForQuestion: question
        fromJSON: emptyQuestionsArray],
        @"Don't throw if no questions are found");
}
```

A very simple change to QuestionBuilder passes this test.

```
- (void)fillInDetailsForQuestion:(Question *)question
                        fromJSON:(NSString *)objectNotation {
    NSParameterAssert(question != nil);
    NSParameterAssert(objectNotation != nil);
    NSData *unicodeNotation = [objectNotation
        dataUsingEncoding: NSUTF8StringEncoding];
    NSDictionary *parsedObject =
        [NSJSONSerialization JSONObjectWithData: unicodeNotation
                                        options: 0
                                          error: NULL];
    if (![parsedObject isKindOfClass: [NSDictionary class]]) {
        return;
    }
    NSString *questionBody = [[[parsedObject
        objectForKey: @"questions"] lastObject] objectForKey: @"body"];
    if (questionBody) {
        question.body = questionBody;
    }
}
```

With all that in place, the question detail view finally looks like what the customer wanted, back in Chapter 5, "Test-Driven Development of an iOS App."

Ship It!

That's the sample application complete—well, it's very rough around the edges, but the functionality is all there. The app was built by writing 182 unit tests, which all run (on my Mac, anyway) in about a second.[5] No code was added to the app without a failing test being written first; at no point did we move on before ensuring that all tests passed.

Despite the slightly artificial way in which the app was built, with each "layer" being completed before moving on to the next, the integration step undertaken in this chapter to convert a collection of independent classes into a working app with useful features was incredibly straightforward. Because the behavior and interface of each class in the app had been carefully specified by the tests, when it came time to put all those classes together, they worked well—with few problems.

There was no sleight of hand in the way code and problems have been presented over the last few chapters. The (mercifully) small number of bugs and regressions on display represent every such problem I encountered, and the order in which classes, tests, and implementation code are introduced in this book truly represent the order in which I built the app. The race condition described and addressed earlier in this chapter is the only time in the whole project that I needed to use the debugger, and for me this is the biggest benefit of test-driven development. Throughout this project I had a very good view of the capabilities and limitations of the code I had written: Anything that passes a test has been done, anything that fails is broken, and anything I don't have a test for doesn't exist. This visibility, and the capability to make changes to the code and see the effect of those changes, combine to give developers great confidence over their coding.

In the next chapter, I'll reflect on the BrowseOverflow project, taking the specific problems we solved in writing this app to make general points about applying test-driven development to Cocoa apps. The project work is complete and won't be added to in future chapters. You may want to carry on improving it yourself, using the application code and test fixtures as a basis to practice test-driven development. A hint to get you started—if you browse to the same topic's list of questions twice, you're likely to find that questions get duplicated in the list. That probably shouldn't happen. If a question appears once in the StackOverflow website, it should appear once in the app.

---

5. Not all of the 182 tests are shown in this book, refer to the sample code on GitHub for the complete test suite.

11

Designing for Test-Driven Development

In the preceding six chapters, we've taken the specification for a product and turned it into a working iPhone app, using the principle of test-driven development. It's time to take a step back, look at what we've done, and see what general guidelines can help in designing classes that will be implemented using a test-driven approach.

Design to Interfaces, Not Implementations

Whenever you're writing a test in a TDD project, you're designing a part of the class that is being tested: what setup it needs, how its API can be used, and what the class does in response to its API being used. It's best to stay away from decisions about *how* the class does what it does when writing the test, and defer these decisions until you're trying to make the test pass. If your code relies on an object implementing a method or property, your test should reflect that requirement. It should not make assumptions about how that method or property is provided.

If you think in this way when you write the test, you leave open the possibility for different implementations to be used in different contexts, and you make it easier to change the implementation that's used in production if you discover problems with performance, security, or other characteristics. You're designing to the interface, not the implementation.

The main benefit of designing to the interface in TDD is that it makes it very easy to replace dependencies on complex systems with fake or mock objects. This is a pattern we've seen throughout the development of BrowseOverflow. For instance, the `StackOverflowCommunicator` object relies on receiving certain callbacks from `NSURLConnection`, but doesn't have any dependency on how the `NSURLConnection` object is implemented—so it's possible to use those callbacks out of context to test them. In its turn, the `StackOverflowCommunicator` sends messages to its delegate, but it doesn't care what the delegate does with these messages. In the real app, the delegate is a `StackOverflowManager` that takes the data, constructs model objects out of it, and then messages a view controller to update a data source and refresh a table view. In the tests, all that is ignored and the delegate is a simple object that records whether it has received the delegate messages.

The way this independence between an object and the implementation of its collaborators has often been expressed, both in Apple's frameworks and in the BrowseOverflow code, is through the use of protocols.[1] The NSURLConnection class knows that its delegate implements the NSURLConnectionDataDelegate protocol, just as the StackOverflowCommunicator knows that its delegate implements the StackOverflowCommunicatorDelegate protocol. All these objects know about their delegates is that they implement the methods specified in the delegate protocol; they do not need to know about what the delegates do as a result of receiving those methods. The flip side is that all the delegates need to know is that they will receive the messages documented in the protocol declaration; they do not need to know what goes on in order to produce those messages. That allows us to test our delegate classes by messaging them from a test fixture instead of a production class.

Delegates are not the only way to design to an interface. In fact, it's a technique that can be used anywhere one class needs to communicate with another. Consider a hypothetical future version of the BrowseOverflow app, where you've decided to change the model implementation to use Core Data. That means setting up managed object contexts, persistent stores, and so on. But you already have a lot of controller classes that implement the logic this app will need—they just talk to "plain old" Objective-C objects rather than NSManagedObject subclasses. That's not a problem. As long as anywhere that needs, for example, a Question instance knows about the "Question-ness" of that object—its title, body text, relationship to a person and so on—it can use any implementation that provides those properties. To keep tests simple, you may choose to carry on using the non-Core Data implementations of the model classes in unit tests so that the tests don't need to deal with the complexity of Core Data.

You can create tests where an object communicates with a "fake" implementation of a protocol, and tests where the real implementation is exercised by generating protocol messages from a "fake" source. In the real application, the real implementation will be exercised by the real source. You could even have a situation where the objects on *both* sides of the interface are fakes, so that fake messages are being consumed by fake receivers. Would that ever be useful?

There's no case in unit testing where you'd want to do that, because it would result in a test that wasn't actually testing any production code. A situation where you would want to put an assembly of fake objects together is in performance testing. If you're designing the architecture of a complex application and want to know something about its performance characteristics—for example, whether it can process incoming data at a particular rate—you could produce a test app that follows the same architecture but where each component does no real work. So you may hypothesize that the network code will take 0.1s to process each message, and create a class that listens for incoming data, then

---

1. Protocols are not the only way to do this, and in older code (before optional methods were introduced in protocols) you may see "informal protocols," which are categories defined on NSObject that declare, but do not define, the interface methods.

waits 0.1s before messaging the next component. In this way you can tweak parameters, such as the frequency of incoming messages or the way in which they are queued, and see the resulting behavior of the overall system.

Tell, Don't Ask

If you have classes that are designed to use any implementation of a particular interface, you need to be able to choose which implementation is used in any context. You want your lightweight implementation that signals which methods have been called to be used in your tests, but you want to use an implementation that performs some useful work in your app.

It is easier to swap collaborator implementations if you configure which collaborator an object should use at runtime, instead of coding that object to choose the object for itself. This principle is known as "tell, don't ask": You tell an object what data and objects it uses; it doesn't ask its environment for the things it needs.

We've seen the difference between these two approaches—telling, and asking—in developing the BrowseOverflow app, particularly in dealing with notifications. The `QuestionListTableDataSource` class is told what notification center instance to use: In the app, this is always the singleton `-[NSNotificationCenter defaultCenter]` object. In tests, it's simple to set up the object to use a fake notification center that offers the visibility needed to make the tests possible.

Conversely, `BrowseOverflowViewController` always asks for the singleton instance, so the tests cannot swap in a fake notification center. Instead, the tests have to go through the complex (and fragile) contortions of using the Objective-C runtime to replace (or "swizzle") method implementations before the tests can be executed. Tests that are too "clever" can be harder to read and understand, and more likely to fail due to changes in the environment. Perhaps a future release of the iOS SDK will change the implementation of `-[NSNotificationCenter defaultCenter]` in a way the tests haven't anticipated, or a future release of OCUnit will attempt to execute multiple tests in parallel. These tests were built this way to show how much harder it can be to rely on shared classes, even though it seems like a way out of constructing a fake object.

Singleton classes are a leading cause of asking rather than telling: It's all too easy to get the default `NSFileManager`, or the shared `UIApplication`. Where the singleton class exposes complicated or environment-dependent behavior (as is true with each of these two examples), tests exercising this code can become either difficult to construct or nondeterministic in outcome. It's always best in these cases to tell the application code what object to use, and pass it the singleton in the app. As explored in Chapter 10, "Putting It All Together," consider whether your own classes really need to be a singleton, or whether it just happens to be the case that there's one instance of the class in the app.

Small, Focused Classes and Methods

A quick search through the application source for BrowseOverflow shows that the longest method in the whole app is about 35 lines of code. Most methods are 10 lines or fewer in length. Stepping back a bit to see the bigger picture, most classes declare only a few methods and properties; each of the class and protocol header files fits comfortably on a single screen in Xcode on my laptop. The application's behavior is the result of the rich interaction of a large number of small classes, each responsible for a single facet of the desired functionality.

This organization of the code into small, highly cohesive classes is as much a side-effect of test-driven development as it is a principle to follow. Because you have to write a test for each aspect of the app's behavior before you can write the app code, the inclination is to write as little code as possible for each aspect so that you can get on to writing the next test and adding the next piece of behavior.

There's a lot of value in writing highly specific tests to achieve as close to a 1:1 mapping between test and app code as is feasible. If one thing goes wrong in the app, the best outcome is that exactly one test fails, so that you can see the one problem and reason quickly about its solution. Conversely if one bug leads to a lot of test failures, you have to stop and think about what all the failing tests have in common so that you can try to identify the root cause of the multiple failures.

In addition, if one test is responsible for specifying the behavior of a large swathe of app code, the likelihood that any of a number of problems can cause the test to fail will increase. This, like the case of multiple test failures, slows you down when you come to analyze the failure and try to determine which part of the code under test is causing the problem. Taking these two conditions together, we see that having small methods that are each responsible for a limited amount of the app's behavior is beneficial to maintaining the app's unit tests (and, by inference, the app itself: The tests are there to support the quality of the application, after all).

Just as it makes sense to keep each method short and focused on a small aspect of what the app does, it's best to keep each class small and responsible for a limited number of things. Having multiple responsibilities in a single class means that it's possible for the code related to different responsibilities to become interdependent, perhaps using the same instance variables or relying on common private methods. That makes it harder to change the code for one of the application's responsibilities without affecting other behavior, which is undesirable because it makes code harder to maintain.

Clearly the optimal number of responsibilities for any class is one, as described by Robert C. Martin in his Single Responsibility Principle. With only one responsibility, the possibility for the code in a class to break the behavior of some other feature is greatly reduced. The code in the BrowseOverflow app follows the Single Responsibility Principle. It might seem that "fetch questions from stackoverflow.com" is one responsibility, but on closer inspection there are two: downloading data from the server and parsing that data to produce a representation that can be displayed in the application's view. That's why the code is broken into the separate `StackOverflowCommunicator` and `...Builder` classes, all coordinated by the `StackOverflowManager`.

Similarly, although UIKit provides the `UITableViewController` that can act as both a view controller and a table view's data source, this combination of responsibilities violates the Single Responsibility Principle. Indeed in the BrowseOverflow app, it proved possible to use a single view controller class to control three different table views, just by changing the data source.

Encapsulation

A useful addition to the Single Responsibility Principle is that if a class is given responsibility for some aspect of the app's behavior, it had better be entirely responsible for that aspect. Although having multiple responsibilities in the same class can lead to complicated coupling between those responsibilities, having a single responsibility spread between multiple classes makes it hard to understand how that responsibility works, because you need to jump between multiple source code files to see how it's implemented.

From the perspective of a developer trying to write code in a test-driven approach, if a responsibility is not encapsulated behind one class, it becomes harder to test the behavior of each participating class in isolation. The reason comes back to the idea of designing to an interface: If a responsibility is spread across many classes, the likelihood is that the implementation of any of those classes depends on the implementation of the other classes. Conversely, if a single class is entirely responsible for performing a task, getting that task done in a different way is as simple as switching out that one class.

Behavior in the BrowseOverflow app is encapsulated into classes that each completely implement the work they're responsible for. In Chapter 9, "View Controllers," I started to design separate `UITableView` data source and delegate classes for each view, thinking that these were separate responsibilities and deserved to be in separate classes. It turned out that this design didn't lead to encapsulated classes; the delegate classes always needed to use objects in the data source, so the two classes were tightly coupled together. I decided to combine the classes into a single class that was both the table view's data source and delegate. The new, combined class still has a single responsibility—managing the table view—and is now well-encapsulated.

Use Is Better Than Reuse

Although many of the preceding design principles have put a lot of emphasis on creating classes that can be interchanged with different implementations or reused in multiple contexts, the first and most important factor to be sure of is that the class is needed in the single context of the app you're trying to write before you even design the tests that exercise it.[2]

Through the process of developing BrowseOverflow, I frequently referred back to the app's requirements to see what was needed when designing a particular class or collection of classes. I wrote the app with the goal of satisfying these requirements, and

---

2. You could think of this as the Non-Zero Responsibility Principle.

although I looked for opportunities to reuse code within the context of the app (as with the example of `BrowseOverflowViewController`, which acts as the view controller for three separate views), I didn't worry about generalizing the created classes beyond the app's requirements. For example, the `QuestionListTableDataSource` is useful for displaying a list of Stack Overflow questions, and not for much else.

This comes back to the principle introduced in Chapter 2, "Techniques for Test-Driven Development," called Ya Ain't Gonna Need It. Any time you're editing code in test-driven development, you should be adding something useful—whether that's writing a new test to document some expected behavior of the app, writing the application code that passes a test and adds new functionality, or refactoring to improve the readability and maintainability of the code. Anything else is unnecessary, so you probably shouldn't be doing it.[3]

Think back to the System Metaphor: the high-level model of what features you need to provide and how they fit together into the app. If you're working on code that doesn't fit into your product's system metaphor, that code probably isn't responsible for anything in the app, and as such won't be needed.

Testing Concurrent Code

Testing code that's designed to run "in the background"—meaning on any thread that isn't the UI or "main" thread—can be hard. We've seen that in testing the preparation of the BrowseOverflow app's user interface, where some of the cells rely on the `UIWebView` class to display some content. `UIWebView` loads and renders its content asynchronously, which means that we're forced in the test to wait for it to finish before checking whether its content matches our expectations. We could potentially hook into the `UIWebView`'s flow and have the test watch for it completing its rendering, but that would just be a more clever way of waiting for it to finish. We'd also have to be sure that any "clever" approach to the test wasn't going to get stymied by the test framework tearing the fixture down before the background code had completed.

Threading, or asynchronous behavior of any form, is one of the application's responsibilities, so according to the Single Responsibility Principle it should be put into one class. That's not always easy, because reasons often exist for code running on different threads to be temporally cohesive. Examples include the need to communicate updates to the UI on the main thread, and synchronization to ensure that collaborating code on different threads always has a consistent view of any shared data.

Although it may not be straightforward to encapsulate asynchronicity entirely in a single class, patterns are available that simplify the construction (and, as a result, the testing) of concurrent code. A very powerful pattern is the Producer–Consumer pattern, in which the producer is responsible for requesting that asynchronous operations be performed, and the consumer is responsible for observing and executing these requests. The iOS SDK provides the `NSOperationQueue` class as an implementation of the consumer,

---

3. You shouldn't be adding it to the app, anyway. Writing code to research an algorithm or third-party API is valuable, but that research code shouldn't be shipped.

with the associated NSOperation class modeling the work units that are scheduled from the producer. NSOperationQueue is built on a lower-level library called Grand Central Dispatch, which also implements the Producer–Consumer pattern.

Producer–Consumer provides a natural interface that we can use to investigate the behavior of concurrent code. In testing the producer, we need to ensure that it adds work (or NSOperations) to a queue, so we can provide it with a stub queue and discover whether the queue receives the operations. We can implement each operation as standalone code and test that this operation functions correctly in isolation. Finally, we could test the queue's logic for dispatching or scheduling operations, although this won't be necessary if you use the Apple-supplied NSOperationQueue.

Every part of the concurrent system can be tested separately, without needing to rely on complicated scheduling tricks in test fixtures to wait for background code to complete. However, this ability to completely unit test concurrent code says nothing about its behavior in the integrated system, and it's still possible for resource contention or scheduling problems to exist in the code. The only way to detect these is to test the whole concurrent system in a variety of environments—a problem that is beyond this book's scope.

Don't Be Cleverer Than Necessary

Brian Kernighan, co-inventor of the C programming language, co-wrote a book called *The Elements of Programming Style*, with P. J. Plauger, which contains this quote:

> Everyone knows that debugging is twice as hard as writing a program in the first place. So if you're as clever as you can be when you write it, how will you ever debug it?

Test-driven developers can reduce the amount of time they spend stepping through code in the debugger, by creating a suite of tests that automatically tests their code and tells them whether it does what they expect. But that doesn't remove the need to write debuggable code. As we saw when integrating the BrowseOverflow app, there are still times when the debugger comes in handy. Besides, the reason for keeping the suite of unit tests around is to make it easy to find regressions; if you can tell what's going wrong but not where or how to fix it, some of that utility is lost.

Your own opinion of what language features or tricks count as "too clever" will depend on your experience and comfort level, but some things are more likely than others to generate code that works in tests but not in production. In the previous section, I described how code that works in the (usually) single-threaded world of a test suite can have concurrency problems that show up in a multithreaded app. Code that changes the (global) Objective-C runtime state is likely to cause these problems: For example, if you dynamically exchange method implementations on a class, code running in two different threads could have different expectations of what a method will do. This problem was noted in Chapter 9, but because the method exchange (or "swizzling") was being done in the single-threaded environment of the test suite, concurrency problems were not going to be encountered.

Prefer a Wide, Shallow Inheritance Hierarchy

Classes that are tightly coupled to other classes are difficult to test in isolation. There is no tighter coupling than inheritance, which connects the interface and implementation of two classes. Not only does the code in the subclass depend on the internals of the superclass behaving correctly, but superclass code that works when you test that class can be broken by the changes in behavior introduced in the subclass.

If you want to introduce an inheritance hierarchy in your own classes, consider whether alternatives are available. If the inheritance relationship would provide custom behavior in the superclass's workflow, a callback interface via either a delegate or block parameters is a way to separate the customization from the original workflow. None of the application classes in BrowseOverflow subclass other app classes, so there is minimal coupling between the implementations of the various classes in the app. The only place where classes defined in the project are subclassed is in the test suite, where some subclasses (such as the `NonNetworkedStackOverflowCommunicator`) have methods stubbed out to limit the amount of superclass behavior invoked in the test.

Sometimes you're forced into subclassing somebody else's class by the behavior of their code: For example, all the entities in a Core Data stack must be instances of `NSManagedObject`, and all the objects in a view hierarchy must be instances of `UIView`. In these cases, the only possible course of action for performing some tasks is subclassing; do so with care and consult the class documentation to find out what the limitations are.

Conclusion

The general approach to test-driven app design is to make each component of the app as independent of everything else that's going on as possible. In this chapter, patterns for removing dependence on other classes, on the code's environment, and on other threads have all been explored.

12

Applying Test-Driven Development to an Existing Project

Y ou've seen a full-featured app developed from inception to completion in a test-driven fashion. Many of you won't be coming into this from scratch, though; you'll have existing apps with code that has grown organically from the first beta version you gave to testers, through major releases and bug fix revisions to the state it's currently in. Does TDD offer you anything? This chapter provides answers to that question.

The Most Important Test You'll Write Is the First

Your app code probably works, for the most part: You wouldn't have released it to your customers if it hadn't at least passed some basic usage tests. But does any particular method in it satisfy all its requirements, or work when faced with the whole range of possible inputs? Those are the sort of questions you can use unit tests to answer.

Each test you add will prove that one more little piece of your app is working as you expect, and the first test takes you from no proof to one little piece of proof. That's an infinite enhancement in your confidence about the code, so it's the most important test you will ever write. It's also the test that will need you to set up a test fixture target and to ensure that you can build parts of your app code in the test fixture, so in that respect, it's the most important test, too. Furthermore, it'll prove that adding tests to this venerable project is possible and does help, so that also makes it the most important test.

But how should you approach writing that first test? What should it test? The answer to that question is simple: What is the next thing you need to change? If you have a bug you need to work on, write a test that fails while this bug is still present and that will pass when you fix the bug. If the next thing you need to do is to add a new feature, start thinking about how that feature will work and capture the first requirement as a new test. Starting by writing that first test will help get you into the "test infected" mindset and onto writing the second test, and then the rest of the test suite that will grow and develop with your app.

A great place to start is by examining the compiler warnings, and the results of Xcode's static code analysis (press Cmd-Shift-B in Xcode, or choose Analyze from the Product menu). Both of these reports describe problems that are already present in the application code, that could potentially cause issues at runtime, and are usually localized and easy to fix. Projects that have been under development for a long time often accumulate warnings or analysis issues, even through no fault of the developers: For example, the static analyzer is a fairly recent addition to Xcode so your past self couldn't help you out by using it. Cleaning up these problems will give you immediate feedback, as the number of warnings or reports is reduced. This gives you an important psychological boost as you realize that you're cleaning up your source code and making things better.

Refactoring to Support Testing

The first problem usually encountered when you start adding unit tests to an existing project—after you've worked up the motivation to write the first test—is difficulty in getting any of the classes to work on its own. With no particular pressure to isolate each class, it's easy to get complex systems of dependencies and coupled behavior between multiple classes so that instantiating any one class in the fixture ends up re-creating almost the entire app. How can you overcome this complexity and separate the app into testable parts—remembering that you cannot yet rely on tests telling you whether anything has broken?

It may not be necessary when you start testing a class to remove every single connection it depends on; if you can break out a few classes into an independent—but internally coupled—subsystem, you can test that subsystem on its own and worry about cleaning up its innards later.

The first step in this process is to identify "inflection points" in the software—places that seem like they could almost be the interface between two separate components. Natural inflection points include the boundaries between the model, view, and controller layers. Others depend on the capabilities and architecture of your own app. These inflection points will not necessarily already represent clean breaks between separate modules; the important part is to identify where they are and what you could do to completely separate the concerns of each module.

After you've found an inflection point, you need to make the smallest changes possible to tease the two connected subsystems apart. The changes need to be small because you cannot (yet) test their impact on the app's functionality, so you're potentially introducing risky changes at this point. The risk will prove worthwhile after you have a greater ability to write automatic tests of your app's code, but for the moment it's necessary to tread carefully. If there's a point where a test can be introduced for even part of the interaction, take the opportunity to reduce the risk associated with further changes.

A change[1] that's often useful at this point is to find a method on one side of the inflection point that uses lots of properties of objects on the other side, and push it across

---

1. Strictly speaking, it's hard to call these changes "refactoring" because there's no proof that the code's behavior isn't being modified.

the boundary. Perhaps it can be converted into a single call to a method on the other side of the boundary, or a method on one side that relies on delegate-style callbacks across the boundary. Making this change enhances the encapsulation of each module by removing the need for classes on each side to know about and change the properties of classes on the other side. If one class is frequently making use of properties defined on another class, consider whether the property should be moved to the class that's using it or whether the classes are sharing some responsibility and should be merged.

If the two modules are now communicating only via messages, there could be an opportunity to introduce a protocol or other interface that describes these messages and protects the modules from each needing to know how the other is implemented. Where the messages sent by one module are received by multiple classes in the other, a Façade[2] object can be used to collect the messages into one class and then a protocol defined to expose the methods on the façade.

After one of the subsystems is communicating with a single interface on the other subsystem, the second subsystem can be replaced in a test fixture by a mock implementation of the interface. The first module can be instantiated in the fixture and made to communicate with the fake version of the second, so you can document and verify expectations of the interaction.

The specific techniques or changes you'll need to employ depend very much on both the organization of your existing code and the intended architecture you have in mind. Michael Feathers discusses a variety of possible approaches in his book *Working Effectively with Legacy Code* (Prentice Hall, 2004); the code examples are in Java but are easy to follow, and it's the principles rather than the specific source code changes that are important.

Real-World Inflection Points

I once worked on a Mac app that had all the hallmarks of having provided a long and illustrious service for its programmers. The APIs used ran all the way from ancient third-party GUI frameworks designed for Mac OS 8 to the latest Cocoa additions. Any architecture that had originally been designed was now long lost under the additions and changes that had been made over the years, in much the same way that Tudor manor houses are sometimes extended and remodeled so much that it's a surprise to find an original wall or roof timber somewhere deep in the center.

It was still possible to identify separate responsibilities in this app—some code did logging, a few functions (there weren't really many classes in the code) managed the file system and so on. These related functions were all grouped into source files, so that, for example, the logging code was all in `app_logging.c`. This meant that the inflection points were clear, because each of these responsibilities could be treated as a separate module. Getting to the point where they could truly be used separately was going to be difficult, because the various functions relied on global shared state, and in some cases needed to be called in a certain order for that state to be set up correctly.

2. The Façade pattern is described in the "Gang of Four" book: *Design Patterns: Elements of Reusable Object-Oriented Software*, by Gamma, Helm, Johnson, and Vlissides, Addison-Wesley 1994.

> To break this coupling, I first created local accessor functions in each of the modules that returned the global variables, and changed the existing code so that all the functions used these accessors instead of reading the globals directly. Then I defined a structure inside each module that had an element for each of the globals and made the accessors look up the global state in these functions. Finally, I gathered all the initialization code into a single function that populated each module's state structure.
>
> Each of these steps was separately very small and had no effect on the overall behavior of the app, but the combined result was that each module was completely separated from the others and depended on a single structure being filled in before the module's functions were used. It became possible to build test drivers that linked to just one of the modules and configured the way that module behaved by changing the elements of the module's state structure. In other words, each module in the app could now be tested in isolation from the rest of the application.

Separating the classes inside a tightly coupled module works in the same way as separating the modules did. Decide what responsibilities the module has, and which class should take on each responsibility. Then, working carefully, reorganize the code into the new classes so that each class depends only on the interface of its collaborators, not on their implementations.

Testing to Support Refactoring

After you're in a position where classes or groups of classes in your app can be instantiated in a test suite and tested independently of each other, you can really pick up steam. It's now possible to specify exactly the required behavior on each class, and that means you're free to make any changes you want to how the classes are implemented. You know that you'll be able to see quickly whether you've changed what the class does, and you don't have to commit to anything until you've seen all the tests pass.

That sort of confidence makes it possible to think about wholesale changes to an app that don't seem possible—or at least not worthwhile—when you aren't supported by the collection of tests. My experience of working on projects that aren't supported by tests is that architectural decisions made early on tend to outstay their welcome. If the code almost works, then continual patching and tweaking when bug reports are made seems preferable to making any larger-scale changes, because the potential benefits seem outweighed by the high probability of introducing regressions or getting lost and ending up with an unbuildable, unworking mess.

The only solution available to address this crumbling code edifice that's collapsing under its own weight often seems to be the nuclear option: Wipe the code out and start again from scratch. That would still mean being in a situation where the code is unreleasable until it does everything the original, messy version does. What are all the capabilities of the original version, anyway?

Many programmers accept that code they wrote six months ago is low quality in comparison with the code they write today, and that in another six months today's code will look poor in comparison with what they will then be able to do. Wouldn't it be great to support adopting the knowledge of your future self, by leaving a collection of notes explaining everything the code you have today does; notes that let programmers change and improve the code without any fear? That's what a unit test suite allows you to do. The suite of tests is that collection of notes, telling your fellow developers and future selves what you did and why, and whether what they're doing functions in the same way.

Code that is well covered by unit tests is very easy to change, because much of the risk associated with making changes is removed. If part of the architecture needs to be replaced, you can make that replacement—there's a set of tests to let you know what your new version needs to do. Do you want to take some existing behavior and move it onto a new class? Edit the tests for that behavior so that they exercise the new class, and then get them back into a passing state. Changing the algorithm used to implement an app feature? You don't need to change the tests at all; what you already have will tell you whether the new algorithm covers all the cases needed in the app.

Do I Really Need to Write All These Tests?

As I said at the beginning of this chapter, the first test is the most important because it's the one that proves you can write unit tests for your existing project. The previous section shows that after you have a collection of tests in place for a class or feature, you can make even large architectural changes with confidence because you always know where you are, what doesn't work (yet), and what you need to fix.

One possible interpretation of this situation is that it's time to initiate the "write a load of unit tests" project, spending—how long? A week? A month? Three?—doing nothing but writing tests and making changes needed to support the application code running in the test suite. Not only is this not necessary, but I would argue that it's actually harmful to your project.

The main downside to doing nothing but writing tests is that it's demoralizing: You're spending lots of time writing code but not actually adding any new features to your product, and that makes it feel like time wasted. A demoralized developer is a less-productive developer, so the time needed to finish this "project" will increase, and then you may not feel like going back to working on the app after you're done—assuming you are ever "done" and don't just give up in disgust, vowing never to write another unit test for the rest of your professional career. However, it also comes back to the point made in Chapter 2, "Techniques for Test-Driven Development." The principle benefit of the red–green–refactor workflow is that you're thinking about the code's requirements at the same time as the code itself, as two aspects of one small problem that's relatively easy for one person to solve. The "improve test coverage" project destroys this relationship between the code and the tests, and therefore removes this important benefit.

The best approach to testing a legacy app is the same as the approach taken to test a brand new app: Write the tests as you need to make changes. Some developers swear by the "boy scout rule" of programming: Always leave the code cleaner than you found it (the analogy is with the Boy Scouts of America's rule—always leave the campsite cleaner than you found it). If you need to work on a particular class, doing the work needed to support test-driven development on that class's code creates an important and useful improvement to your project—and probably helps you to understand more about how that class behaves and what you need to do to get your work done.

13

Beyond Today's Test-Driven Development

I hope that this book has enthused you about the possibility of writing test-driven iOS apps, shown you how to get started, and convinced you that even the most gnarly of legacy projects can benefit from a test-driven approach after you do a bit of groundwork to get started. This chapter wraps things up by looking at techniques and technology related to TDD. Some of these things are already available but are not in common use yet; others are not available now, or work in other environments but not Cocoa Touch. These are all concepts and technologies you could be using for your apps soon.

Expressing Ranges of Input and Output

Many of the tests created for the BrowseOverflow app used a specific result to stand in for a general case. For example, if a table view data source constructs the first cell in a table correctly, perhaps it will create all cells correctly. If a question presents two answers in the correct order, perhaps it will order all answers correctly.

The reason for making these conceptual leaps ultimately comes down to life's being too short to do otherwise. We have to trust ourselves (or whoever will write or maintain the app code) to avoid taking shortcuts, to understand that the test represents an unwritten general rule, and to write code that satisfies the general rule rather than merely passing the test as written. To do otherwise would involve an explosion in the number of tests, because a wide enough collection of examples would have to be considered before special-casing the code to make each test pass became harder than writing the general solution.

It would be great if there were an easy way to write a test that expressed "for each of these inputs, the following outputs should be produced" or even "for any valid input, the following should be true of the result." You could do that today in OCUnit, by defining a collection of inputs and outputs—perhaps a dictionary that maps an input onto the expected result—and creating a test that loops over the collection, testing each result. Although that works, it means cluttering up tests that use this technique with code that implements the loop rather than expressing what the test is supposed to be telling you.

Other unit test frameworks have ways of abstracting this collection of values out of the test, so that the test fixture is responsible for preparing the inputs, and each test is responsible for verifying that for a given input, the expected result occurs. A test in this situation can pass and fail multiple times in the same run, if the expectations are met for only part of the input domain.

An example of this form of testing is available in the JUnit framework, where it is called Theories. The test fixture provides a method that generates an array of datapoints to be used as inputs for the tests; each test encapsulates a theory that should hold for any input condition. The framework takes on the responsibility of running each test once for every datapoint supplied by the fixture, and for distinguishing successful and failing instances of the same test.

Behavior-Driven Development

The workflow involved in TDD can be described in the following way: Find out what your app needs to do, express it in executable form, and then make it work. Behavior-Driven Development, or BDD, takes this approach to writing software and applies it more generally, so that customer requirements are documented as executable test cases from the start.

BDD is not just about tool support and a test framework; it also requires that the customer needs be captured in a standard form, where each requirement also functions as its own acceptance test. Part of this standardized requirement form is the *ubiquitous language*, a glossary of terms from the problem domain used in the same way by everybody in the team. The point of defining a ubiquitous language is that it reduces some of the ambiguity in communicating between customers and users—who are usually experts in the problem domain but not in software—and developers, who are usually experts in software but not in the problem domain.

Many developers will create a *domain-specific language* (DSL), a programming language that exposes software behavior in terms of the ubiquitous language. It's this DSL that allows customers to review the executable test cases in terms that they understand, and to confirm that they accurately capture the software requirements.

BDD tests follow a very similar pattern to TDD, although because the tests are a communication aid and not just a developer tool, there is more emphasis on making them readable. The tests are usually referred to as "specs" because they are the specifications for features in the finished app. A spec in the Cedar[1] BDD framework for Mac and iOS follows this format.

```
describe(@"Deep Thought", ^{
    beforeEach(^{
        //... set up the environment
    });
```

---

1. https://github.com/pivotal/cedar and http://twitter.com/cedarbdd

```
it(@"should solve the great question", ^{
    //... test code
    expect(theAnswer).to(equal(42));
});
});
```

Notice that the naming and ordering convention of the test macros promotes reading the success criteria as if it were an English language sentence: expect the answer to equal 42. This is done using "matchers"; macros that separate the description of a test condition from evaluation of its result.

In Chapter 4, "Tools for Testing," you saw the big collection of macros defined by OCUnit, and the similarly large collection defined by the Google toolkit. The problem with OCUnit-style test frameworks is that whenever you want to express a new type of test, you have to construct a new STAssert...() macro, which leads to duplication and increased effort of learning and using the framework. Matchers reduce the duplication— you would still need a new matcher, but evaluate it in a standard way—and the improved readability of the test reduces the cognitive load associated with using matchers in tests. They have the useful side-effect of being easier for nonprogrammers to understand, too.

A common form for matchers is Hamcrest; and an Objective-C implementation called OCHamcrest can be found at http://code.google.com/p/hamcrest/wiki/TutorialObjectiveC. Hamcrest matchers can be used in OCUnit tests to make the tests easier to read; they are not tied to BDD frameworks like Cedar.

Automatic Test Case Generation

Chapter 12, "Applying Test-Driven Development to an Existing Project," showed that it is possible to add unit tests to an existing project; there are challenges, but it can be done. One of the problems is knowing when your tests express all the different conditions. Because you're taking the implementation and trying to work out the requirements, how do you know what all the supported inputs are? Do they represent all the required inputs?

It would be useful, at least as a starting point, to use the code as a guideline—to read through a method, making a note of every decision or loop, and looking at the conditions needed to go down each branch. After you had mapped out all the conditions, you would know what input states are supported by the method and what it does in response to each state. You would know that executing the method with each of the different input states in turn would represent a complete test of the method's functionality. Armed with this knowledge, you could decide whether the app needs to support all the inputs the method provides, whether the method behaves in the correct way for any given preconditions, and whether it needs to support any additional states.

Building this table of possible input states would be time-consuming even on a comparatively short method, and as with all time-consuming tasks, it would be great to get a computer to do it for you. That's where klee comes in. Klee is a tool based on the

LLVM compiler used in Xcode that analyzes your compiled code[2] to construct this table of input conditions. To use klee, you instrument your code to tell it that some of the variables are symbolic. Klee executes your code in a virtual machine, and whenever the code tries to access a symbolic variable, klee keeps track of all the possible values that variable could have. For example, if klee encountered the line:

```
if (x > 0)
```

where x was symbolic, it would know that there are now two paths the code can take, but in subsequent lines of the function, if klee took the true branch of the `if` condition, x will now only ever be greater than 0; and if it took the other branch, x will only ever be less than or equal to 0. It can also discover conditions that would lead to app termination, such as the code dereferencing a `NULL` pointer or accessing an array beyond its bounds.

Klee's output is a collection of files, one for each of the possible paths through the app code. For each case, klee records an example of the values the symbolic variables must take to execute that path. This file can be used as input to a klee runner, which sets the symbolic variables to the specified values and executes the code, allowing you to see what the result of executing that condition is. Klee cannot tell you whether the result is correct, of course; its purpose is to produce the minimal set of tests that express the total range of code behavior.

Klee has its limitations; it can test programs that use the standard C library (part of `libSystem` on iOS) by providing its own implementation of the functions in that library. It can't currently be used to generate tests for an iOS app, and the more complex the code you're examining is, the more conditions klee will discover and report. It's a useful tool for analyzing small functions in isolation, and as it matures will become a useful aid in understanding legacy code.

Similar tools in other environments are more capable. A lot of academic software engineering research is focused on the Java language, and tools that can generate tests from symbolic execution of Java bytecode, or that can analyze UML diagrams to produce Java test code, are comparatively mature, although they are mainly still research projects. Examples of improvements on "blind" path execution include Directed Automated Random Testing[3] and using knowledge of how objects usually interface with each other to prune unlikely or nonsensical code paths.[4]

Automatic test case generation tools like klee are also useful in cases where you have unit tests, even where you've been using test-driven development and so have entirely grown the code using the tests as a specification. By completely analyzing all possible paths of execution, the generation tool can point out conditions that can be met in the code but that are not covered by tests. Examples include methods that can be passed

---

2. More precisely, it analyses the LLVM bitcode, an intermediate representation of the compiled code from which the compiler creates a machine language binary.

3. http://dl.acm.org/citation.cfm?id=2001425

4. http://ieeexplore.ieee.org/xpl/freeabs_all.jsp?arnumber=5770597

NULL as a parameter and methods that can be called in a different sequence than is expected in the test fixture.

Automatically Creating Code to Pass Tests

When we have tools like klee to automatically generate test coverage from executable code, a question naturally arises: Can we go the other way? Given a collection of tests, could a computer automatically provide code that satisfies all the requirements in the tests? In TDD it's our set of unit tests that express what the code should do in computer-readable form, so perhaps it's possible to turn that representation into a running app in the same way our forebears turned human-readable C into machine language with their compilers.

On the surface, it seems that for all of its benefits, TDD introduces a certain amount of redundancy into the development process. You first write a test that describes to the computer how the app *should* behave, then you write the app code that describes to the computer how the app *does* behave. Effectively, you express the same requirement in two ways (three, if you count the refactoring step where you write the same app code again in a more pleasant form). If you could get a compiler-like tool to go from a test fixture to a running app, you could remove some of this redundancy but still get to design each class's API and specify its behavior.

To some extent this is already possible, although that extent is very limited. For systems whose operation can be completely specified in a formal grammar like Z,[5] it's possible to construct the software entirely from the specification—in reality, this is not much different from "programming" the software in the Z language though.

There's a very wide gap between a specification constructed in Z and a collection of unit test fixtures. Unit tests, while being executable code, are ultimately produced for the programmer's benefit. They tell you what you need to know about writing the app; they don't tell the computer everything it needs to know to do the same. In part, that's deliberate: By designing each class to be independent of the others, and each method to be testable in isolation, we knowingly leave out information on how the methods and classes are hooked up to each other. Another reason unit tests aren't a complete specification of an app's behavior is that it's easy for people to rely on tacit knowledge to write tests that, despite being incomplete, are unambiguous to the people who need to read them. For example, you and I know that -[UIViewController viewWillAppear:] gets called before -[UIViewController viewDidAppear:], so we don't need to document anything about their ordering in our tests. If a computer were to generate app code from the tests, though, it would need to be told that.

It would probably be possible to provide some of this tacit information via the frameworks themselves, just as the framework documentation tells us developers about ordering and other requirements. For the moment, though, generating an application entirely

---

5. http://sdg.csail.mit.edu/6.894/scanPapers/UsingZ2.pdf: The Z notation is a combination of mathematical set theory and predicate logic that can be used to precisely specify software behavior.

from a test specification remains more complicated than writing the tests and the code in parallel.

Conclusion

The features Apple supplies in Xcode's OCUnit framework are sufficient to build full-featured apps using TDD, but do not represent the cutting edge of software engineering. Newer features, extensions of the technique and helpful tools all exist, and are in various stages of readiness for iOS developers. As these become available to and adopted by iOS developers, they will become useful strings in our bows as we write and ship quality apps.

Index

X-Y-Z

Test-Driven iOS Development

Graham Lee

Developer's Library

FREE
Online Edition

Your purchase of *Test-Driven iOS Development* includes access to a free online edition for 45 days through the **Safari Books Online** subscription service. Nearly every Addison-Wesley Professional book is available online through **Safari Books Online**, along with over thousands of books and videos from publishers such as Cisco Press, Exam Cram, IBM Press, O'Reilly Media, Prentice Hall, Que, Sams, and VMware Press.

Safari Books Online is a digital library providing searchable, on-demand access to thousands of technology, digital media, and professional development books and videos from leading publishers. With one monthly or yearly subscription price, you get unlimited access to learning tools and information on topics including mobile app and software development, tips and tricks on using your favorite gadgets, networking, project management, graphic design, and much more.

Activate your FREE Online Edition at
informit.com/safarifree

STEP 1: Enter the coupon code: WKFNLCB.

STEP 2: New Safari users, complete the brief registration form.
Safari subscribers, just log in.

If you have difficulty registering on Safari or accessing the online edition,
please e-mail customer-service@safaribooksonline.com